THE
DEVELOPMENT
OF
CONSCIOUSNESS

A Confluent Theory of Values

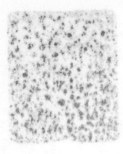

THE
DEVELOPMENT
OF
CONSCIOUSNESS

A Confluent Theory of Values

Brian P. Hall
Assisted by Patrick Smith

Consultant Author
Eileen Cantin

A CEVAM Book

PAULIST PRESS
New York, N.Y./Paramus, N.J.

Library of Congress Catalogue Card Number: 75-34843

ISBN: 0-8091-0201-3 (cloth)
ISBN: 0-8091-1894-7 (paper)

Published by Paulist Press
Editorial Office: 1865 Broadway, New York, New York 10023
Business Office: 400 Sette Drive, Paramus, New Jersey 07652

Printed and Bound in the United States of America

ACKNOWLEDGMENTS

Page 160: Allport, Gordon W., *The Nature of Prejudice.* Menlo Park, Calif., Addison-Wesley Company, 1954. Used with permission.

Pages 195-196: Asch, Solomon W. and Henle, Mary, eds., *The Selected Papers of Wolfgang Kohler.* New York, Liveright, 1969. Used with permission.

Pages 153-155: Beck, C.M., Crittenden, B.S. and Sullivan, E.V., *Moral Education.* Toronto, University of Toronto Press, New York, Paulist/Newman Press, 1971. Used with permission.

Page 189: Bell, Daniel, *The Coming of Post-Industrial Society: A Venture in Social Forecasting.*© 1973 by Daniel Bell, Basic Books, Inc., Publishers, New York. Used with permission.

Page 226: Berger, Peter, *The Sacred Canopy: Elements of a Sociological Theory of Religion.* New York, Doubleday & Company, 1967. Used with permission.

Page 188: Bronowski, Jacob, *The Ascent of Man.* Boston, Little, Brown & Company, First American Edition, 1974. Used with permission.

Page 6: Brown, George, Unpublished Manuscript. University of California at Santa Barbara.

Page 4: Clark Kenneth, *Civilisation.* New York, Harper & Row, 1969. Used with permission.

Page 157: Erikson, Erik H., "Identity and the Life Cycle" © 1968 W. W. Norton & Company, Inc. Used with permission.

Page 22: Freire, Paulo, *Education For Critical Consciousness.*© 1973 by Paulo Freire. Used by permission of The Seabury Press, Inc., New York.

Page 49: Freire, Paulo, *Pedagogy Of The Oppressed.*©1970 by Paulo Freire. Used by permission of The Seabury Press, Inc., New York.

Page 21: Fromm, Erich, *Escape From Freedom.* New York, Toronto, Rinehart and Company, 1941. Used with permission.

Page 191: Frondizi, Risieri, *What Is Value? An Introduction To Axiology.* Translated by Solomon Lipp. Reprinted by permission of The Open Court Publishing Company, LaSalle, Illinois.

Page 66: Glasser, William, *Reality Therapy: A New Approach To Psychiatry.* New York, Harper & Row, 1965. Used with permission.

Page 220: Goulet, Denis, "An Ethical Model For The Study Of Values" from *Harvard Educational Review,* Volume 41, May, 1971.© Harvard Educational Review, Cambridge, Mass. Used with permission.

Page 73: Kohlberg, Lawrence, "The Concepts Of Developmental Psychology As A Central Guide To Education: Examples From Cognitive, Moral and Psychological Education." Cambridge, Massachusetts, Harvard University, Institute for Human Development. Used with permission.

Page 74: Angyal, Andras, "A Theoretical Model of Personality Studies." Duke University Press, *Journal of Personality*, September, 1951. Used with permission.

CONTENTS

PREFACE

History knows of no time in which man has not been concerned with the issue of values. People have examined their values, written about them, legislated in support of them and expressed them in their artistic creations from time immemorial. Then why another book on values?

Because there is something new to be said. The value issue has once again found itself front and center on the educational scene due to the attention given it by educators interested in Value Clarification and in moral development. In recent years both Sidney Simon and Lawrence Kohlberg have become commonly cited authorities in values education circles across the land. But each of these men works in rather narrow and confined areas.

There is a need to put their contributions, which are significant, in perspective. Simon and his followers receive criticism for leaving teachers with a classroom full of students who may have clarified their values but are now wondering what to do next. Kohlberg comes in for criticism because his efforts are centered too exclusively on the cognitive domain. This is like criticizing Edison for not inventing the jet engine. A man is entitled to put parameters on his field of inquiry and focus on the problems he thinks deserve such scrutiny.

What this book attempts to do is situate the efforts of men like Sidney Simon, Lawrence Kohlberg and others in the larger human enterprise of promoting human growth. This book is meant to be a force for integrating the efforts of all who are dedicated to education whether administrators, counselors, teachers or parents. It examines the history of human development, from value clarification, and from those dealing with human development in moral reasoning and then formulates a theory which seeks to integrate all these varied endeavors.

The resulting construct is called a confluent theory of values. As the word "confluence" suggests, this theory brings together many streams of thought that have been following their own separate courses. It argues for a holistic approach to education, refusing to see the cognitive/affective education debate in terms of either/or.

It focuses on the value question because of the author's conviction that values are, in fact, by their very nature forces which integrate a person's many activites into a unified life plan. They can have the same unifying effect on the educational process with its diverse disciplines and sometimes competing rationales.

A book like this is much needed by classroom teachers who can only be confused by the mass of material on values currently available to them; it provides them with a framework for organizing this material as well as a critical base from which to evaluate it.

Hopefully professional educators, theorists and evaluators will respond to this work by criticizing it and helping to reformulate the theory where that seems called for. It is from such constructive exchanges that progress usually comes. This confluent theory is offered in the spirit of inquiry. It is intended as only a step in the direction of integration, not as a final solution to that issue.

I would particularly like to thank various people that have helped me with this work. Special acknowledgement goes to Eileen Cantin and Pat Smith from the staff for the hours of brainstorming and reflection. This is not to mention the hours of editing and indexing that Pat contributed. And no small addition is the encouragement, criticism and support by two special people, Dr. Richard Kunkel, St. Louis University and Dr. Julius Elias, University of Connecticut; not only their expertise but their friendship helped to make this work possible.

Last but not least has been the encouragement of the Lilly Endowment, through the funding of Project Values—a joint effort of CEVAM and the Education Department at St. Louis University. To the endless list of thanks recognition goes to the vision and encouragement of Kevin Lynch and Richard Payne of Paulist Press.

Brian P. Hall
September, 1975

CHAPTER I

THE CONFLUENT APPROACH

LOPEZ ANAYA, Fernando *Mermaid*. 1942. Etching with granular surface treatment and roulette, printed in dark green. Pl: 23 5/8 x 14 7/8''. Sh: 29 7/8 x 21 3/4''. Collection, The Museum of Modern Art, New York. Inter-American Fund.

The problem of man and his becoming is particularly urgent for parents, teachers, school officials, and citizens concerned with conduct of education. To choose soundly what to teach and how to teach it, to judge what educational goals are practicable and what ones are not—such wisdom requires the best possible understanding of human nature and its transformation.

Phillip Phenix

INTRODUCTION

This book is about values. It formulates a theory of values that offers to you the reader an over-all construct that hopefully, will not preempt your own creative input. Rather it is intended to provide a structure out of which you can understand the nature of values and how they may be utilized within the educational process.

The value question is primarily the question of consciousness. Our level of consciousness and the parameters it puts upon our world determine the values, behavioral alternatives and creative life styles we are able to act out.

Consciousness always entails a continuous interplay between the person and the environment. It is the environment impinging on consciousness that shapes and reinforces and at times retards an individual's growth.

An Old Problem

The question of value of course is not a new one, because it is and always has been the essential question confronting man. In times past we may not always have used that word but we were facing the same basic value issue. From the very beginning values have been tied up with man's continual interaction with his environment.

The City and Man

Lewis Mumford in his book, *The City in History*, talks about the beginning of the city and the demise of the primitive village community in the following manner:

> The order and stability of the village, along with its maternal enclosure and intimacy and its oneness with the forces of nature, were carried over into the city: if lost in the city at large, through its over expansion, it nevertheless remains in the quarter of the neighborhood. Without this communal identification and mothering, the young become demoralized: indeed, their very power to become fully human may vanish, along with neolithic man's first obligation—the cherishing and nurturing of life. What we call morality began in the Mores, the life-conserving customs, of the village. When these primary

bonds dissolve, when intimated visible community ceases to be watchful, indentifiable, deeply concerned group, and the "We" becomes a buzzing swarm of "I's," the secondary ties and allegiances become too feeble to halt the disintegration of the urban community. Only now that the village ways are rapidly disappearing throughout the world can we estimate all the city owes to them for their vital energy and loving nurture that made possible man's further development.

What Mumford describes is the beginning of the development of man as it coincided with the movement of neolithic man from the village to the city. What is important is that from the early stages of human history the values and morals that issued in life-conserving customs were developed by the human community in relationship to its over-all environment.

VALUES

To value is to make a choice and act upon it. The choices and acts of man constitute his history. But as a man chooses and acts on values he also seeks meaning—meaning making and valuing are for all intents and purposes aspects of the same reality.

The act of valuing appears in the history of art each time artists make meaningful statements through external representations such as painting, sculpture and architecture. Think of the impact felt by a person wandering through medieval Europe! Serfdom, the plague and continual wars abound, then suddenly there appears rising out of the shacks and rubble of a small town in southern France a magnificent cathedral. Cathedrals express in stone images the values of security, confidence and hope in a better world. To enter these magnificent places, to be caught up in their loftiness with statues of heavenly figures and massive murals of other worlds painted upon their walls was to enter into an act of valuing.

Such an environment shaped the values of many people in medieval Europe as do many of our functional office buildings today. These buildings may be no less beautiful, but their projected values are certainly different, namely those of achievement, success and production.

History of Ideas

The valuing process clearly was at the heart of many of the great philosophical struggles of history. For example Reformation Europe presented a picture of a people trying to clarify through theology and culture which values from tradition they considered to be priorities in their own development. They were engaged in the process of value clarification and value development.

An interesting commentary on this process emerges from the development of encyclopedias and dictionaries in 18th century France. Kenneth Clark comments as follows:

> The aim of the Encyclopedia seems harmless enough to us. But authoritarian governments don't like dictionaries. They live by lies and bamboozling abstractions, and can't afford to have words accurately defined. The Encyclopedia was twice suppressed; and by its ultimate triumph the polite reunions in these elegant salons became the precursors of the revolutionary politics. They were also precursors of science. (P. 257.)

Clark is talking about a community of intellectuals who met at salons in Paris before the Revolution and whose collaboration came to fruition in the publishing of encyclopedias and dictionaries. Such books were largely devoted to the clarification of words and ideas and therefore the inherent values. Those that emerged guided the very life of France itself and contributed to the Revolution.

Value Education

There are many teachers who have gone through their own process of revolution because they used value-clarification techniques and then had to deal with the reaction of their students! The process often promoted as much growth in the teacher as in the student. Here we only want to emphasize that the process of valuing, of value clarification and morality itself is as old as man himself.

The subject matter we call value education is simply a structure that helps us to understand better how the consciousness of man develops. That is to say it helps students get a handle on what it is they are doing. It also gives us some novel strategic methods that can be employed in a variety of educational settings. The word education here is used very broadly to mean the pursuit of learning and the acquisition of the skills necessary to utilize that learning in a creative manner.

VALUES—The Subject Matter Today

Education and learning in general have gone through a number of cycles both in the educational and therapeutic service-related fields. At various times there are exponents of behavior modification, those who stress the "affective domain," and those who emphasize the cognitive side of learning.

The behavioralists would claim that therapeutically a *1.* person adjusts to life and behaves well if he is shaped by a society that carefully monitors and modifies behavior; in the view of such educators, that is the most effective way of training or educating humans. Many educators feel that their primary task is to teach the basic skills that a person needs to function well and fit into society. These skills may range from reading, writing and arithmetic for some to character formation for others.

Those who stressed the affective domain in the past few *2.* years placed major emphasis on emotional and imaginal development. They believed that a person's feelings and imagination need considerable attention and that this should be the primary stress of education. Carl Rogers would be an example of this approach.

Finally there are those who stress the cognitive domain. *3.* They have always been in the majority because for hundreds of years most people have viewed education as a cognitive process. In this approach the intellect—the reason of man as an objective observer of reality—has been the center of attention. Information processing along with skill training are considered of primary importance. Piaget is a key person here.

CONFLUENT EDUCATION

By confluent education we mean an educational theory that integrates both method and discipline from a wide variety of sources. Educators should not simply choose between cognitive or affective or behavioral approaches to learning, but rather they should integrate all these approaches into a holistic theory of education. One of the reasons why value education is important is that values are essential to the person and as such are integrating forces that tend to bring all these elements into focus. Thus a value-centered education is confluent education.

George Brown, professor of education at the University of California at Santa Barbara has this to say:

> Confluent education seeks to integrate, in teaching and learning, the realm of emotions, attitudes, and values (affective domain) with that of thought and intellect (cognitive domain). It views this integration as essential to meaningful relevant education, to intelligent and mature behavior, and to a person taking a responsible and creative place in a democratic society.

Historically then there has been a process of some educators stressing the cognitive on the one hand with other educators like Rogers trying to counteract this movement by stressing affective and emotional education. There is an urgent need for a more integrated approach.

VALUE EDUCATION: ITS FOCUS

The Hall Report from Canada and the Plowden Report in England have greatly influenced education in the United States and presently stress this more holistic view of education. Both highlight the necessity for training teachers in both child and human development. As a consequence of this the field that we generally call value education, whether in public education or in social services, can be divided into three areas.

1. Value Development:

This is the study of how values develop in individuals, of what values and priorities are essential for man's mental well being and growth and of what values contribute to society's development. Some questions that need to be introduced here are: How does one enhance and develop a sense of self-esteem in an individual? How does one provide security in the classroom, a value that is so necessary for the development of any child? How do we develop leadership that will foster the creative authority of an individual and those working under him? These questions deal with this issue.

2. Moral Development:

This is the study of how people make rational cognitive judgments concerning what is right and what is wrong. Of particular influence here is the work of Lawrence Kohlberg of Harvard University. Kohlberg has pointed out that the moral choice—the choice as to what is right or wrong—is developmental. Depending on his level of development a person will make different kinds of rational judgments from a cognitive base. In the view of this writer the ability to make moral judgments is one of the skills resulting from value development. Moral and value development deal with what values an individual "ought" to have. We say that an individual needs certain values in order to survive in society, but society needs him to have certain values if that society is to become creative and provide a creatively reinforcing environment for its citizens. The value requirements here would be those that we say individuals "ought to have."

3. Value Clarification:

This is in contrast to the developmental areas in that it only deals with what "is." It is primarily an educational method to be employed by the educator and counselor. It makes no moral judgments concerning what values "ought to be" but rather places before the person the values that he "does" have. Our assumption is that people are usually not aware of their underlying values and therefore are not conscious of the forces that cause them to behave as they do. We also assume that for people at a particular stage of development to clarify where they are is most important as a part of their maturing and decision-making processes.

The point that we want to make is that all three of the above take on a meaningful structure only as they are *seen in relationship to the individual's development of "consciousness."* That is what this book is about.

THE IMPORTANCE OF VALUE EDUCATION

The question often raised in conferences is: "Why is it that value education and value clarification are so prominent at this time?" The current interest in value questions is usually attributed to the present moral crisis in our country, indeed in the whole world. To answer this question at a deeper level the reality of a rapidly changing society and the consequences of future shock demand that we make choices that are both accurate and logical if we are to survive into the future. The most reliable guide to such choices is our awareness of what our values are.

World Issues

In recent years even more complex problems have loomed large on the human horizon, such as "overpopulation." The planet undoubtedly is moving towards a crisis arising from the presence of too many people and the absence of too few resources. And not only this but the problem of waste due to the random production orientation of some nations, in particular the United States and Japan, is causing problems of which the energy crisis is only one example.

An increasing number of nations are aware of the necessity for world planning and for more interdependent operations at the international level. However this is of no use at all unless such values as interdependence and harmony filter down into the very fabric of our own national structures, our politics, the manner in which we administrate schools and hospitals and ultimately into our individual lives.

The accomplishment of these ends requires the education of peoples to a new consciousness in a new world. This means understanding that certain types of value priorities are essential to the survival of mankind if the life span of the human species is to exceed that of the dinosaurs.

Value and Human Potential

Clarification of values reveals our potential and equips us with the knowledge that enables us to make logical choices regarding the future—a skill that every person needs to acquire. As such it is not a skill that stands apart from those needed in the sciences, but rather integrates the sciences and simply brings all our present knowledge into a more holistic focus. This is what we mean by confluence.

The acquisition of this skill is no easy task. Any person

who wishes to become adept at clarifying his own values and bringing to consciousness precisely how he makes choices must overcome obstacles. Life is confusing and complex, sometimes even overwhelming. To confront life's conundrums on a day-to-day basis a person must be confident that he is master of his own destiny.

Two problems in particular make this a challenging and demanding enterprise. One is the feeling of powerlessness many *1.* individuals feel in the face of life's complexities. The other problem is the intricate and complicated network of rela- *2.* tionships to the rest of reality that each individual experiences. He must deal with the physical and cultural environment and relate to his family, his friends, his authority figures and a wide range of human institutions. It is because the individual is enmeshed in such an entangling web of relationships that we speak of the individual as system.

Let us briefly look at these two value-related obstacles that impede an individual from easily controlling his own fate.

1. Powerlessness and Power:

One of the undeniable facts about teaching values no matter at what level they are taught, whether one is talking about moral development or value clarification, is its demand that people make choices for themselves and act upon them.

Simon on Value

We need to pay tribute at this time to the publication by Raths, Harmin, and Simon in 1966 of a study called *Values in Teaching*. This popular book maintained that the thing chosen is not a value unless all seven of the following conditions are met:

1) a value must be chosen freely
2) from alternatives
3) after thoughtful consideration of the consequences of each of the alternatives
4) the person must be happy with the choice
5) must be willing to affirm the choice publicly
6) the person must act on the choice
7) the person must have done it recently and repeatedly.

The last definition has some shortcomings but credit must be given to the authors for what it offers. They want to stress that values are chosen, not given. For hundreds of years traditional education has stressed the opposite.

Freire and His Banking Concept

In his *Pedagogy of the Oppressed* Paulo Freire characterizes traditional educational methodology, which he calls the "Banking Method," as follows:

a) the teacher teaches and the students are taught
b) the teacher knows everything and the students know nothing
c) the teacher thinks and the students are thought about
d) the teacher talks and the students listen—meekly
e) the teacher disciplines and the students are disciplined
f) the teacher chooses and enforces the choice, and the students comply

The Value Method

Here Freire is clearly reacting with his usual forcefulness to that long revered educational attitude that views children as empty vessels waiting to be filled with the wisdom of the learned teachers. From such a perspective educators frequently confuse "to know" with "to receive the right kind of information." At the time this method was developed it served some useful purposes and still is one ingredient of the educational process. The early European immigrants to the United States did need to learn to converse in English, to read and to write their names. By modern standards the methods used were a bit crude but effective. Education was strictly utilitarian, developing needed citizenship skills. Values were transmitted within the family framework rather than through the educational system.

By contrast the above definition of the valuing process of Raths, Harmin and Simon assumes that education includes character training and has to do with over-all human development. For them the what, how and why of valuing is an integral part of the educational process. By this definition they are claiming that students do not learn or know something simply by soaking up information like so many sponges. Values involve an internal choosing by the student, not an external giving by the teacher. Values education attempts to subject this valuing process to the conscious reflection of the students.

It is evident from this that if one chooses freely from alternatives one is actually prioritizing values. This definition led teachers in the classroom to utilize a simple method that informed people they did not have values unless they were happy with their choices and were willing to commit themselves publicly and to act on them.

Example Strategy

At this point it would be helpful to engage in a specific value-clarification strategy that highlights some of the issues we are considering here.

I.   First examine the following five value definitions. The strategy will work with them.

1. Power: The sense of one's own authority and the ability to initiate action in certain areas of competence. A person with this as a value places priority on accomplishing his own goals, on success and achievement.

2. Interdependence: Cooperation is more important in the long run than acting independently. Here a person emphasizes group creativity and yet works from a solid base of self-confidence.

3. Instrumentality: Technical competence in specific areas, such as TV repair, writing, building. Such a person puts his priority on getting the job done and seeing results. He generally likes to work with his hands, use machines or do painting.

4. Expressiveness: Communicating one's feeling, ideas and imagination. A person with this as a priority likes to discuss and plan and is less concerned with goals and end results than with the process itself.

5. Duty: Doing what one should, being responsive to those who have authority. A person who is duty-oriented is concerned with determining and meeting his obligations. Expectations of the boss, the church and the law loom large in decision-making.

II.   Now attempt to determine which of these values provides your life with its basic structure. What really determines the main choices around which you organize your day-to-day behavior?

The best way to do this is to take a typical day (if you have any days that are typical) from the preceding week and see which of these values played the major role in your decision making. Did you generally choose actions that originated in your need to be your own authority (power), in your yearning to communicate your feelings and ideas (expressiveness), in your desire to cooperate with others (interdependence), in your concern for meeting your responsibilities (duty), or in valuing your own technical competence (instrumentality)?

To get at this issue construct an instrument like the one below that has a column for each of these five values.

DIAGRAM 1

POWER	DUTY	EXPRESSIVENESS	INSTRUMENTALITY	INTERDEPENDENCE

Put in the appropriate column those activities and the time devoted to them that were behavioral expressions of that particular value. Add the time totals in each column; the resulting figures should indicate how you rank those values behaviorally. You may also discover that a considerable number of activities from the day selected do not fit any of these values. This is to be expected. We have chosen these five values because they relate to the issue of power/powerlessness.

III.   There is no right or wrong ranking of these values; we are all different in the way we do things. But our rankings do not normally vary greatly over long periods of time. The emphasis might change but not the value attitude behind the ranking. To be accurate in filling in the above chart one must answer honestly some difficult questions. Suppose for example on the day in question I spent a fair amount of time with my children. Then I must determine if my behavior towards my children was sparked by expressiveness, power (as defined above) or sense of duty. It is only then that I can assign the time to the appropriate column.

Sometimes a crisis pushes a value to a position of priority that is not typical. If my son falls and breaks a leg while hiking, instrumentality (getting the needed help) will probably come first no matter what my usual preference is.

Let us look at some possible rankings for various types of people. Take the case of two architects:

> Architect A
> > Ranks—Duty
> > > Instrumentality
> > > Expressiveness
> > > Power
> > > Interdependence
>
> Archictect B
> > Ranks—Expressiveness
> > > Power
> > > Instrumentality
> > > Interdependence
> > > Duty

Architect A is most concerned with doing what his boss or client expects and then with having the instrumental skills to do the expected job. Only then do his own expressiveness and personal power become factors in his behavior.

Architect B is most concerned with his own expressiveness and power. Instrumentality is important because it gives him the skills needed to express himself. Duty is a value, but in taking a job he is concerned with getting the client to allow him to do it in his own way. Architect B actually demonstrates more power than Architect A because his expressiveness shapes his duty rather than the opposite.

Now look at your own ranking and ask yourself if you really value this ranking. Check by measuring your ranking against the following criteria.

1) Do you choose it freely?
2) Consider the consequences of the other choices, namely ranking the values in different orders. Do you still stick to the choice you have made?
3) Do you understand how this ranking affects your behavior?
4) Does your ranking have a creative rather than a destructive effect on you and on others?
5) Are you satisfied enough with your choices to share your ranking with another person?
6) Does this represent a repeated pattern in your life? For example was the day typical?

If you answer yes to all of the above it would be a true value-ranking. To know what I choose, to reflect on my choice and to act on it gives me a sense of power and control over my life.

The process of valuing teaches people the necessity of ownership (controlling their own lives) and responsibility and thus contributes greatly to the development of their sense of power and authority. One of the essential reasons why this definition is so popular is that it gets to the heart of our primary social problem, namely the feeling of powerlessness of people in our society.

This powerlessness leads to a sense of meaninglessness, a consequence of an inability to make meaningful choices in one's life. Of course the business of choosing meaningfully is not simply a problem of one's personality or one's individual personal authority or psychological development; it is also a problem of one's environment. Often the environment imposes on a person a situation in which choice-making is impossible.

Meaninglessness

Meaninglessness makes a person feel trapped by existence itself, and imprisons a person in his own helplessness. For such a person values no longer exist. Why? When one comes to the point where it is impossible to choose or act, valuing becomes impossible. Life has become meaningless.

Studs Terkel said the following about the working conditions of ordinary people:

> Even a writer as astringent and seemingly unromantic as Orwell never quite lost the habit of seeing working classes through the cozy fog of an Edwardian music hall. There is a wide range of similar attitudes running down through the folksy ballyhoo of the Sunday columnist, the journalists who always remember with admiration the latest *bon mot* of their pub pal "Alf."
>
> Similarly, on our shores, the myth dies hard. The most perdurable and certainly the most dreary is that of the cab driver-philosopher. Our columnists still insist on citing him as the perceptive "diamond in the rough" social observer. Lucky Miller, a young cab driver, has his say in this matter, "A lot of drivers, they'll agree to almost anything a passenger will say, no matter how absurd. They're angling for that tip." Barbers and bartenders are probably not far behind as being eminently quotable. They are also typical. This in no way reflects on the nature of the work so much as on the slothfulness of journalists, and the phenomenon of tipping. "Usually I do not disagree with a customer," says a barber. "As that's gonna hurt business." It's predetermined his business—or work—being what it is.
>
> Simultaneously, as our "Alf," called "Archie" or "Joe," is romanticized, he is caricatured. He is the clod, put down by still others. The others, who call themselves middle-class, are in turn put down by still others, impersonal in nature —The Organization, The Institution, The Bureaucracy. Who you gonna sock? You can't sock General Motors . . . Thus the "dumbness" (or "numbness" or "tiredness") of both classes is encouraged and exploited in the society more conspicuously manipulative than Orwell's. A perverse alchemy is at work: the goal that may be found in their unexamined lives is trans-

muted into the dross of banal being. This put-down and its acceptance have been made possible by a perverted "work ethic" (P.114).

Terkel illustrates how few people are really pleased with the work they are doing. He illustrates the sense of powerlessness of so many people. But there is another side to this dreary story: "I was constantly astonished by the extraordinary dreams of ordinary people." This of course relates to the "meaning" question. Dreaming, seeing alternatives to things as they are, produces the power to choose and act on something that is seen as making sense. Terkel ends by quoting Tom Patrick a Brooklyn fireman who makes sense out of life in this way: way:

> The fucking world's so fucked up, the country's fucked up. But the firemen, you actually see them produce. You see them put out a fire. You see them come out with babies in their hands. You see them give mouth-to-mouth when a guy is dying. You can't get around that shit. That's real. To me, that's what I want to be.
>   I worked in a bank, you know, it's just paper. It's not real. Nine to five and it's shit. You're lookin' at numbers. But I can look back and say, "I helped put out a fire. I helped save somebody." It shows something I did on this earth.

This illustrates that a person can enjoy a sense of accomplishment and be satisfied that his actions are worthwhile if he perceives his life as meaningful. Only then does he have a sense of power. Powerlessness and meaninglessness accompany one another and frequently lodge themselves in an individual's consciousness when he has become confused by life's complexity. This leads us to consider the second obstacle in an individual's self management, the intricate network of relationships that surround him.

2. Individual as System

In recent years, particularly through the Fifties and Sixties, the psychotherapeutic sciences have placed considerable stress on the importance of becoming a person in reaction to the general feeling of powerlessness in society. Carl Rogers in particular has been an exponent of the importance of the individual as a person, as in this passage:

> I have pointed out that each individual appears to be asking a double question: "Who am I?" and "How may I become myself?" I have stated that in a favorable psychological climate a process of becoming takes place; and here the individual drops one after another of the defenses or masks with which he has faced life; then he experiences fully the hidden aspects of himself; then he discovers in these experiences the stranger who has been living behind these masks, the stranger who is himself. I have tried to give my picture of the characteristic attributes of the person who emerges; a person who is more open to all elements of his organic experience; a person who is developing a trust of his own organism as an instrument of sensitive living; the person who accepts a locus of evaluation as residing with himself; a person who is learning to live (in) his life as a participant in a fluid, ongoing process, in which he is continually discovering new aspects of himself in the flow of his experience. These are some of the elements which seem to be involved in becoming a person (pp. 122-23).

This emphasis on the importance and value of person and his becoming through his personal choices and through trusting his own experiences reflects the kind of definition of the process of valuing that Raths, Harmon, and Simon spoke of.

The negative side of the emphasis on individual as person has led to negative behavior, particularly in people who are becoming acquainted for the first time with the sacredness of person! Often they will emphasize independence as consisting of the choices they make and that they regard as sacred and for which they therefore owe no explanation, nor have any responsibility to share with other persons. I have heard this often from persons in a marriage conflict who decide to separate on the basis of "I just feel this is right for us."

This type of behavior often is well-illustrated in teenagers and in those who are experiencing independence for the first time. They want to be free. They want to do their own thing. Yet they do not always have the perception or the skills to see how this affects others with whom they are related.

Person and the Environment

The study of values continually clarifies not only the power of the individual but also recognizes that person and environment are in a continual interactive process. Because of this complex interaction we will speak here and in the remainder of the book not so much about the sacredness of "person," valid as that is, but rather about the "individual as a system." I think this is well illustrated in the following section of a story from an unpublished manuscript, which emphasizes how confusing it is to make choices in an environment crowded with other people, each inviting the individual to act in a specific way.

The Story

I found myself present at a gigantic tribunal. I was being judged. The hall around me was vast like some Gothic cathedral. Before me high upon a rostrum was a podium made of iron. Upon it sat a judge. The judge was Satan.

The evil one sneered and with a grin pointed a long scrawny finger at me and shouted words that echoed through the vast hall. The last echo tinkled and fell upon my ears. "You are to be judged, you are no more, because you listened to too many voices. Your fault is that you trusted others." He screamed a cackling laughter. "You trusted and you will become a fragmented nothing," his laughter became louder and my very bones felt cold. I breathed and trembled. "Sir," I said, "all my life I have struggled to become me." He sneered like Captain Hook, tapping his fingers impatiently upon the podium.

"I struggled all my life to make decisions to be strong and persuasive in my direction and then. . ."

"And you trusted, fool," he screamed—but with a tinge of uncertainty.

"No! No! I will not have that. There was the struggle."

"Struggle?" returned this judge in a low monotonous voice.

"I wanted to bring others in to share my ventures, my business, my life. I needed them but so often they hurt me."

The judge sat up in an almost caring manner. "So what have you learned my boy?"

"Some responded to my questions and used them against me, some like thick clay did nothing, did not even acknowledge my presence, but one or maybe two responded and cared for my words and actions."

He laughed heinously and then stopped suddenly. And then he said quietly, but in crystal clear fashion like the tinkling of a bell, "So few among so many? What are they my boy? They are nothing?"

There was an ominous silence, a total quietness where nothing moved, not even the breeze.

"But, it wasn't trusting that was the problem." The judge's eyes became dark. He blurted "What. . .?"

"It was the not knowing. Not knowing when it was time to trust them and time *not* to trust me. Not knowing when to trust me and not to trust them!"

The judge became deathly still and in that moment a high wind blew through the hall and with a sickly screech the tribunal in its darkness withered away. I looked around; the great hall was bare, and there was a hole in the roof through which the sun's rays came and in which the sparrow's nest rested. The floor all around me teemed with life. Insects basked in the sunbeams, life was present everywhere and that was good.

In this story the individual under judgment traces that part of his history in which he has been struggling to be himself. It describes a person-centered approach to the individual that is valid within its own context and indeed necessary to human growth.

Satan laughed at him, condemning him for his trusting in other persons. That is to say that an individual who naively trusts can be and has often been destroyed by others or as we often say "the system."

As the story goes on the subject becomes aware of the development of his consciousness. He moves beyond the naive view of life which says one should trust all people to a new position that states it is not always a question of trusting others but sometimes a question of trusting one's self. The problem may even be knowing when to trust oneself and when to trust others.

This involves the individual in the acquisition of a new

series of skills. The ability to know when to trust another means that one has to have insight into other people's personalities, into other systems of influence in order to discern when they (the others) have the skills and the ability and the inclination to respond to one's own request in a creative manner. To assign a person a responsibility or a job that is beyond his ability is of course destructive. There are not many Davids who defeat their Goliaths in their youth.

Thus as one matures in life and becomes aware of what growth entails one realizes that it has to do with knowledge and intuitive insight into persons and systems external to oneself, their skills and their ability to respond to oneself. So one moves not in a dependent relationship to them or even an independent one, but rather one strives for a genuine *interdependence*. This is the way to put order into the chaos that surrounds an individual in today's world.

Freire

In *Education for Cultural Consciousness* Paulo Freire speaks to both the issues we have just been treating, the powerlessness of modern man and the tendency of the individual to surrender control to the many forces surrounding him.

While not explicitly dealing with values, Freire still sees this powerlessness as the central problem of our time. He maintains that the way a person handles the power/powerlessness dilemma determines how he views himself. It is then a question of consciousness. The individual can view himself either as a subject freely controlling his own life or as an object at the beck and call of others. These alternate ways of living and conceptualizing one's self are designated by the terms integration and adaptation.

> *Integration* with one's context, as distinguished from *adaptation*, is a distinctively human activity. Integration results from the capacity to adapt oneself to reality *plus* the critical capacity to make choices and transform that reality. To the extent that man loses his ability to make choices and is subjugated to the choices of others, to the extent that his decisions are no longer his own because they result from external prescriptions, he is no longer integrated. Rather, he has adapted. He has "adjusted." Unpliant men, with a revolutionary spirit, are often termed "maladjusted."

We would add to Freire's comments that the values problem is at the heart of the integrative/adaptive approach to reality. The adaptive person organizes his consciousness around core values that contrast drastically with those central to the mental world of the integrated person. Passive obedience, conformity, external approval and reliance on the directives of others characterizes the adaptive person, while independence, creativity, self confidence and self directedness are typical of the integrated person.

Erich Fromm

In this connection Freire cites the following passage from Erich Fromm's *Escape From Freedom*:

> (Man) has become free from the external bonds that would prevent him from doing and thinking as he sees fit. He would become free to act according to his own will, if he knew what he wanted, thought and felt. But he does not know. He conforms to anonymous authorities and adopts a self which is not his.

Some of the ideas we have treated above in discussion on Individual As System, Freire considers in a section devoted to the way men deal with historical epochs. We stressed the confusion with which the complexities of contemporary life surround the individual. He speaks of the forces and movements in society that constitute the themes of any historical epoch.

In Freire's terms the individual will be a subject in history only if he recognizes the themes of his epoch and participates in them creatively and actively. Many men are merely spectators to history as the following clearly indicates.

> But unfortunately, what happens to a greater or lesser degree in the various 'worlds" into which the world is divided is that the ordinary person is crushed, diminished, converted into a spectator, maneuvered by myths which powerful social forces have created. These myths turn against him; they destroy and annihilate him. Tragically frightened, men fear authentic relationships and even doubt the possibility of their existence. On the other hand, fearing solitude, they gather in groups lacking in any critical and loving ties which might transform them into a cooperating unit, into a true community.

This describes the situation of many persons today who have no mastery over the direction of their lives. Freire passionately devotes himself to trying to help men develop what he calls critical consciousness that will allow them to become subjects or active participants in history.

This book has a similar purpose. Developing a critical consciousness that probes behind and beneath the currents of history—individual and social—is a value-related undertaking. Our conviction is that a person's consciousness at any point in his development is organized around values. As an individual becomes aware of what his behavioral values are he takes the first step towards controlling his life. Then and only then a growth pattern can be developed. Our confluent theory of value development deals with that growth pattern and with the skills needed for attaining autonomy and self-mastery that in turn opens the door to other important values. But before we can come to grips with the issue of value development we must begin by answering two basic preliminary questions:

1. What is a value?
2. What is the nature of the valuing process?

CHAPTER II

VALUE AND ENVIRONMENT

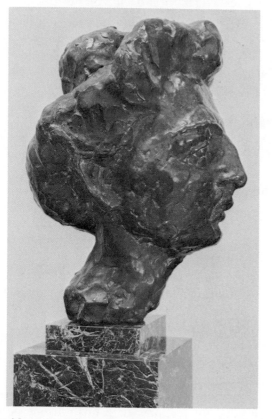

MATISSE, Henri Jeannette, I (Jeanne Vaderin, 1st state). (1910-13). Bronze, 13″ high. Collection, The Museum of Modern Art, New York. Acquired through the Lillie P. Bliss Bequest.

Far back in the neighboring mountains, alone in a log cabin with no running water and only a single fireplace for heat, lives an elderly lady. She draws her water from a well; she raises her own vegetables in the spring. Even though her own husband died several years ago, and one side of her body was later paralyzed due to a stroke, Aunt Arie refuses to leave. With her husband's clothes still hanging inside, washed and ready to wear, her home has become a sacred place over which she alone must now keep watch.

Aunt Arie

INTRODUCTION

Before we can talk about consciousness and a confluent theory of values we had best decide on our definition of a value and how it relates to the valuing process. Is it subjective? Is valuable what I decide is valuable? Is it objective? Is it outside me altogether in the environment somewhere, posited in some place totally external to me? What is and where is the value—that is what this chapter is about.

Value Definition

Any person, relationship or object which when freely chosen and acted upon contributes to the self's meaning and enhances its growth.

There are several observations to be made about this definition:

1. Not everything chosen by the self qualifies as a value. A value must aid the self in its meaning/seeking and must foster the growth of the person. Because of what it can obtain materially and do psychologically the pursuit of money might normally be a value. Yet if in an individual life the quest for money is obsessive and inhibits growth it is not a value for that person. So the definition does have a moral dimension to it in that a value-choice must contribute to growth.

2. This definition is developmental because what is needed for meaning or growth at one point in a person's life is not necessarily desirable at a later stage of development. Also the content of the same value changes as a person develops. The pursuit of security in the adult responds to a different set of concrete needs than those experienced by the security-seeking child.

3. This definition arises from a confluent approach to value development because what contributes to meaning or enhances growth is never simple. Both the cognitive and affective sides of a man are present and operative when he chooses a value. And some values such as intimacy can be achieved only by persons who are highly skilled. Thus this definition cannot be ap-

preciated fully unless one understands that a wide variety of skills are necessary for the realization of certain values.

4. The ontological foundation of any value is outside of but not apart from the self as subject. Values then are rooted in the objective order giving them commonality and making them public. They are there for everyone. Yet persons, relationships and objects are values only as a result of interaction with a self. Schlegal writes in his article, "Quantum Physics and Human Purpose":

The set of human values then has even its ultimate basis for validity both in man and in the broader natural world because the features of that world are not without dependence on man's own interaction with it.

5. The value character of a person, relationship or object receives something real when the subject chooses it. The act of choosing lifts it from the world of indifferent realities and makes it a value to a particular chooser. When a person chooses a house to be his home he does not alter the ontological status of the house but he does introduce the house into his history. It has a significance it did not have prior to its selection. Its ontological structure is unchanged, but it has begun a new history. It has entered into a dynamic relationship with the new owner.

The following diagram focuses on this dynamic interaction between the self and the object-become-value.

DIAGRAM 2

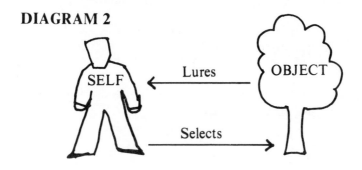

The object as value exercises an attraction on the subject by relating to some need of the subject. The subject in the act of valuing adopts a stance towards the object as a value. The object is viewed as being there for the self or in relationship to the self. The act of the self viewing the object as need-satisfying and choosing it contributes something to the object becoming a value. Still if the object did not lure the self in its direction it would not be seen as a value by the self.

For example a man may see a beautiful woman. He sees her and he values her. If he were not looking at her she still would be beautiful. But at the same time when she is in the picture and when he does see her obviously there is something about the beautiful woman that attracts him. It is in fact the dynamic interplay between the two that produces the valuing operation. The object lures, self selects and both are changed. This leads us to a second definition.

The Act of Valuing:

The act of valuing is the stance the self takes towards the environment such that the self acquires meaning and the creative development of both the self and the environment is enhanced.

The word "stance" requires considerable elaboration, but first the meaning of "self" and "environment" need clarification.

THE STANCE OF THE SELF

The Self

The self is a complex entity. Frank Kimper, in a private paper, defines the self in the following manner:

> The "self" is a dynamic center of being, center of consciousness, actively willing change in the direction of becoming the free and individual entity one is potentially.

He goes on to say that it is a "purposive core I have learned to trust in myself and in others."

The Ego

The psychological term "ego" nearly expresses what we mean by "self," but, as Tillich pointed out, it entails more than the term "ego" normally and technically has included, that is, self includes the subconscious and unconscious basis for the conscious ego.

The Child's Viewpoint

In the early stages of the development of a human being, ego and self are not distinct. The child is self-centered, seeing the universe as being made for him. His own feelings, his thoughts and fantasies, everything that he experiences in his environment is perceived globally in an undifferentiated fashion.

A.A. Milne in writing his famous *Winnie the Pooh* stories wrote from the perspective of the child. The child is quite naturally and beautifully self-centered. The following illustrates this point from the story called "An Enchanted Place," taken from *The House at Pooh Corner*.

> So they began going there, and after they had walked a little way Christopher Robin said:
> "What do you like doing best in the world, Pooh?"
> "Well," said Pooh, "what I like best—" and then he had to stop and think. Because although eating honey was a very good thing to do there was just a moment before you began to eat it which was better than when you were, but he didn't know what it was called. And then he thought that being with Christopher Robin was a very good thing to do, and having Piglet near was a very friendly thing to have; and so, when he had thought it all out, he said:
> "What I like best in the whole world is Me and Piglet going to see You, and You saying 'What about a little something?' And Me saying, 'Well, I shouldn't mind a little something, should you, Piglet,' and it being a hummy sort of day outside, and birds singing."

The perspective from which Milne wrote was that of the child. In the last paragraph Pooh's world begins with Me with a capital "M." The perspective of the child is that the world is created for the individual who sees himself at its center. This is not an act of selfishness but rather the natural beginning of development of individual consciousness.

Self in the Child

This experience of unity that is the child's is of course primitive and naive in its formation. Feeling and intellect are not distinct in the ego and because he is unaware of their presence he can be controlled by either of these aspects of his personality. A variety of forces can control his behavior, fear or some other emotion, the need for food or whatever fleeting purpose demands his present attention. In such instances the ego is the same as self.

Self in the Adult

Part of the maturing process is the separation of the self from the ego. Because the child is controlled by drives that are segmented, as well as by a variety of compulsions and circumstances, there is no major direction to his striving.

The function of the self in the mature adult is to integrate and give a basic direction to the many drives the person experiences. This is what separates the adult from the child or the mature person from the immature. For example the child might be overwhelmed by a feeling of anger because he does not get what he wants. He may scream for his mother's attention. The mature adult would not simply deal with anger by pushing it down and withdrawing, but would have hopefully gained skills in which that anger could be expressed spontaneously and in a nondestructive manner.

The self in the mature adult then is purposeful and able to make creative choices in the service of long range goals. He has acquired the skills that prevent circumstances from dominating his life. Interaction with the environment has been a learning process. It is through education that the individual begins to recognize the roles of feelings, of objective reason and of creative imagination in decision-making. These elements, often referred to as affective and cognitive domains, are not separate entities in the personality but are dimensions of the dynamic whole that is the self.

The mature person deals with these dimensions in such a way that he can reflect on them objectively. In other words such a man differs from the immature in that he is not at the mercy of these dimensions in his personality but rather controls them through reasonable reflection—reflection that is goal-oriented.

The following dream was reported to me by a counselee who was in the process of creative growth, and who was at a stage in her life when she was becoming independent and recognizing her own inner authority.

A Dream

"I was on a journey and found myself sinking into a huge ocean. The water was fairly clear and I had a moderate sense of fear and adventure as I explored. Around me were all kinds of fish, beautiful rocks and plants that I had never seen before. Occasionally a rather large fish would come and I would feel a little fear as I wondered whether it would see me, but it always looked at me curiously and then went away.

A Story about the Self

As I walked I came upon a ledge overlooking a large valley in the ocean. I lay for a moment on the ledge and looked down below. Suddenly to my surprise I saw a machine. It seemed at first to be a rather beautiful globular aluminum vessel with a large window in the front with four large mechanical legs. As I looked more closely there were also arms coming from the machine that reached out, picked up rocks and plants and examined them and put them back in their place, stopped occasionally and then went on its journey.

The machine seemed neither dangerous nor destructive but rather appeared to be one that was examining curiously and even lovingly the ocean floor. As I continued to observe, the machine came close to the ledge where I was lying. I was able to see a large oblong window and there inside was an individual operating the machine.

I climbed to the bottom of the ledge and peered in through the window. There was a moment of fear and then one of elation and life as I recognized the individual operating the machine was myself."

In quoting this example I would never of course want people to get the impression that I am suggesting that the self is the little individual inside of us operating a machine. This is hardly the purpose. What is important is the symbolic impact for the individual who had the dream. It was the sudden recognition that there was a dynamic purposeful center, her real self in control of her body, intellect and emotions. This center made her holistically responsible for her own behavior. She experienced fear as she suddenly recognized that all she did in her life was really her own responsibility. She was no longer a dependent child but rather an adult liable for her own actions, challenged to create her own future.

The self then is the dynamic control center of the person, bringing together the imagination, the feelings, the intellect, and the accumulated skills of the individual in a holistic manner as he or she relates to the total environment that confronts the self.

Thus only a confluent approach to man is realistic, one that integrates rather than fragments by focusing on merely one element like the intellect or the feelings. The self is the control center that links a person to the external environment. In fact, environment is not really external to a person but rather is something that the person himself is a part of. The following diagram presents the complexity of the self and thereby highlights the need for a confluent approach to man.

DIAGRAM 3

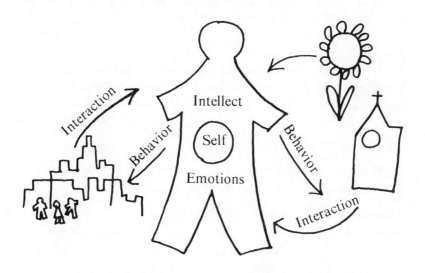

The diagram simply represents the interactive flow between man's environment that is external to him and that internal environment that makes up his person. Various factors in human behavior like emotions, imagination and intellect are not separate independent entities but one integrated whole united by the dynamic purpose that the self sets up as a goal. The self, the human being in the world, experiences continual conflicting tensions and strives to achieve meaning in the face of these contending forces throughout his life.

THE STANCE OF THE SELF
TO THE ENVIRONMENT

Environment

Environment is the self's field of experience. It is the totality of man's surroundings, internal and external. It is the planet earth in itself and as modified by man, galaxies and the stars, the sun and the moon. It is the material world external to yet partially shaped by man on the one hand and all the feelings, impulses and fantasies internal to the person on the other. It is the thought atmosphere present in any society. It is the political and cultural world.

Self and Creative Tension
        The self, the individual person, is constantly faced with polarities in his life development. Self then becomes a dynamic center of interaction, as illustrated in the following:

DIAGRAM 4

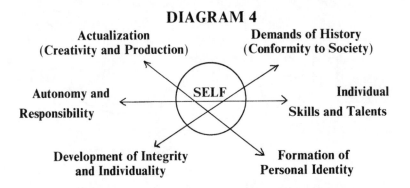

The diagram illustrates some of the creative tensions with which each individual has to struggle in order, to find meaning in his life development. It presents only the main conflicts a person must resolve.

1)   The tension between developing a sense of integrity and individuality on the one hand versus the demands made by history (tradition) to conform in certain circumstances to the demands of society. Cicero held that freedom is given by the law of the state. The function of the law of society was to provide the citizen with enough security to maximize his freedom. There is then a continual tension between conformity on the one hand and individuality on the other.

2)   The creative tension between individual skills and talents that are peculiarly one's own versus responsibility to society and to fellow man. Skills are then not developed in a vacuum, they are not simply for one's own personal survival but relate to the survival of one's family as a meaningful value-seeking organism.

3)   The tension between the personal formation of one's own identity on the one hand and the need to actualize this identity concretely through creative production in society. Clearly a person could become so production oriented, so obsessed by the need to gain more material things or the need to produce in order to become successful that his own identity could be lost. This is often the case in large factory complexes where a person may have a meaningless, repititious job on a production line that does not enhance his creativity and even slowly destroys his personal identity. This is a tension.

Experience

The point is then that the self has an awareness field, an experience of life, and is able to reflect on its own fantasies, feelings and ideas as well as on those things external to itself. The field of experience covers many things: other persons, human organization in institutions, plants, flowers and other growing things, disorders in nature, human and nonhuman. The self seeks to find meaning through the tensions and questions with which these realities confront it. All these things are environment but are perceived by the self accurately or in a distorted fashion by the screening of the senses. External environment then is not immediately present to the self. It is screened and perhaps misrepresented by the many factors involved in human consciousness.

Exercise in Conflict

A good exercise to illustrate how we misinterpret things by screening things out is to ask a group of persons to reflect on a conflict and share it with one another. Simply think of a time when you were very angry with someone and where finally the conflict was resolved. Examine the following questions:
1) At the height of my anger how did I view the other person or persons?
2) After the resolution of the conflict and we had listened to each other how did I view the person?
3) What were the discrepancies and what does this say about our natural screening processes?

How a person perceives his environment is conditioned by his own level of development and consciousness. Thus the environment is always a mixture of internal and external realities. While this mixture forms a unity (we speak of environment as a single thing) it is only the mature self that has the ability to differentiate the various components of the environment and deal with them individually.

A School Environment

A friend who worked in a public-education office that dealt with the funding of local public-school districts told me the story of the building of a modern school in a rural area that was completely designed on the open classroom concept. Prior to the building of this school the students had attended school in an old building in the downtown section of a moderate-size city in a midwestern state. The school had no playground and had two entrances, one for black students and one for white.

For the past half century then this school had teachers who dealt with students who were segregated and who caused them no difficulty whatsoever during recess because there was no playground, and the students would walk from the school onto the street and usually spend most of their recess time in a local drugstore. Although this environment must have caused some difficulties the teachers had adjusted and had been able to deal with the situation over the years.

Suddenly in the early Seventies the school board was given money, and with great enthusiasm they built a new school on the outskirts of the town. They were happy with the fact that the new school would have a playground and would be in an area where students could be controlled during recess, thus reducing the possibility of accidents and making life, so they thought, more pleasant for everyone.

Open Classroom

The new school was built. The learning areas were large and were not sectioned into small classrooms for a mere thirty students, as had been the case previously. The emphasis was to be on individual learning with large numbers of students at various grades all in a large room; the idea was that students would then be moved around by creative teachers in order that they could each learn at their own pace.

This new environment however caused tremendous problems for the teachers. My friend reports that he visited the school six months after it opened and found that the teachers had sectioned off the classrooms, forming the large learning areas into traditional classrooms by blocking off footage with filing cabinets, false screens, literally anything that they could get hold of.

In addition they were having tremendous problems in human relations because now they were confronted head-on with a black-white conflict. Previously the students had been segregated, and now not only did they come through the same entrance they came in the same bus and played together on the same playground. The problem was more that of the teachers than the students. The teachers of course could not be blamed. They simply had not been trained and did not have the skills to deal with the new environment.

Environment as Active

Thus environment is not passive or inert. It resists being managed in an easy fashion. It can move against and restrict the freedom of the self. The very existence of the external environment not to mention the forces let loose by society limits what the self can do. If the self is creative and skilled it can manage the environment so that it promotes life-enhancing experiences. Or of course the self can be overwhelmed by the environment as in the example above.

As we begin to examine how man can deal with this complex environment it will become evident that only a confluent approach takes sufficient account of that complexity.

THE STANCE

In our original definition we talked about the "stance" of the self to the environment. Stance describes the complex of subjective and objective attitudes whereby the self attempts to manage its internal environment and to relate constructively to the external environment.

Self on Two Fronts

In other words the self in stance-taking must operate on two fronts, each demanding different kinds of skills. Activities on the internal front require skills like emotional control, pain tolerance and the ability to handle selectively internal impressions coming from the external world. To deal with the external environment a person must have interpersonal and instrumental skills plus a creative imagination. As a person develops the skills that he needs vary. These skill variables will be discussed in detail in Chapter V.

So the stance is the way the self deals with the environment. It is never a simple response to a value; it always involves a more or less complicated procedure of value ranking. Implicit in the word stance are both the individual's meaning system and his world view, both of which furnish him with the criteria he needs to rank values: to chose this value rather than that one. The following passage clarifies this:

Value Ranking

Usually we view the world through sets of priorities that we have. It may be that friends are very important to us. But if I am the type of person who places high priority on studying, I may have little time for friends. In this example the ranking would have been as follows:

1. Studying
2. Friends

In such an example the value of study is important. The value of friends can also be very important. However, consider an individual with the opposite ranking, namely:

1. Friends
2. Studying

In each case, both values are very important, but the reverse order would, in fact, change the behavior of the person. The latter individual would spend more time with friends. This person might, for example, be more of an extrovert and more social in his thinking, whereas the former individual would probably be more inward-thinking and more happy living in a world of ideas rather than people.

The stance a person assumes toward his environment at a particular moment is a concrete expression of his level of

consciousness. In that instant he has ranked values, he has engaged his meaning system and activated his world view. The
way he ranks his priorities alters his behavior, his feelings and
may even have a concrete effect on his intellectual stance.

A proper evaluation of what occurs in that moment entails some familiarity with the general typology of consciousness.

While the consciousness of no two men is ever exactly
alike there are certain elements of consciousness common to all
men. These dimensions of consciousness structure the way the
self approaches environment.

THE STANCE AND TIME

The temporal dimension of consciousness covers the
way a person is mentally in touch with his past, present and future, and how these are present to his consciousness. The following diagram illustrates this dimension of consciousness.

DIAGRAM 4
TIME AND CONSCIOUSNESS

TIME PAST	TIME PRESENT	TIME FUTURE
MEMORY	'NOW' AWARENESS	IMAGINATION
1. What happened: Fixed forever.	1. What is: Fixed for now.	1. What might be: Unfixed
2. How I View It:	2. How I View It:	2. How I View It:
Rational: Comprehension Emotional: Guilt or Celebration	Rationally: Comprehension Emotionally: Acceptance or Frustration	Rationally: In process, Incomplete Emotionally: Anxiety, Fear or Hope and Construction

←—— REMEMBERING ——→ "NOW" ←—— FANTASIZING ——→

The Past

Memory is the faculty that puts me in touch with my past. The "what happened" aspect of the past is beyond conscious control—it refers to the past event as it happened, an extra-mental reality. But the "how I view it" aspect of the past is within my conscious control. The way I view the past can be changed. For example guilt is a present attitude toward the past.

Guilt

If I feel guilty today about spanking my six-year-old child in anger that is a "now" feeling about a fixed event that happened yesterday. But I can do something about the guilt I feel "now" by apologizing and doing something for the future by dealing with how I use my anger.

It can be changed first of all with regard to comprehension. How fully and deeply do I understand what happened? Do I see all the factors that were interrelated in the past event? Factors internal to me? Factors internal to other participants in the event? Factors stemming from the broader aspect of the environment? As a person's consciousness expands he sees more and more and what he sees he grasps more thoroughly. A child is hardly in touch with his past and what contact there is is superficial. An older and more mature person not only is in touch with his past but is able to explore it at some depth and survey its many dimensions and selectively incorporate it into his present and future.

The Person

In the above diagram my consciousness of the present comes under the heading "Now Awareness." "What is" is beyond my control; it is extra-mental reality. It is not as finally fixed as the past because at every moment the present is open to the future.

As with the past I can control how I view the present. I can increase my comprehension/extension. I can develop my consciousness so that I see more and understand what I see more fully.

My emotional response to the present is under my control. I may feel frustrated or bored. Or I may feel alive and interested as I view the present. Just how I feel toward the present is much influenced by how I view the past and the future. If I am guilt ridden as I face the past and anxious and fearful as I face the future I will not be happy with the present.

The Future

My imagination puts me in touch with my future and its creative possibilities. Mounier in *The Character of Man* maintains that all time has a future point of reference.

> Life presents itself to us as a creative future; memory is knowledge of the past in the service of the future; present, the place from which action starts towards the future. The future is not alien to space; we speak of it being 'wide open' before us, as offering wider or narrower horizons (p. 79).

What will be is not fixed. It is partially determined by what is, because the future springs not from a vacuum but from the present with all its limitations. Creative dreaming about the future differs from aimless dreaming precisely in this respect, it takes account of the limits the present imposes on the future.

It is in the way they view the future that creative people differ from the unimaginative. The creative person tends to see the limitations of the present as not final. He is concerned with alternatives. The unimaginative see the future as an extension of the present and define their future in terms of fitting into present structures. The development of the imagination is the development of a perspective that sees alternative futures. If I am guilty about yesterday's angry behavior I must learn to express my anger more creatively in the future. This is primarily a skill that coincides with the development of consciousness. Let us take the following interview as an example.

The Case of John Henry

In the following interview J.H. was a counselor in a private agency. At the time he was the only counselor and had only a part-time secretary. E. stands for the educator in this case, a guidance counselor.

J.H.: I'm feeling miserable about something and I'm so tired all the time. It's the job of mine.

E.: Tired and miserable. You sound somewhat overwhelmed.

J.H.: That's it. I feel there is no future. I simply can't cope with my work. I worked ninety hours last week and my wife's going to kill me.

E.: Why don't we look closer at the values and see what alternatives there might be.

J.H.: (Somewhat emotional) Values! There's only one value. Work, Work, Work!

E.: You mentioned your wife.

J.H.: Okay. Number one, work; number two, wife.

E.: Your wife sounds a long way off if you're working ninety hours a week. What about the work? What are its elements?

J.H.: Well I like it. I mean my life is my work, but it turns out to be too much at times. Okay. There is counseling, mainly group counseling. I really like that. Then there is secretarial work. I have a secretary. She only works part-time and I end up doing a lot of it. That is very annoying, And there is the administrative and public relations work. That takes about half my time. Finally there's teaching. I really like the teaching partly because my wife and I team teach, but I really don't have time to do it properly. The whole thing is damned impossible! I'm living like the only thing in the world is surviving.

E.: Surviving. You only make just enough money to live on with all this work that you're doing?

J.H.: No, as a matter of fact the board has voted me a raise and money to get additional personnel but I'm so bogged down I never seem to get down to it. I guess I'm not quite sure what I need.

E.: It's not really survival? It's almost as if you're overwhelmed with so many alternatives—too much stuff.

J.H.: That's it exactly.

E.: I'd like you to dream a wild dream. Imagine that you're in a perfect world in the future sometime. Now just relax and try to imagine how you'd like things to be.

J.H.: Well, I'd like my wife to be in the picture. Maybe the first person in the picture. Then work second.

E.: What would that mean in terms of how much time you'd have to work?

J.H.: (Getting anxious) That means I'd have to work about fifty hours a week and it's impossible.

E.: If in this perfect world you could rank all these different things that you mentioned in your work, regardless of time or problems, how would you rank them?

J.H.: Well, number one teach—I do this with my wife. Number two, my counseling. Number three, the administration and public relations. Number four, secretarial work.

E.: Well, if we put these down on a piece of paper they would look like this:

Present	*Future or Desired*
1. Administration	1. Teaching
2. Counseling	2. Counseling
3. Secretarial Work	3. Administration
4. Teaching	4. Secretarial Work

E.: John, is this accurate you think?

J.H.: Yes that seems accurate to me. I guess that's what I've got to do.

E.: Now just a minute. Before we move on I'd like you to consider that you have four things ranked there and how you rank them will change your behavior. But because there are four things this means there are twenty four alternatives. So perhaps now instead of why or how you convert from one to another it might be better to ask yourself, "Which of these alternatives would I like to do?" basing it on your present limitations and existing reality. In other words we can't really jump to some future dream that we've been talking about until we have looked at what could be possible in the first few months if you really worked at it.

J.H.: Well the actual bread and butter money comes from the counseling so that should be number one. And following that I'd really like to teach because it's something I do with my wife and it brings us together much more, and we like to do that. And then administration followed by the secretarial, which I shouldn't be doing anyway.

The above interview took place over several weeks. And as we proceeded beyond this point John was able to discuss and work out with the counselor/educator a time schedule whereby he could begin to employ additional persons. First of all the conversation dealt with the kind of additional persons and all the alternatives involved in that. For example did he need a secretary who could do some of the administrative work? Did he need someone who should help with the counseling?

In the complicated process that followed it turned out that he really needed a counselor/administrator and a good secretary. In addition to this, because he needed his wife more involved with himself he gave her the job of finding a full-time secretary. In time the counselor/administrator was found and John was able to reduce his hours of work.

Anxiety vs. Hope

As we examine the interview above you will note that when the counselor moved too quickly towards the future John became anxious. The negative side of the future is anxiety. Anxiety is the apprehension that something bad is going to happen. It is the fearful side of the imagination.

Coping and Support

This was really an educational process of extending the person's creative imagination to see alternatives that he could handle with a process that gave him the support needed to cope with the alternatives. By ranking the values or in this case the priorities he was able to see more than twenty-four alternatives. This could in some cases be overwhelming for an individual. The counselor/educator must stay and be supportive to the person so that he chooses alternatives within his skills realm. If this individual had cut back his work immediately he probably would not have been able to cope.

The second thing to note is that initially the individual was unable to see any alternatives except work versus wife, which is a combination of two alternatives. By looking at the underlying priorities in the work he was able to expand those alternatives at least twenty-four fold so that they could be chosen more easily. Of course one could have put wife along with the priorities but that would be another method and another way of doing things.

The main point we are trying to make here is that this was a process in developing an individual's imagination and in developing the skills to deal with it.

It is especially in the way they view the future that people demonstrate different levels of consciousness. A small-minded person can only see the immediate future and sees it as limited, restricted opportunity. His comprehension of future possibilities is superficial, not deep. His mental horizons give him only restricted areas in which to operate. A person with a more developed consciousness enjoys his future prospects because they offer him so many possibilities. He has a sense of freedom as he looks forward to creating his own future. His mental horizons are wide enough that he has no sense of being hemmed in by them.

People's emotional attitudes towards the future differ depending on their levels of consciousness. This brings to mind the fact that consciousness encompasses more than intellectual stance. A person's IQ (often stressed in educational quarters) is only one factor in the mental makeup. The person who views the future with fear or anxiety is mentally impoverished regardless of how intelligent he is.

A sense of hope and enthusiasm *vis-à-vis* the future is an essential constituent of the creative imagination of a well developed consciousness. To be able to choose hopefully and design one's own world is the process of meaning-making. This then is not simply a question of consciousness, but is also one of skill development.

Next then let us look at space as another dimension of that stance of self to the environment.

THE STANCE AND SPACE

There are two basic categories of space that influence one's consciousness of the world or world view: 1) insignificant or meaningless space, 2) significant or meaningful space.

1. Insignificant Space:

This is the space that does not concern or interest a person. It is where one does not operate mentally or actually. The early pioneers in the United States may have known of the existence of Russia, but it did not vitally concern them. Many today are aware of the Third World and its social and political problems, but it does not interest them. For them it is not a theater for personal action. It is then insignificant space. The child even as he grows in awareness of space in the world around him interests himself only in that space that supplies satisfaction for his bodily needs—food, warmth, security.

2. Significant Space:

This is all the space that interests a person. It is the field of consciousness and action. It tends to expand as one grows. It is of many different kinds:

Different Types of Space
   a) Bodily Space. That space that supplies satisfaction for bodily and personal needs. It is the only significant space for the infant. It is also a reality for adults, involving needs such as food and warmth.
   b) Private Space. It is the space used for the things one does or seeks to do alone, as where one works on one's hobby, where one reads and thinks.
   c) Work Space. It is where one does one's job and where one prepares himself to do his job, such as traveling to and from work. It includes the people with whom one works.
   d) Cultural Space. It is a place where one follows cultural pursuits—at home, the theater, the symphony, school—

and again the people with whom one shares these activities.

e) Recreational Space. It is where one plays and recuperates. It may include things like tennis courts, golf courses, where one travels, where one dances and where one partys. Again it includes the people with whom one does these things.

f) Intimate Space. It is a space one shares with others with whom one has the type of relationship in which one shares one's deepest thoughts and feelings. Family space is probably a sub-division of this, but is in some instances separate as a category.

g) Social Space. It is where one lives one's non-intimate social life with friends and peers; it cuts across some of the categories like recreational and institutional space.

h) Economic Space. It determines to what extent one can be active in cultural, recreational, social and institutional space. If one is economically poor one's freedom to explore new space is severely restricted.

i) Institutional Space. This includes all those institutions that are significant in one's life—state, church, the political arena and the school.

j) Sacred Space. This has a number of unique dimensions of its own because it relates particularly to the area of meaning-making.

    i. Space where one experiences the presence of the Other in solitude, sometimes in an organized setting.

    ii. Ritual space where one's relationship with the Other is structured by ritual.

    iii. In the life of a mature person it coincides more and more with total space.

    iv. It supplies a reference point for orienting and organizing all other activities.

Sacred Space

Sacred Space is particularly important in that it is an environment that is structured for the purpose of helping people to find meaning within defined limits. For example a church or synagogue is an environment that is sacred because its purpose as a building is to provide for activities that will help people make sense out of their lives. Within that building the act of ritual is an act of meaning-making.

But no less important as a sacred environment is a court of law, for example, which orders chaos and makes meaning out of a criminal act. It does so by limiting destruction in society. It limits the destruction of another person's meaning. The home itself is a sacred environment in that its particularity to a specific family gives the members meaning by providing the values of security, belonging and appreciation. So it is then that space itself is a meaning-maker.

CONCLUSION—THE CENTRAL POINT IN CONSCIOUSNESS

In *The Sacred and Profane*, Eliade writes of a reference point at the center of sacred space around which experience is organized. An example is the totem pole, which joins together the component areas of the universe. The totem pole, while it exists extra-mentally, symbolizes a reality that is internalized and becomes a central point in consciousness both in time and space around which mental life revolves. Eliade cites the example of a tribe of primitives who laid down to die when their totem pole was destroyed—they had lost their sense of meaning. In our society, everyone has his own totem.

For far too many that totem is constituted by the job they have. The point here is that at every level of consciousness there is a central reference point around which experience is organized. This point is the stance of the self to the environment, that is to say the self's valuing process. The particulars that become important to us at that reference point are what we call values.

For some people, like Willie Loman in *Death of a Salesman*, the major reference point was work, which comes out of a particular level of consciousness. It was the core value. For a small baby the stance that he takes in the world is one in which he wants his needs satisfied. The primary values that are evident in his behavior will be the acquisition of warmth, physical satisfaction and the mother's breast. Needs in particular play a large part in determining a person's level of consciousness, especially at the earlier stages of life. In this regard the need for meaning is primary and is something that continues throughout human experience.

The person who has never had his security needs adequately met in much of his activity regardless of its specific nature will be seeking security because it is so basic a need. This need will become the central point of his consciousness and the acquisition of it will be that which gives him meaning. If a man is an accomplished chemist or a physicist and still hungers for security even his professional life will be organized around that central need.

We have looked at the concept of value and valuing as being those choices behind the acts we perform. To value is to prioritize so that we give meaning to our lives. We noted that the stance of the self is one of prioritizing rather than the picking out of the specific value. We looked extensively at what stance means to the environment and self. But central to the valuing operation is the process of meaning-making that enhances the development of man.

The question of meaning-making is central to all the valuing process and gets at the heart of the question of the development of consciousness. Those choices that enhance man are basically those choices we would categorize under "ought," all those choices we would designate as moral. In order to understand more deeply the relationship of meaning to our needs and to those values we ought to choose for the creative enhancing of man we have to look at the development of consciousness. That is the purpose of the next chapter.

CHAPTER III

THE DEVELOPMENT OF CONSCIOUSNESS

GIACOMETTI, Alberto *Chariot*, (1950). Bronze, 57 x 26 x 26 1/8″. Collection, The Museum of Modern Art, New York. Purchase.

To achieve critical consciousness of the fact that it is necessary to be the "owner of one's own labor," that labor "constitutes part of the human person," and that "a human being can neither be sold nor can he sell himself" is to go a step beyond the deception of palliative solutions. It is to engage in authentic transformation of reality in order, by humanizing that reality, to humanize man.

Paulo Freire

INTRODUCTION

Consciousness

In order to get at the heart of what values and valuing is about we have to understand human consciousness. The fact is that the way in which we choose values, the very values that we choose, how we rank them and the way we define a particular value is dictated totally by our perception of the world around us. The manner in which we perceive the world is what we call consciousness, which changes with the maturing process. That is to say consciousness is developmental. There are four phases of development of consciousness.

Needs

Man's most basic ongoing enterprise is building his own world. This is equally true whether one thinks of mankind as a whole or of the individual man. First, man enhanced his world by modifying the environment to meet his own needs. And that process has continued uninterrupted to our own time. Buildings, cities, states and social institutions of many varied purposes are external expressions of man's unending devotion to world construction.

For the individual man, world construction is largely an internal mental operation involving both cognitive and affective faculties and relying upon whatever skills each man brings to this task. Each man originally enters a world constructed by others but eventually involves himself in either a remodeling operation or in major reconstruction. The world each man builds takes its shape from that man's values, his meaning system and his world view. In a word it takes shape from that man's level of consciousness.

Perception

Any attempt at understanding a man's behavior then must deal with his perception of the world, which is developmental and subject to continual reassessment. The way in which one views the world at age five and the values that one chooses will hardly enable one to perform productively in an adult world. The meaning system of an Australian aborigine will be of little use to a 20th century New Yorker in coping with the complexities of his chaotic environment. A pre-Copernican mind set is not suitable for a post-Darwinian man.

World View of the Child

Imagine the world view of a young child. His interest is restricted to those things that can satisfy his self-centered needs. Consequently his world is narrow, need oriented and very physical. He prizes (values) his own security and all that contributes to his bodily well-being. Hopefully his world view will someday undergo considerable expansion. His interest in the immediate and self-centered will give way to cosmic-centered long-range goals. His values will not be generated by selfish needs but by a genuine enthusiasm for the welfare of society.

Phases of Consciousness

Such transformation cannot happen simply or suddenly; it involves a complex process of human development. It is because of this complexity that only a confluent theory of value development is adequate for the task of accounting for the imagined transformations. For the child with his now egocentric perspective to become a well-developed adult with a cosmic perspective will require the gradual acquisition of many varied skills, skills that equip him to function productively in society, skills that enable him to live fruitfully with other men and most importantly a skilled imagination that puts him in touch with creative alternatives to the existing order.

The acquisition of these skills in the transformation process can be achieved slowly only by passing through a number of phases of development. We call these "Phases of Consciousness," and each has its own set of values and its own meaning system reflecting its world view.

THE DEVELOPMENTAL PHASES OF CONSCIOUSNESS

A Story

The following story will serve to illustrate the phases.
There was once a small boy by the name of Galahad

who was locked in a small bare room in a tower of the west wing of a huge red and yellow granite castle. He had been confined there since birth. As he grew older his yearnings to escape increased. The room had but one door and a barred window that overlooked a beautiful blue sea. Every day he would look out of the window with awe at the long yellow beaches and the sea breaking upon the sand. He would gaze across the bay and watch the trees bending in the wind. Each year he would wait for the flowers to grow around the castle.

Each day as he grew older he tried vainly to open his room door, which appeared to him to be held fast by a solitary sliding latch on his side of the door. But the latch would never budge. Then one day his efforts met with some slight success— the latch moved about an inch. Each day thereafter it gave a little more until one day it released completely and the door came open.

Galahad timidly and apprehensively went through the doorway into a very large hall that at first glance seemed to have no exit. He examined each wall, searching for some escape hatch, when he spied an opening that appeared to be a laundry chute. He crawled into the opening and fell for what seemed to be an endless distance and landed unhurt in a dark moist tunnel. Slowly he edged his way along a wall of the tunnel for what seemed like hours until again he fell headlong and landed on firmer ground. He saw a light coming from a room ahead.

When he entered the room he discovered he had stumbled into a gigantic kitchen at the far side of which was a sizable window. Worn out from his efforts to get free and fearless of the consequences he dived out of the window.

Galahad's glee in discovering himself sprawled on a sun-drenched beach found expression in unrestrained yells of delight. He leaped to his feet and romped along the beach nearly delirious with delight at the experience of freedom amidst the limitless expanse of sand and sea. No walls controlled his direction now.

Finally an exhausted Galahad threw himself down on the sand and looked back toward the castle. To his amazement he discovered that it was a sand castle only two feet high and that three young children were just putting the finishing touches on it. At that moment a huge wave came rushing ashore and destroyed it. The children were quite upset and ready to give up on their castle-building project.

Galahad suddenly felt master of the situation and went up to the children, confident that together they could build a new castle that the sea would not destroy.

After the new castle was completed he sat down and enchanted the children with his storytelling. And so it was that his fame grew and he became known as the storyteller of the beach.

Stages of Consciousness

The story is a symbol of one person's process of growing up; it is a symbolic experience of a journey through consciousness. We put it here because it illustrates a developmental view of the phases of human consciousness which follows:

Phase I

The consciousness of the small child who encounters the world as mystery is depicted by Galahad's wonder as he stares in awe at creation from his window in the castle. He has no way of dealing with it or understanding it but is struck by its beauty. Also this primitive world view is typified by the children of the beach who lack the skills needed to cope with the world that they are creating, namely the castle they are building. So this is the world of consciousness of the child who greets the world continually as new and surprising, looking at it with a sense of awe and wonder. The world rather than the child is in control.

Phase II

As the child develops he begins to view the world as a problem with which he can deal only if he acquires certain basic skills. It is a world full of difficulties. The individual at this phase of consciousness struggles through life controlled by forces outside of himself. Existence itself is a struggle to solve life's problems. This level of consciousness with its many puzzles appears in the dream of Galahad locked in the room and wandering through the labyrinthe of tunnels, attempting to escape from the castle. The several falls he takes symbolize his lack of control over life's direction.

Phase III
The third phase of consciousnes is reached as the individual achieves and experiences freedom and independence. At this stage a person becomes self-directed, no longer living like a puppet on a string in the grip of outside forces. The dream symbol for this phase of consciousness is Galahad's escape from the castle and his joyful cavorting along the beach.

Phase IV
In the final phase of consciousness, pictured by the individual's awareness of the universe in its entirety, he sees his total life as a sand castle with which he can play. The beach symbolizes the whole world, the castle being only a part of that world. This is the first time that he sees the totality of reality in perspective. But the new child is a child reborn with the skills of the adult, thereby enabling him to cope with the world. At this stage of consciousness the person devotes himself to constructing a new world. Obviously Galahad achieves this level as he helps the children build a new castle and shares his imagination by becoming a storyteller.

THE FOUR PHASES
Let us now view the phases in more detail. First we need to be conscious that the phases of consciousness in the story are value-related. As a person grows he rearranges his value priorities; faced with a problem of escaping from the castle, Galahad had different priorities from the children playing in the sand simply because his view of the world—his consciousness—was different.

The Value Process

In the previous chapter the value process was defined as follows: "The process by which self, responding to various environments (people, objects and so on) takes a stance and selects its priorities expressed through its behavior in such a way as to find meaning and enhance the development of man." This definition is developmental in that the person's perception (consciousness) of his environment changes, as in the story. His process of selecting priorities and his behavior undergo adjustment. At any given moment in a person's life his phase of consciousness is expressed in a particular value-stance towards his environment.

The following diagram helps us to see this in a little more detail.

DIAGRAM 5

World View or Basic Perspectives	Basic Needs	Basic Values
World as Mystery	Food	Security
P		
H Physical/Existence	Warmth	Survival
A I		
S Self as Center	Physical Affection	Pleasure
E		
	To explore	Wonder
World As Problem	Approval	Belonging
P		
H Social/Interaction	Skills	Work
A II		Self Competence
S Self As Belonging	Success	
E		Self Worth
World As Project & Invention		
P	Personal Authority	Independence
H	Freedom	Equity-Rights
A III Conscious/Acting	Dignity	Service
S	Integrity (honesty)	Creation
E Self as Independent		
World As Mystery Cared For	"Convivial" Technology	
P	Wholeness	"Convivial Tools"
H	Community	Harmony
A IV Interdependence/	Ecology-Personal	Interdependence
S Making	Community	Intimacy
E Selves as Life Giver	Congruence	Synergy

With these dimensions of consciousness in mind we can now examine the four phases as diagramed above. They represent four phases of consciousness, and are a mental construct based on observation of human behavior. A phase of consciousness as presented here has to do with the way a person orders his experience, to what he gives priority, what needs control his attention and how he makes sense of his life. It is the individual's perception of the world. Thus his world view indicates a person's stage of development, and each phase produces a distinct world view.

Before we review the phases in depth let us keep the following in mind in reference to the above diagram.

1. The phases are developmental I through IV. This means that a person will not develop the second or third phase of consciousness until he has first fully experienced the first phase. That is to say the Phase IV consciousness is only possible after the progressive experience of the first three.
2. The four phases can be differentiated on the basis of age, maturity (mental and emotional) and skills. Phase I thus normally corresponds to the first stage of development of a young child, taking into account both maturity and skills. A child normally passes beyond this phase by the age of six. A person usually cannot move out of the second phase until he is at least sixteen. It would be unusual for anyone to reach the fourth phase before the age of forty; so Phase III covers a wide age span from the late teens on. In our society few people ever move beyond the third phase; in fact most people remain at an upper phase two position.

   Although there could be other phases beyond the fourth phase they are not within the vision of our society at this point in history so the first phase depicts the most primitive phase of development of an adult and also the first stage of the child. On the other hand the fourth phase depicts the most developed persons in society, characterized by those ideals that most societies acknowledge as worthy of pursuit. These would be people like a Ghandi or a Socrates.
3. The above diagram also shows the basic needs operative in persons at the particular phase of consciousness and gives some examples of the kinds of values that a person of that phase would choose. These particular aspects will be dealt with in detail in the next

chapter. They are placed here in order to illustrate the fact that consciousness, needs and valuing are interrelated and never in fact are separable. Let us now look at the phases of consciousness in more detail.

Phase I—The World as Mystery—The Self as Center

This is generally the level of consciousness of the young child. His perspective is egocentric and he sees the whole world as there just for him. There is a scene typifying him in A.A. Milne's *Winnie the Pooh*.

Winnie the Pooh

The little round bear is hungry and is looking for his favorite meal—honey. He looks up and sees a bee. He says to himself, "If I follow the bee to the tree, I will find honey for me." Winnie then goes on to conclude that if there is honey in the tree, because he likes honey, "the honey must be there for me." As the story proceeds the little bear climbs up the tree and of course gets stung by the bee and has to run for his life.

The point of the story is that it depicts what we mean by the self-centered act. The self as center here does not mean that the individual is selfish in any moral sense; rather it indicates the person feels that the world was created for him. Winnie the Pooh concluded that because there was a bee and a tree and honey and because he liked honey those things must have been for him!

A similar experience familiar to many of us is one's going into a friend's house with a small child who then helps himself to candy. The child does not think this is wrong. Because there is candy in the house and he likes candy, it must be for him. At the age of one or two, this is not a moral question or a question of bad discipline but rather a fact of consciousness of the child.

The Copernican Revolution

In the history of science it was Nicolhas Copernicus who around 1500 demonstrated that the sun ruled the family of the planets and was at the center of our system, not the earth. Early Greek astronomers, particularly Ptolemy, had stated that the earth was situated in the middle of the heavens. In short Copernicus started the revolution that denied the centrality of both the earth and man in the universe.

The world at this level is perceived as being mysterious. One is struck by the awesomeness of nature. I remember several years ago visiting Tepotzotlan in Mexico. The small village stood at the foot of a gigantic rock. One might describe it as a mountain that was sheared flat on one side. At the top was an old wooden cross that one could see on clear days. The feeling as one walked into the village was one of being overwhelmed by nature itself. One experienced the awesomeness of the creation itself, a quality that is natural to the child and hopefully maintains itself in the adult.

In the world of the child, when he is very much the center of his own reality, all the dangers and things that might overwhelm him are sublimated into his own delightful fantasies. It is the world of the child where everything is related to his or her own delight. This of course is wonderfully portrayed in *Alice in Wonderland* by Lewis Carroll. We remember for example the Mad-Hatter's Tea Party.

The Tea Party

There was a table set out under a tree in front of the house, and the March Hare and the Hatter were having tea at it: A dormouse was sitting between them, fast asleep, and the other three were resting their elbows on it, and talking over its head.

"Very uncomfortable for the Dormouse," thought Alice; "only, as it is asleep, I suppose it doesn't mind."

The table was a very large one, but the three were all crowded together at one corner of it.

"No room! No room!" they cried out when they saw Alice coming.

"There is plenty of room!" said Alice indignantly, as she sat down in a large armchair at one end of the table.

"Have some wine," the March Hare said in an encouraging tone.

Alice looked around the table but there was nothing on it but tea. "I don't see any wine," she remarked.

"There isn't any," said the March Hare.

"Then it wasn't very civil of you to offer it," says Alice angrily.

"It wasn't very civil of you to sit down without being invited," says the March Hare.

"I didn't know it was your table," says Alice; "It's laid for a great many more than three."

"Your hair wants cutting," said the Hatter. He had been looking at Alice for sometime with great curiosity, and this was his first speech.

This world of wonder and mystery where attention spans are short and nothing is really threatening is the world of innocence. This is a world incidentally that has often been carried into the adult world. We should be reminded however that such innocence, while suitable in the child who in an accepting way lacks the skills to cope with his environment, becomes a problem for an adult.

The following essay on *Naive and Sentimental Poetry* by Schiller reminds us of the fact.

There are moments in our lives when we dedicate a kind of love and tender respect to nature and plants, minerals, animals, and landscapes, as well as to human nature in children, and the customs of country folk, and to the primitive world, not because it gratifies our senses, nor yet because it satisfies our understanding and taste (the very opposite can occur in both instances), rather, simply *because it is nature*. Every person of a finer cast who is not totally lacking in feeling experiences this when he wanders in the open air, when he stays in the country, or lingers before the monuments of ancient times; in short, whenever he is surprised in the midst of artificial circumstances and situations by the sight of simple nature.

Phase I—Adult

The power center at this first level of consciousness is outside the self. Needs are dominant in determining one's behavior. An adult on this level may freely consent not to follow impulse, but he is so influenced by these egocentric impulses that he rarely resists them. The person has few skills, either personal or environmental. As a result the choices of an adult on this level center on survival, security and physical pleasure. As a self-centered being the person is aware primarily of the self and its preservation. When he is not threatened he is aware of the self and its satisfaction. That drive for satisfaction becomes visible in curiosity and wonder and the need for physical affection.

Spy Movies

Many of our modern spy movies, those with James Bond and Matt Helm, are built on the psychology of Phase I attitudes towards life. The keynotes of a good spy movie then are sex as physical affection, danger, survival and a sense of meaning and accomplishment by overcoming one's enemy and gaining security.

The Protectors

A typical example of this was a popular television series from England called *The Protectors*. All the introductions to this series, which was a half-hour spy thriller, started the same way. First the viewer heard the dramatic music and then saw a picture of a hero looking out a window and tucking a revolver into his belt. The gun of course symbolized survival. He was basically at war. The main emphasis was preservation. He was at the same time well dressed and affluent, personal meaning coming from the fact that he was held high in the opinion of government officials and was much sought after. In the next scene a car came roaring down the street, turned, rolled over and burst into flames. This symbol of danger placed the viewer in the grip of the need to survive.

In the very next scene we saw our hero beating some eggs and sitting down to a hearty breakfast. Instantly this was followed by a picture of a beautiful woman with whom he walked. The image of course is of sex and food, the basic gratification of physical needs. In short we had here a Phase I psychology that blended the excitement of wonder with the basic needs for survival and physical gratification.

Greek Tragedy

A survival-oriented consciousness centering around the need to preserve one's life is of course basic in literature in the great tragedies, such as those written by Shakespeare and the early Greek writers. The following quotation is from *Electra*, the work of Euripides written about 413 B.C. The story is one of deep emotions revolving around a history of survival and war, specifically the war of Greece against Troy. Agamemnon is the general-in-chief of the Greeks. His wife, Clytemnestra, had been false to him and with her lover Aegisthus planned his murder. The old general however had two children, Electra and Orestes, who managed to escape. In the play Electra was given to a farmer who looked after her. She has now grown older and is soon to meet her brother Orestes. Together they plot revenge and kill the queen mother. This is a theme found in many fantasies down to our present time even in a fairy tale like *Snow White and the Seven Dwarfs*, both stories incarnating evil in a wicked woman. The following passage is the opening soliloquy by the farmer who has Electra under his protection.

> Argos, old bright floor of the world, "Inachus" pouring tides
> King Agamemnon once on a thousand ships hoisted
> the war god here and sailed across to Troy.
> He killed the monarch of the Land of Illium,
> Priam; he sacked the glorious city of Dardanus;
> He came home safe to Argos and high on the towering shrines
> Nailed up the massive loot of Barbary for the gods.
> So, over there he did well. But in his own house
> He died in ambush planned for him by his own wife
> Clytemnestra and by her lover Aegisthus' hand.

And so we see in the beginning of the farmer's address that the scene is set. The general, a war hero, returning home out of this whole atmosphere of survival is killed by his wife's lover. One is then introduced to feelings of violence and injustice. The farmer continued, referring to Electra:

> Electra waited motionless in her father's house
> but when the burning season of young ripeness took her,
> then the great princess of the land of Greece came begging
> her bridal. Aegisthus was afraid. Afraid her son
> if nobel in blood will punish Agememnon's death.
> He held her in the house sundered from every love.
> Yet, even guarded so, she filled his nights with fear
> less she in secret to some prince might still bear sons;
> he laid his plans to kill her. But her mother though
> savage in soul, then saved her from Aegisthus' blow.
> The lady found excuse for murdering her husband
> but flinches from killing a child, afraid of the world's contempt.

Later Aegisthus framed a new design. He swore
to any man who captured Agememnon's son
running to exile and murdered him, a price of gold.
Electra-he gave her to me as a gift, to hold
her as my wife."

Self Preservation

This world of preservation so well depicted in the tragedy points clearly to the dynamic interrelationship between the
self and the environment that we spoke of previously. The environment of war and violence has set the scene for the ensuing
tragedy; the dominant level of consciousness of the characters
in Phase I and the need for preservation assuming primacy.
This theme is carried on so well by Shakespeare and in the
opening monologue of *King Richard III* or *Macbeth* in its entirety.

Survival in the Corporation

In these works of Shakespeare, as in *Electra*, we see a
tragedy of violence, of survival set up by a war environment.
This points to an underlying truism, namely that values are
reinforced by the environment. Put in a modern setting, Robert
Townsend, writing for the Center for the Democratic Institutions, has the following to say about some of the reinforcing attitudes of modern corporations. Concerning the development of
an executive in some of these corporations he says the following:

> The best two guarantees that the chief executive officer will
> work full time are hunger and fear. He has to hunger for the
> company to succeed; and he has to have so much of his own
> money and ego tied-up in the company that fear of failure is
> constantly with him. Given those circumstances, almost any-
> body can become an excellent chief executive. I have seen
> three cases recently where people with no previous manage-
> ment experience became outstanding chief executives. But all
> three, in addition to having required hunger and fear, com-
> pletely abandoned their former specialities and devoted them-
> selves totally to listening to other people and making deci-
> sions.

Summary

In conclusion the Phase I world view is centered around:

    1) Self in its need for basic sense gratification

    2) Self in its need for preservation

    3) Self as innocent without skills

The need for meaning at this level is tied to the need for survival and security. In other words things make sense to a child or adult at this level when they fit his need to survive. About the only significant space is bodily space.

Basic Needs

So anything that contributes to the satisfaction of the basic needs is a value to a person of this level—food, warmth, affections and the mother who supplies these things.

The person on this level is innocent of any long-range planning. Actions are reactive rather than creative. Goals are immediate and concrete. Activity involving others tends to be manipulative, such as of the mother when needing to be fed or eliminating enemies by murder in the tragedies. Even the explorative activity of the child in response to a sense of wonder tends to be egocentric.

Most of the conflict in the child's life results from the fact that in reality the world is not just there for the child but others as well; for example a mother's involvement in other things of interest to her prevents her from responding to the child's every need or desire. Or the child encounters another child who takes away his toys. These are growth experiences that aid the child in moving to the next level where the world now is seen as there for others too.

Adults still functioning largely at this phase view things egocentrically. Intellectually they may be aware that the world is there for others too, but they do not let that awareness interfere with their need-oriented behavior. They tend to deal with others in a manipulative way by being insensitive to other's needs. In this regard they differ from the child only in that their manipulative skills are superior. This was well illustrated in *Electra*.

A Story Line

We might imagine Phase I consciousness in its most creative stage as a man standing naked and newborn in a friendly environment of grass, trees and shrubs. He is curious about what he sees; everything is new and interesting to him. Then the winter comes and he is confronted by an environment that is no longer passive but moves against him and threatens his very survival. This level then is depicted in the twofold experience of mystery and awe on the one hand and the need for preservation on the other.

But man is a rational intelligent being. He differs from the animal in that as his consciousness developed he was able to recognize that survival required cooperation. So he moved beyond the physical realm to a level of social cooperation. Let us now look in detail at the second level.

DIAGRAM 6

		World As Mystery	Food		Security
P					
H		Physical/Existence	Warmth		Survival
A	I				
S		Self as Center	Physical Affection		Pleasure
E			To Explore		Wonder
		World As Problem	Approval		Belonging
P					
H		Social/Interaction	Skills		Work
A	II				
S		Self as Belonging	Success		Self Competence
E					Self Worth

Phase II—The World as Problem—Self as Belonging

At this phase the person sees the world as a problem to be solved. The basic problem that man faces as he attains this level of consciousness is how to get on in the world—how to belong and how to acquire the skills to survive and achieve.

World of "Them"

This phase of consciousness then is an extension of the first phase, but from self-preservation the person moves to the problem of coping with and controlling the environment. This is the world of the child five and six years of age and up. The world is seen by this person as being controlled by "them." If it is a child "they" tend to be parents and teachers. As he grows older the adult at this phase will see "them" as being the politicians, the bishops, those in "authority." To be successful a person therefore needs "their" approval.

It takes little imagination for a person to realize that the best way to win "their" approval is to acquire the skills and the self-competence that school, society and parents approve.

World as Social

A central characteristic of consciousness at Phase II is that the person's world is enlarged beyond his self-centered needs to include the social dimensions of life. The world is now there for others as well as for himself; in fact a major constituent of the world is the way it is perceived by others, both by individuals, and at a later stage by institutions. The world that enters his consciousness is one established by others into which the individual must fit himself if he is to experience a sense of personal worth.

Self Esteem

The central reference point in consciousness arises from the basic need for self esteem, which is achieved by becoming useful as a participant in the regular activity of the existing order. So belongingness and being accepted by others are key values. The person organizes his experiences around this need to achieve self esteem by meeting the expectations of significant others: family, peers and established institutions. The pursuit of this central need gives life meaning and order.

Here is a portion of a letter from the *Fox Fire Book* that is an expression of this phase of consciousness:

> we had our crib full. that lasted till the next fall. everybody in the neighborhood come and my mother cooked a big dinner for the crowd. seams as every body was happie to. i remember when my mother had to cook one the fireplace. we played out out biggest Snow ever com. we had a Spring to cary out watter from and my dad had to take his Shovel and ditch out a way through the Snow for us to get the Spring. the Snow was waist deep. (The periods were added to make it more understandable.)

Glasser: Basic Needs

This quotation from a letter illustrates the sense of

belonging that is so much a need in every family. William
Glasser has built up a system of pyschotherapy around this
need factor and calls it "Reality Therapy." He speaks of the
basic needs of the human being in the following manner:

> "The fulfillment of the physiological needs of food, warmth,
> and rest are rarely the concern of psychiatry."

This would be a Phase I operation. He continues:

> Psychiatry must be concerned with two basic psychological
> needs: the need to love and be loved and the need to feel that
> we are worthwhile to ourselves and others. Helping patients
> fulfill these two needs is the basis of 'Reality Therapy.'

Elsewhere Glasser introduces this subject of basic needs in the
following manner:

> Before discussing the basic needs themselves, we must clarify
> the process through which they are fulfilled. Briefly we must
> be involved with other people, one at the very minimum, but
> hopefully many more than one. At all times in our lives we
> must have at least one person who cares about us and for
> whom we care for ourselves.

Playing by Rules

In the world perceived as established and run by others
a person must play by the accepted rules if he is to be successful in the eyes of others. Not the least of those rules is that
everyone must contribute in a productive way to society's well-
being. In this regard a person feels a need to develop his interpersonal and instrumental skills and to engage in a useful and
marketable activity.

Thus work as productive labor is a high value at this
stage. This makes a person feel useful and provides him with a
conviction that he has earned his right to belong. The combination of the approval of significant others and his own awareness of being skilled produced in him a sense of self worth. But
as at the first phase power and authority are judged to reside
primarily outside the self in "them."

Skills for Growth

The person at this phase is still in a dependent relationship to his environment. He begins to seek to control the environment through work by developing the appropriate skills. Society and a good educational pedagogy provide a secure setting for the child through such institutions as schools and hospitals.

Meaning is not acquired through the satisfaction of his senses but rather through the experience of cooperation with others that is reinforced through social approval. Thus a child goes to school where good behavior is rewarded, and at the same time where he is taught the skills to become a competent individual, to cope with and manage the environment on his own.

Central to this phase of development then is the value of self-esteem, a combination of a sense of competence and adequacy and an appreciation of one's own intrinsic worth. The person learns that he is of value both in himself through his sense of belonging and as a professionally competent individual through his educational experience. He learns to feel "at home" in society.

Reinforcing Values of Work and Success

The problem that can arise at this phase of consciousness is that a person who lives in a society that reinforces the kinds of values typical of that stage may fail to reach the next phase. In other words if too much emphasis in placed on success and producing results a person may conclude that self-worth comes only from work. This kind of distortion sees competence in work as the way to achieve a sense of belonging. This is well described in the story *Nog's Vision*, set in a land of strange creatures called "Pricklies." They are little round creatures with pricklies sticking out, very much like a porcupine.

> Another odd thing about Pricklies was that they all came in different colors depending on what their job was. A Pricklie's job was the most important thing in the world to him. It was so important, in fact, that a Pricklie's job was what his name was.
>
> The King was white with red pricklies and he was called —well, King Pricklie. He was the only red and white Pricklie in the land. The three king advisors were gray and, yes they were called Advisor Pricklies.
>
> There were several Doctor Pricklies. They were all

white and sat all day in the hospital making babies and putting casts on broken Pricklies. Those who were pink wrote newspapers or made the movies and television shows; they are called Telepricklies. All the brown Pricklies were policemen and they kept law and order and made sure no foreigners came into the valley. The Pricklies who build the buildings were silver, while purple Pricklies made clothing for Pricklies to wear. Food was grown by the green Pricklies.

It was a most pleasant land. Everybody knew his place. Everybody did something. In fact, everybody was quite, quite satisfied. But it had not always been that way.

You see, many, many years ago when the first Pricklies lived, they weren't quite so satisfied. They were so prickly it was difficult to make friends with each other. Why, Pricklies couldn't kiss or even shake hands because their pricklies got in the way. So over the years they learned not to sit close to each other.

One might evaluate Pricklies with the familiar saying "all work and no play makes Jack a dull boy." The point is that our society, through its advertising and the Protestant work ethic, has emphasized the importance of work, imbalancing the other major needs at this phase like the sense of belonging and community that are equally important.

Space

It is evident that at this level significant space expands considerably. Social and work space are especially important, as is institutional space. Sacred space, at least at the ritual stage, is generally prized because it represents institutions that are concerned with one's sense of self-esteem. In many churches the sense of belonging is a major component of the Sunday morning service.

Initially a person at this phase devotes himself so totally to learning how to attain a sense of self-esteem and competence in the world as established by others that he has little time or interest in considering alternatives to the existing order. Once his skills enable him to feel at home in the present order he is free to contemplate alternatives to the world as constituted. He is then ready to consider a move to the next phase.

A Story Extended

At the first phase of development man was naked in the

environment, born as it were into an Eden, awed by the beauty of nature. As winter came and the elements moved against him, he moved into a condition of survival that called for social cooperation that forced him into the second phase of development.

The second phase of development is a new consciousness, as we have seen, a consciousness of the need for social interaction and cooperation, a need for interpersonal skills, a need for a sense of one's own value in order that one might cope with the environment in a constructive manner. This phase of consciousness is quite different from the first in that the choices made by an individual are based on social cooperation and not on ego needs.

So as we progress now and try to understand what the next phase will be, we see that this man has minimally satisfied his needs to cope with the environment. He must find meaning elsewhere. He then begins to find himself advancing into the third phase of consciousness. He experiences a need to move beyond the decisions and requirements of "they" to independent action where he makes his own choices and decisions.

DIAGRAM 7

	World as Project and Invention	**Personal Authority**	**Independence**
P		**Freedom**	**Equity-Rights**
H	**Conscience/Acting**		
A III		**Dignity**	**Service**
S			
E	**Self As Independent**	**Integrity (Honesty)**	**Creation**

Phase III—World as Project and Invention—Self as Independent

At this phase a person ceases to be so dependent on what is in the world as established by others. This happens basically because a person no longer needs self worth as affirmed by others since that value is now an internalized part of his system. He finds meaning no more in an environment supplying the kind of reinforcement necessary to develop a second phase of consciousness. As a source of meaning living up to the expectations of others assumes less importance than being what he himself wants to be. Internal and personal expectations replace external ones. The self begins to take charge.

Self Directed

The point around which consciousness revolves at this phase is the need to be self-directed. Doing something simply because another expects it or orders it ceases to be meaningful and is no longer a value around which to organize one's life. A personal sense of power and authority replaces institutional control or behavior. Consequently creativity and imagination are prized. A new-found sense of honesty makes conformity hypocritical.

Space Widened

At this level of consciousness space has been widened. At the first phase space is restricted to those things, those objects, those places that supply one's needs. At the second phase of consciousness the person is very much aware of that space that gives him a sense of belonging. The person is aware of family and peers and those involved in his success at work. But now for the first time the person's choices originate within, and as a consequence his choices expand his world. A person now becomes sensitive to the rights of others and acquires a concern for justice. He literally expands himself into a larger society.

Ira Progoff writing (in *The Symbolic and the Real*) about Socrates, that great Greek figure who continually challenged the mind with his questioning, says the following of him in reference to his defense in the court at Athens before his final condemnation and death:

> Socrates there described his intimate feeling of why it was important for him to live his life as he had been living it. It was not a question of intellectual philosophy, but of a calling that came to him from two sources, an outward source and an inward source, which Socrates understood as ultimately not separate at all from one another. The outward source of his calling was the gods of the Greek Pantheon; and to this the Oracle at Delphi testified. The inward source of his calling was the oracle within himself. He described this as the "divine faculty

of which the internal oracle is the source." To Socrates the inward and the outward were two aspects of a single principle. It was in the light of this unity that he could state his belief "that there were gods in a sense higher than any of my accusers' belief in them."

Conscience

Progoff is speaking about that time in life when individuals have to be themselves, have to make statements because an inner voice calls them to a mission to be true to themselves rather than being guided by external voices in society or by the majority opinion.

In terms of the phase of consciousness we would say that the person can do no other because he has moved beyond that level that gave him meaning through the approval of others. Meaning is only present to him when he listens to his own inner voice. It is then at this phase that the consciousness develops for the first time. The following diagram illustrates this in terms of the four phases:

DIAGRAM 8

PHASE I	PHASE II	PHASE III	PHASE IV
Ego (Dominant) + The World	"They"	"I"	"We"
Authority outside self		Authority within self	

In viewing the four phases of consciousness we see a tremendous difference between the first two and the last two. Meaning for the first two comes basically from what is given from without. At the last two phases authority is from within and consequently what is meaningful to the person also comes from within. We have to be careful here not to confuse internal authority with a lack of cooperation. This does not imply a radical independence in which one does not listen to any other individual, but only that one must consciously assume responsibility for the final decision himself.

Kohlberg

Lawrence Kohlberg points to this clearly in his levels of moral development. He refers to Level III (our Phase III) as the post-conventional autonomous or principled level and says the following of it:

> The individual makes a clear effort to define moral values and principles to have validity and application apart from the authority the groups or persons holding these principles, and apart from the individual's own identification with these groups.

He then goes on to speak of the social contract legalistic orientation. At this level a person listens to the voice of law and order, but only after criticism and careful evaluation. A person is beginning to make meaningful acts of his own. Kohlberg then talks about the conscience stage as follows:

> The universal ethical principle orientation. Right is defined by the decision of conscience and in accord with self-chosen ethical principles that appeal to logical comprehensiveness, universality, and consistency. These principles are abstract and ethical. (The Golden Rule, the categorical imperative); they are not concrete moral rules like the Ten Commandments. At heart, these are universal principles of justice, of the reciprocity and equality of human rights, and of respect for the dignity of human beings as individual persons.

This phase of consciousness is one that covers the condition of human development that we normatively speak of as maturity. It is the stage where a man honestly and clearly is able to evaluate himself and to make moral decisions out of his own conscience.

It is a phase of consciousness where authority is primarily interior, which means that one has the skills and self-confidence to accept one's own goodness. One is beyond the need for approval from others and has achieved sufficient security and all those other attributes of the first two phases of consciousness that equip one to make clear and responsible decisions of one's own. A person at this phase of conscience begins to move towards others and concerns himself with the justice and rights of society.

Andras Angyal puts it as follows:

The over-all pattern of personality functions can be from two
different vantage points. Viewed from one of these vantage
points, the human being seems to be striving basically to assert
and to expand his self-determination. He is an antonomous
being, a self governing entity that asserts itself actively instead
of reacting passively like a physical body to the impacts of the
surrounding world. In an objective fashion this tendency can
be described as follows, the human being is an autonomous
unity that, acting upon the surrounding world, molds and modifies it. His life is a resultant of self-determination on the one
hand, and the impact of a surrounding world, the situation, on
the other. Its basic tendency, the trend toward increased autonomy, expresses the person's striving from a state of lesser
self-determination in greater situational influence to a state of
greater self-determination in lesser situational influence.
    Seen from another vantage point, human life reveals a
very different basic pattern from the one described above.
From this point of view the person appears to seek a place for
himself in a larger unit in which he strives to become a part. In
the first tendency we see him struggling for centrality in his
world, trying to mold, to organize, the objects and the events
of his world, to bring them under his own jurisdiction and government. In the second tendency he seems rather to strive to
surrender himself willingly to seek a home for himself and to
become an organic part of something that he conceives as
greater than himself.

This illustrates the crossroads that this phase of consciousness represents. First of all it represents a new consciousness of self as having authority within (see Diagram 8) and second it represents a new expanded consciousness of mankind.

It represents the self for the first time transcending itself
and indicates a movement towards justice and rights for mankind. For example liberation, freedom and independence have
become far more than matters for personal development. They
are also matters for group social action and national liberation.
A clear expression of this mentality is expressed in the Declaration of Independence written 200 years ago.

When in the course of human events, it becomes necessary for
one people to dissolve the political bonds which have connected them with another, and to assume among the powers of the

earth, the separate, and equal station to which the Laws of Nature and of Nature's God entitle them a decent respect for the opinions of mankind requires that they should declare the causes which impel them to the separation.

We hold these truths to be self-evident, that all men are created equal, that they are endowed by their Creator with certain unalienable Rights, that among these are Life, Liberty and the pursuit of Happiness.—

That to secure these Rights, Governments are instituted among men, deriving their powers from the consent of governed.

That whenever any Form of Government becomes destructive of these ends, it is the Right of the People to order or to abolish it, and to institute new Government, laying its foundation on such principles and organizing its powers in such form, as to them shall seem most likely to effect their Safety and Happiness. Prudence, indeed, will dictate that Governments long established should not be changed for light and transient causes; and accordingly all experiences hath shown that mankind are more disposed to suffer, while evils are sufferable, and to right themselves by abolishing the forms to which they are accustomed. But when a long train of abuses and usurpations, pursuing invariably the same Object envices a design to reduce them under absolute Despotism, it is their right, it is their duty, to throw off such Government, and to provide new Guards for future security.

DIAGRAM 9

		World as Mystery Cared For	"Convivial" Technology	"Convivial Tools"
P			**Wholeness**	**Harmony**
H				
A	**IV**		**Community**	**Interdependence**
S		**Interdependence/**		
E		**Making**	**Ecology-Personal Community**	**Intimacy**
		Selves as Life Giver	**Congruence**	**Synergy**

Phase IV—World as Mystery Cared For—Selves as Life Giver

At this phase the person's world undergoes a gigantic expansion and enters consciousness as a series of interrelated tasks to be performed in conjunction with other like-minded men. There is complete transcendance of the self. A person now always acts interdependently in conjunction with other selves.

Self Transcended

The person sees the world as unfinished, its present constitution not nearly as important as its future potentiality. This viewpoint implies no disregard or lack of concern for existing persons or communities even though they too are viewed in their potentiality as much as in their actuality.

The world is seen as a mystery, but one for which man now takes authority. Man chooses, creates and enhances the environment. That is to say man takes authority over the creation and works in a cooperative manner with others and with nature itself in a common interdependent action seeking harmonious balance.

At this phase of consciousness independent actions opposed to interdependent action is no longer seen as valid. At Phase III the human being was viewed very much in terms of person and individual, while at Phase IV the individual is viewed as system. The key to this phase of consciousness is that more than ever before there is much more of a unity between man and tools, and between mankind and his technology.

Eileen Cantin writing on Mounier expresses this as follows:

> The most basic mode of transcedence and the one which paves the way for higher modes is production. By modifying the world around him and making it more and more an objectification of himself, the person extends his physical and, through it, his personal being. He gives himself a new and more extensive body and he gives something of his own humanity to impersonal reality. Transformation of matter implies not only its personalization, but also provides new opportunities for the emergence of the human spirit. As the condition of matter is transformed so are the conditions for the expression and the emergence of the human spirit heightened.

Cantin goes on to say that Mounier admitted that humanity has not yet integrated the experiences of the technological revolu-

tion but insisted that given time this integration will occur.
Mounier also spoke of a second level of transcendence.

> The second level of transcendence is that of which is achieved
> through interpersonal relations. The person is called to surpass
> himself by sharing himself with another person.

That is further put into context in the following:

> A community of persons find its cohesion within a We which
> is itself a Person. The We emerges from the community in
> much the same fashion as the I emerges from its material con-
> ditions, i.e., in response to a call.

In the latter quotations the distinction between "I" and
"We" parallels the distinction between the third and fourth
phases of operation. The point that I want to make here is that
at this fourth phase of consciousness there is a transcendence of
person in the individual sphere moving to a community operation which is related directly to an overall technological revolution.

The key to consciousness at this phase is the integration
of mankind. In education the lines and separations between the
sciences and the arts and so on become nonoperable. There is
an increased need for integration and interdependence. In particular the relationship between personal growth and technology, rather than being separate entities treated in separate
sciences, requires close integration.

R. W. Sperry, in relating future progress to neural advances in science, takes the following stand:

> Advances in the mind-brain sciences of the last few decades
> have substantially narrowed the lattitudes for speculation. In
> particular, accumulating evidence in the neuroscience builds
> up overwhelmingly today to the conviction that conscious
> mental awareness is the property of, and inseparatably tied to,
> the living brain. This is something that modern science points
> to as a sudden reality of our world that we now must face.
> Like the reality of our world that we now must face. Like the
> knowledge of the neurosciences must be taken into count and
> our values and ultimate goals reshaped accordingly. A concept
> of mind and matter emerges that supports a unifying "this-
> world" view of man in nature as a framework of valued guide-

lines. Perhaps more than any other single development, its advances in the last half century and our understanding of the neuro mechanisms of mind and conscious awareness clear the way for a rational approach in the realm of values. This is not to say that the problem of mind-brain relations are fully solved—far from it—but only that by process of elimination the range of realistic answers and the implications has been greatly reduced.

In order for this phase of consciousness to be fully operative technology and the use of tools must become convivial, that is to say every man must become as technically competent as he is skilled in reasoning and personal relationships.

East and West

Critical to this phase of consciousness is an understanding of reality rooted in congruence. The mind sees things in their wholeness and is able to resolve opposites and recognize the presence of harmony as an underlying fact of all natural reality.

Persons at a Phase II consciousness operate primarily on a Newtonian understanding of the world where "every action has an opposite reaction." If we understand enough facts about any given reality we will find that it is somehow mathematically ordered and can be understood in this manner.

Personal Harmony

In recent years with the discoveries in Quantum physics we understand that a constant state of order and balance as static is not necessarily the true state of reality at all! Harmony, which implies movement and tension and not balance or equilibrium, is fundamental to nature. From the East as well as in the growing developments in our Western psychology there comes a great deal of information and numerous practices that can enable a person to find harmony in personal terms. Closely related to this harmony is the value of interdependence that operates on the physical, the social and the interpsychic levels. For example on the physical level one hand operates independently from the other. However they are both interdependent and rooted in the harmony of the body itself.

Socially three men working in harmonious interdependence can do far more than as three independent units. Until recently Westerners never took very seriously the skills of meditation and physical relaxation as taught by the East. Nyanaponika Thera says:

> The Nations of the world seem unthinkingly to assume that their reserves of strength are inexhaustable. Against such unwarranted belief stands the universal Law of Impermanence, the fact of incessant Change, that has been emphasized so strongly by the Buddha. This law of Impermanence includes the fact shown by history and by daily experience, that the external opportunities for material and spiritual regeneration, and the vital strength and inner readiness required of it, are never without limits, either for individuals or for nations.

Publications such as *The Heart of Buddhist Meditation* are very helpful and speak to the anxiety of our times. But clearly history has shown that this method has failed to regenerate the societies where it is practiced. Those countries where the Buddha arose are in incredible trouble because of their material and social needs. One also has to recognize that much of their poverty has been a result of their religious laws. Clearly the religious mind, Eastern or Western, can say much about the need for harmony in the individual life. However one who reaches this phase of consciousness also realizes that this harmony has to be extended to technology and society at large. Inner harmony must be integrated with social harmony through technology.

Technology: Social Harmony

At this phase then the reference point in consciousness around which experience is organized is a commitment to creative cosmic transformation. Cosmos include the "micro" as well as "macro." In other words the person's concern with worldwide problems like poverty does not imply a lack of involvement with people on the local scene. On the contrary this commitment to building a better world begins locally with the fostering of the spirit of mutual dedication among like-minded persons.

Where independence was a key value at the previous

phase interdependence is primary here. Harmony and congruence are cherished as values in one's close personal relationships and in the cosmos as a whole. Another basic value is synergy, the conviction that several individuals may cooperate on a joint creative project with resulting effects that far exceed the sum of their individual efforts.

The bringing together of individual harmony and the technological process is spoken to in what Ivan Illich in *Tools for Conviviality* calls "Convivial Reconstruction." By conviviality is meant the opposite of the need for industrial production. It is a word that means autonomous and creative intercourse among persons and their environment.

> I consider conviviality to be individual freedom realized in personal interdependence and, as such, an intrinsic ethical value. I believe that in any society, as conviviality is reduced below a certain level no amount of industrial productivity can effectively satisfy the needs that it creates among society's members.

Convivial Tools

The basic subject matter of Illich's thesis is "tools." The problem is one of consciousness. Society needs to recognize that tools and technology have moved beyond the capability of the individual so as to impose upon him all sorts of demands. The average man is controlled by his tools.

Illich wants to place the tool back in the hands of the man. He raises some questions as, "Why do we need automobiles that go faster than twenty miles per hour?" When cars go twenty miles per hour in terms of present traffic problems you end by spending twice as much time finding a parking spot. A slower vehicle would reduce pollution, thin out traffic and of course lower the death rate.

His point then is not only that automobiles traveling at twenty miles per hour would free the individual, but they would be simpler in construction and therefore could be maintained by the individual himself. Much more at the heart of his thesis however is his concern about major tools of society like medicine and education.

Illich

Presently a great deal of medicine could be put in the hands of ordinary people through public education. Education itself in the same way decides whether people are educated enough through its intricate system of grading. Education as a tool says Illich, should be placed back in the hands of the people. Illich has the following to say about the tool of education:

> The planning of new educational institutions ought not to begin with the administrative goals of a principal or president, or with the teaching goals of a professional educator, or with the learning goals of any hypothetical class of people. It must not start with the question, "What should someone learn?" but with the question, "What kinds of things and people might learners want to be in contact with in order to learn?"
> Educational resources are usually labeled according to educators' curricular goals. I propose to do the contrary, to label four different approaches which enable the students to gain access to any educational resource which may help him to define and achieve his goals:
> 1. Reference services to Educational Objects—which facilitate access to things or processes used for formal learning. Some of these things can be reserved for this purpose, stored in libraries, rental agencies, laboratories, and showrooms like museums and theaters; others can be in daily use in factories, airports, or on farms, that may develop the students as apprentices on off-hours.
> 2. Skill Exchanges—which permit persons to list their skills, the conditions under which they are willing to serve as models for others who want to learn these skills, and the addresses at which they can be reached.
> 3. Peer Matching—a communication network which permits persons to describe the learning activity in which they wish to engage and the hope of finding a partner for the inquiry.
> 4. Reference Services to Educators—at large—who can be listed in a directory giving the addresses and self-descriptions of professionals, para-professionals, and free-lances, along with conditions of access to their services. Such educators, as we will see, could be chosen by polling or consulting their former clients.

World Consciousness

In conclusion, this phase of consciousness (Phase IV) is

one in which there is a priority placed on reality as being holistic, harmonious and transforming. This phase places heavy emphasis on interdependence both in the personal and the political sphere. That is to say a person with this kind of consciousness is aware of the need for interdependence at a planetary level.

It is interesting that interdependence is a major value-word batted around in international circles. For example the United Nations has an informative newspaper printed in several languages called "The Interdependent." With the recent energy crisis and the ways it is affecting world economy, it has become clear that we are at the point now where world government is visible and consequently extensive interdependence is necessary. We might then conclude this section with a quotation from a report of the Center for the Study of Democratic Institutions written by Harvey Wheeler:

> The time for the introduction of world constitutionalism is at hand. Admittedly, by some measures, nationalism appears today to be at high tide; world order appears to recede ever more remotely into the future. However, today's nationalism is quite different from that of the nineteenth century. Indeed, to the extent that our nationalism—135 nations—survives, each nation, even the largest ones will require a world rule of law to protect themselves from the danger of being finessed into catastrophe by the folly of others. The security of todays' nations can only truly be measured by the strength of the forces making for world order. These forces are stronger than the view from Washington or Moscow would not indicate.

THE MEANING OF THE PHASES

The description of the four phases of consciousness we have just given must be understood before one can go more deeply into the question of valuing. For these world views give perspective to us and open up or limit the values we choose and the manner in which we define them.

This simplified presentation of the phases of development of consciousness enables us to realize how many and how varied are the possible stances of any individual toward his environment. A key factor in determining what level of development a person has reached is his meaning system. This also relates to the individual's phase of consciousness. At every phase of development the need for meaning is central, but at each phase it is tied to different concrete needs. For our purposes this is of great importance because nothing can qualify as a value that does not contribute to a man's meaning.

Consciousness and Meaning

The centrality of meaning seeking in a human behavior is widely recognized. Philip Phenix writes as follows in *Realms of Meaning*:

> The fundamental human motivation is the search for meaning. The human being is a creature whose distinctive life consists in having meanings and whose basic aim is to fulfill them. He can never rest content simply with the biological satisfaction. He is forever disturbed by ones who are alien to animal existence. His real longing is for meaning, and whether he recognizes it or not, his striving, whatever its apparent object, is directed towards the enlargement and deepening of meaning.

Victor Frankl writes in *Man's Search of Meaning*:

> Man's search for meaning is a primary force in his life and not a 'secondary rationalization' of instinctual drives.

Chaos

Man finds meaning when he is trying to discover or construct a friendly universe. The enemies of meaning are the unexpected, the uncontrollable, the unaccountable, the hostile and the purposeless, in a word, chaos. These forces must somehow be conquered if man is to experience his life as meaningful. Man must domesticate his environment.

Domestication

Meaning is experienced when a man feels at home in his world, when he feels a oneness with his world, when he is able to integrate himself into the world process. Before man can domesticate his environment and feel at home in his world he must deal with the enemies of meaning. He has to establish some kind of control over the forces of chaos. This can be done by either an internal mental operation or by external public activity.

The internal operation is essentially the constructing of a

meaning system. Man controls his world internally by imposing mental order on it (what Berger calls Nomos). "Human craving for meaning . . . appears to have a force of instinct. Men are congenitally compelled to impose a meaningful order upon reality."

Only when the world is thus ordered can an individual inhabit it in relative comfort. The hostile or the unpredictable may still be present, but they are now mentally managed and thus pose no serious threat to meaning. The myths constructed by primitive societies are early examples of a meaning-system. For example the story of Adam and Eve allowed man to explain chaos as resulting from the destructive behavior of humanity. This explanation allows men to feel comfortable even though they might be surrounded by chaotic force.

Man can also deal with chaos by trying to modify his environment—to deal with the chaos as a reality external to him. This too is a domesticating activity. Historically the most common method of attempting to do this has been religious ritual. Obvious examples would be sacrifices that attempted to placate angry deities and incantations over the sick or the rites of exorcism.

Ritual and Technology

Ritual is still used in this way but for most people technology is considered the most effective way of conquering chaos. Sick people usually call the doctor rather than the priest. By technology man can modify his environment in such a way that the world is a most comfortable place for him to live. The point of this then is that the acquisition of meaning comes about through the integration of both the internal and the external environment in a holistic manner.

Meaning and consciousness then are interrelated. An individual finds meaning as he develops values that allow him to feel at home in his world. The values he chooses and the manner in which he defines them is rooted in his phase of consciousness.

For example an individual who never succeeded in feeling that he belonged to any social group (Phase II) would never feel at home. Unless the value of belonging were somehow achieved the individual could not survive mentally and would be forced back to a more primitive level of consciousness. An effective way to appreciate the relationship between meaning-making and consciousness is to view it against the background of human development.

Exploration and Domestication

As the human being moves through the phases of consciousness and seeks to find meaning his struggles involve two basic operations:

1. Exploration
2. Domestication.

Comfortable Environments

In the very birth experience itself a child moves from the comfortable internal environment of the womb into an external world where the external less comfortable environment automatically places more demands on him. He is forced to explore this new world. His needs are no longer automatically met. As the mother cuddles him, touches him, the child begins to feel at home in his new environment. He explores and domesticates the new world. If domestication is not achieved growth is impossible.

Meaning-making is central to human development. One of the basic tasks for anyone trying to promote human growth is to find ways of fostering man's ability to successfully explore and domesticate new situations. That is why the environment of the classroom is so important for the young child. It must be one that fosters his curiosity, gives him the freedom to explore and does not overwhelm him with so many alternatives that he is unable to control and domesticate what he finds.

Human life cannot be meaningful if it is not at the same time purposeful and directed to goals. The absence of purpose, especially long-range purpose in the adult, slowly renders the person choiceless and therefore without meaning. It is purposeful behavior that gives a human life order. Without this, life would be just a series of segmented episodes not integrated into a meaningful pattern because it would have no central purpose. This of course has to be examined against the background of development. First let us look at the following diagrams.

DIAGRAM 10

MEANING SEEKING

THE GROWTH FACILITATOR

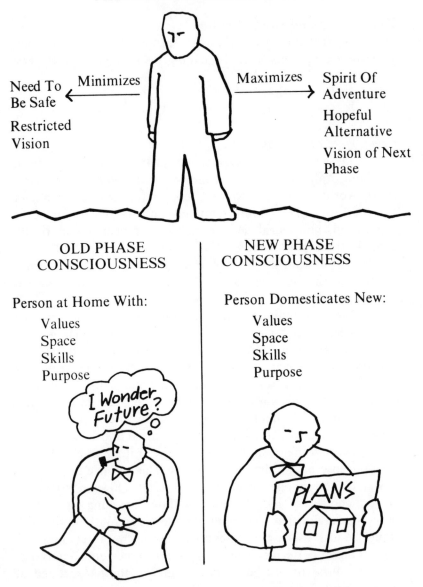

OLD PHASE CONSCIOUSNESS	NEW PHASE CONSCIOUSNESS
Person at Home With:	Person Domesticates New:
Values	Values
Space	Space
Skills	Skills
Purpose	Purpose

Moving from One Phase to Another

Diagram 10 helps us to see the relationship between the development of consciousness and meaning-seeking. In the diagram we see a movement from one phase of consciousness to another. This could be, for example, a movement from Phase II to Phase III, Phase II being the old Phase and Phase III the new Phase. At the old phase we have a person who is feeling at home with the values of that phase. He feels at home not only with the values but also the space and skills and a life purpose consistent with that level. He is comfortable.

He is now beginning to wonder about the future, that is he is beginning to have a consciousness of the new phase. We might imagine a person for example who now wants to take a leadership position in a company. This means that there are going to be new values and new skills and new purposes involved for him. Quite naturally he begins to plan in his imagination for this new stage of consciousness, the fact that he needs all these new skills makes him insecure.

If he is to find meaning at this new phase he must have skills or be given realistic guidance about the next stage with its new alternatives so that he can plan for them properly.

DIAGRAM 11

SUPPORT FOR GROWTH

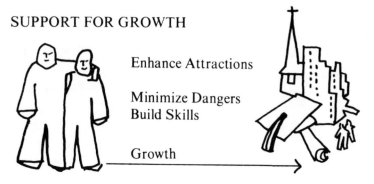

Enhance Attractions

Minimize Dangers
Build Skills

Growth

Diagram 11 simply indicates what is necessary to help a person move from one phase to another. One must enhance the attractions of the next phase and minimize the dangers; one must also help him to build the new skills. There is nothing worse than helping a person to grow without the needed skills.

The small child at the first phase who is very self-centered and yet now needs to expand his relationships must attain a sense of respect for others and accept the responsibility involved in social relationships; but he must be taught those skills quite specifically by teachers and parents. Often children grow up without these skills and never move out of these more primitive phases of consciousness because of it.

Clearly what we are saying is that a person acquires meaning through the values he chooses at his particular phase of consciousness. A person quite naturally reaches a stage when he begins to explore the next phase of consciousness but is only able to accommodate his behavior to that new phase as he is able to let go of his previous phase and domesticate his new environment.

DIAGRAM 11B

MEANING SEEKING EXAMPLE PHASE II/III

PHASE I
CONSCIOUSNESS PHYSICAL

Security
Survival
Wonder

PHASE II
CONSCIOUSNESS SOCIAL

Insecure About:	Self Worth	Secure With:
Values	Belonging	Values
Space	Prestige	Space
Skills	Competence	Skills
	Success	

PHASE III
CONSCIOUSNESS INDEPENDENT

Growing
In
Skill
Space
Imagination

We will now try to increase our understanding or growth through meaning seeking by examining Diagram 11b which looks at the journey of an individual moving from Phase I through Phase III.

The values that are evident at Phase I are security and survival. We see a fine little figure standing at the beginning of Phase II. His memory looks back to the previous phase. He is aware of the need to survive at this stage; he still wants to be a child, to play rather than to go to school. His priorities are wonder, receiving physical attention and security.

His new phase demands that he be competent and successful and involve himself in social relationships. Naturally the young child who is only at the beginning of this phase of consciousness is insecure about these new values and the as yet unexplored space.

As he grows and moves across Phase II by going to school and gaining some competence, he has domesticated his new world. He is now at home in it. We now see him at the end of Phase II.

This phase of consciousness does not give him meaning anymore. He does not find meaning in succcess and prestige any longer. They are helpful and give him the security he needs, but now his explorative imagination begins to look at Phase III. He then moves to Phase III and first as in the beginning of Phase II feels very insecure about the new values. And so he domesticates those values, before moving on to the next phase—Phase IV.

DIAGRAM 12

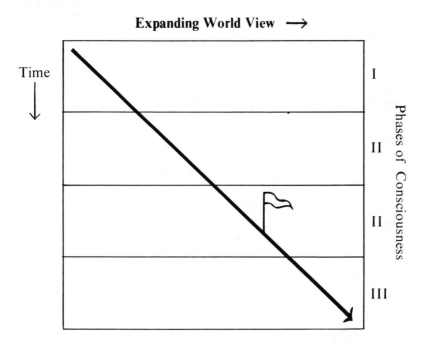

Expanding World View $\longrightarrow$

Time

I

II

II

III

Phases of Consciousness

In Diagram 12 above the line that moves diagonally across the graph is the development of consciousness through time. The further the person goes the more he sees; his world view expands as he develops.

At the point of the little flag on the diagram the vision of reality is vast, extending into the future and its possibilities and penetrating more deeply into whatever is brought to consciousness at that time.

The world views (phases of consciousness) typical of persons at each of the four phases quite predictably are similar to world views expressed throughout man's intellectual history. The originators of the creation myths interpret the chaos in the world of nature as a visible manifestation of the struggle between the uncontrollable forces they have deified. The creator "God" is the conqueror who has produced order by vanquishing the other deities. This clearly expresses a survival orientated world view highlighted by needs and interests similar to the person on Phase I.

People like Martin Luther at the time of his break from the dominance of the Roman Church present a striking picture of a person enduring the pain of moving from Phase II to Phase III. He foresook the status quo and became very much of an independent person even though such a change in his development meant taking on the world. In fact there is little doubt that he had to do this in order to continue to grow in a way that would be meaningful to him.

Past, Present, and Future

As we have indicated the phases of consciousness treated above also constitute world views. My world view is the conscious perception of my immediate reality which includes an awareness of my past with its limitations and the future with its responsibilities. This is further illustrated by the following diagram, an extension of the previous one.

DIAGRAM 13

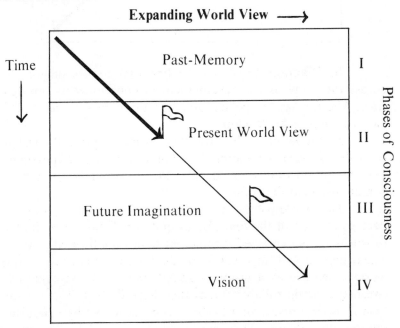

Memory and Consciousness

Let us imagine a person at the first flag on the diagram. His world view puts him in touch with his past and future. Through his memory he has contact with Phase I. In remembering the past a person at Phase II is also remembering a time when he was less skilled and had different interests. For example as a teenager graduating from high school with all the skills to be able to go out and work in the world, one can still remember when one was a small child and very dependent on one's parents. In other words as a mature person at a second phase of consciousness, one remembers a time when one did not have the competency that one has now and when one was dependent on adults and concerned primarily with self interests. Naturally at that time one's world was quite different. Therefore consciousness and memory are related.

Future and Consciousness

At the same time one is beginning to think about the future and so one is aware in the imagination of where one wants to go and what one wants to do. With present skills and present talents this might be quite hard for one. One's imagination of the future, Phase III in the diagram, is something within grasp, something one wants to do. One's imagination is of the future; his dreams will reflect on various future possibilities which at times might even relate to a Phase IV consciousness.

What we are pointing out here is that a person who is at a particular phase of consciousness is at the same time related to the future and the past through memory and imagination. Memory and imagination come together in the present—confluently at a particular phase of consciousness—through specific manifestations of behavior and skills.

A Short Example

A simply strategy to help a group of persons especially young adults discuss some of these questions is: "Sit still, relax, and close your eyes and think about your life as it is, your friends, school or job and family." Now have each person write a few notes on what he thought about.

After a few minutes without discussion have everyone relax once again. "Sit still and relax and imagine yourself in a new location, new school or job. It is your first day. Try to experience the day and some of your feelings." Now have each person write some notes on the experience. If you have time you could have people role-play or make a collage to depict the two situations.

The idea is to try to compare some of the feelings in both situations. In new situations: "What new skills would have to be applied, or old skills dusted off and used again? What could you say about domestication and exploration?"

Conclusion

We have dealt here in detail with the levels of consciousness expressed as individual world views. This is the groundwork for a theory of value development. It is important that we have a clear understanding of the four phases of consciousness. We have indicated how these phases relate to an individual's quest for meaning. As we move back and look at the definition of a value and at the process of valuing in the first and second chapter we see that it includes those choices that are meaningful to the individual and also enhance the development of man. We see how meaning is related to consciousness, but as yet we have not really dealt with that other dimension, namely how the choice should be an act of enhancing the development of man. Just as meaning has been viewed in relation to the development of consciousness so those choices that are meaning-giving will have to be dealt with specifically in relation to value development in the next chapter.

Finally we need to keep in mind that any given value that a person may have as for example work or education will change its definition in terms of the world view of the person. Not only is he going to define the value differently but he is going to rank it differently in the sets of priorities that he calls his own.

The phase of consciousness reflects the world view or the manner in which the person perceives the world in which he lives. But a value is that particular object or relationship that gives the person meaning and is chosen within the context of a series of priorities in order that life in general may be enhanced. This subject matter at hand is specifically that of value development and constitutes the kind of the information needed for creating growth oriented strategies and educational methods. Let us now pursue value development.

CHAPTER IV

THE DEVELOPMENT OF VALUES

STELLA, Joseph (1877-1946) *The Brooklyn Bridge:* Variation on an Old Theme Purchase Acg. #42.15 Oil on Canvas—70″ x 42″ Collection of Whitney Museum of American Art, New York.

Living is learning, and growing is learning. One learns to walk, talk and throw a ball; to read, bake a cake, and get along with age-mates of the opposite sex; to hold down a job, to raise children; to retire gracefully when too old to work effectively, and to get along without a husband or wife who has been at one's side for forty years. These are all learning tasks. To understand human development, one must understand learning. The human individual learns his way through life.

Robert J. Havighurst

INTRODUCTION

This chapter is about the development of values. All that has preceeded this chapter and all that follows it is really an explanation and deepening of this material. The values a person chooses stem from his world view. Consequently we had to deal with the world view question, the phases of consciousness, before we could deal with the matter of value development.

Next, in order to be able to use what we know about values strategically and appropriately in depth with people in various educational settings, we have to know what the necessary environments are for permitting values to develop, and what skills are required for a person to work with these values. These subject matters will be dealt with later.

This chapter will also deal with how values enhance the development of man and as such will conclude the examination of the definition of the value process stated in Chapter I. Finally this chapter is very important to the reader who wants to practice value education or use values material for counseling or administration. Much of the basic material necessary for the understanding of values and especially their practical use will be explored in this chapter.

CONSCIOUSNESS, VALUES AND VALUE INDICATORS

Specific values like love, security or work come out of a phase of consciousness of an individual on the one hand and are expressed through his behavior on the other. In order to understand this we might look at the following Diagram 14. Examining the diagram we see that values are determined first of all by the world view of the individual. So the first thing to think about in any developmental strategy or any approach to values is: "What is the world view of the individual?" This is the same thing as asking what is that person's phase of consciousness.

DIAGRAM 14

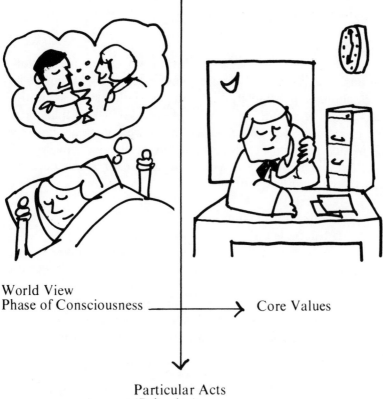

World View
Phase of Consciousness ———————→ Core Values

Particular Acts
(Behavior)
Value Indicators

World View

    The diagram considers a person who is a businessman operating at Phase II. We see him in bed thinking about a cocktail party that he has just left. His primary interest is to be a successful competent individual and that controls the way he views the world. He is concerned about the image he conveys to people, the clothes he wears. He is caught up in the prestige syndrome. He is thinking about the party and the "booboos" he made, worrying about whether or not he upset anybody. His consciousness is centered on what people think. All of this describes his general level of consciousness, a level that views the world as a problem that engages his best efforts. He achieves a sense of meaning by having others see him as a successful and prestigious individual.

Core Values

In the next part of the diagram we see our friend working busily at his desk. It is past ten o'clock at night and he has a telephone supported by his shoulder while at the same time he is studying a book and opening a file cabinet with his hand. We might say then there are certain core values arising from his world view that he expresses behaviorally. Thus his actions, which reveal his phase of consciousness, express his core values. They might be as follows:

1. Work
2. Education (Study)
3. Success

Our friend's values may of course include others besides these, but in the picture it becomes obvious that he is working hard and also studying even at this late hour. It is thus evident that certain values like success, work and education are a part of his particular lifestyle. In other words the particularity of his lifestyle is described by the values that he chooses, the core values.

There is quite a distinction between the core values and the phase of consciousness. The phase of consciousness is how a person perceives the world in general. It is the screen through which he views everything—the world appears as a certain color to him. The core values are those particular values he chooses that give him meaning and shape his lifestyle. They become visible in the concrete choices he makes. They are human motivators. Consciousness and core values are never revealed in one value like work or success but through several values ranked in a particular order.

The individual in the above diagram has three values that are major priorities for him: work, education and success. Obviously he could rank these in a number of different ways. The world view does not necessarily dictate how a person will rank these values but does determine that he values working late into the night. For our friend one would probably conclude that success or work is his first value, although this may not necessarily be the case.

Behavior

So proceeding from the phase of consciousness is the concrete behavior that is a specific indicator of values for the individual. In the case above the concrete behavior points to the value of work. But this does not describe what work means to that individual. He values work but this does not tell us what kind of work he does, what his profession is, what his aspirations and goals are. The manner in which the person works at his job is also specific to the individual.

Value Indicators

The point here is that the particular acts and choices with their emotional content are what we call "Value Indicators." As we shall see later the value indicators are the primary object of strategy development. Strategies should be designed to reveal not only a single value indicator but several and the way in which they are ranked as priorities. They will clearly indicate the underlying core values an individual has, which in turn will reveal his stage of consciousness.

Finally in viewing the diagram above we see that there is movement from what we might say are larger general categories to more particular ones. There is a movement from the most universal (the phase of consciousness) to the individual act at a particular moment on a given day. This act is the value indicator.

DIAGRAM 15

LOCATING VALUES

UNIVERSAL		PARTICULAR
LEVEL OF $\longrightarrow$ CONSCIOUSNESS	PARTICULAR CHOICE $\longrightarrow$ PRIORITIZED CORE—VALUE	PARTICULAR EVENT ACT—VALUE INDICATOR

In the above process we see a distinct way of going about things and how a particular event shapes itself. First an individual comes to a situation with a level of consciousness. He has a particular world view. Then as a consequence of that world view he pre-imagines what it is that he is going to do and finally does it by making particular choices that express a set of core values that he has prioritized in a certain order. Some examples of core values are security, work, self competence. (A list of sixty underlying core values are given later.) So as a consequence of his world view and his pre-imagining a person acts in a specific manner in a particular event. For example he applies for a certain job. He behaves in a certain way in an interview. He joins certain clubs. All these particular events are value indicators.

Educational Design

Later as we start to look at how we design educational strategies and how we use the value event in a clinical manner we will discover that the best order for proceeding is just the reverse of the above. The order is as follows:

1. We start by looking at a particular event. Value clarification is the educational method whereby we examine a particular event. We take a precise moment in the event and using it as a value indicator draw out the underlying values operative in that event and try to see what their priority is.

2. Step two is the discovery and the analysis of the underlying values derived from the particular event. Having discovered those values and prioritized them we need to guide a person in the process of defining in depth each one of the values he has chosen. This will point out the phase of consciousness.

3. The phase of consciousness will be apparent from a person's definition of the values and the choosing and prioritizing of those values out of the particular event.

The process I have described here as an educational method does not have to go through to the final diagnosing of a phase of consciousness; that would depend on the goal of the particular lesson or situation.

If a counselor chooses to go all the way through to discovering a phase of consciousness it is usually to help a person construct a road map that plots where he wants to go in his own development. One might do this in guiding a student or a counselee. The type of information derived from such a process is helpful, even essential, in the planning and developing of an educational program or a specific grade curriculum.

OF PHASES AND STAGES

There are eight stages of value development, two stages for each phase of consciousness, a stage "A" and a stage "B." This is illustrated clearly in the following diagram:

DIAGRAM 16

PHASES OF CONSCIOUSNESS	STAGE OF VALUE DEVELOPMENT
I. **WORLD AS MYSTERY** **(PHYSICAL)**	**A. SELF PRESERVATION**
	B. SELF DELIGHT/SECURITY
II. **WORLD AS PROBLEM** **(SOCIAL)**	**A. SELF WORTH**
	B. SELF COMPETENCE
III. WORLD AS PROJECT AND **INVENTION** **(CONSCIENCE/ACT)**	**A. INDEPENDENCE (FREEDOM)**
	B. BEING SELF
IV. WORLD AS MYSTERY **CARED FOR** **(INTERDEPENDENT)**	**A. HARMONY**
	B. SYNERGY

Primary Values

In referring to a stage of value development we will for example refer to Stage III—B, (being self), or to Stage II—A, (self-worth).

In the above diagram each stage of value development is designated by a particular value. For example Stage I—A is designated by self preservation. Stage I—B is designated by security. The values designated in this table are what we referred to in one of my earlier works (*Value Clarification as Learning Process: A Source Book*) as primary values. The primary value at any stage designates the value that is primarily operative in the life of the individual in question.

In order to have a sense of meaning and to be able to survive in this world a person will need the values we call primary values at whatever stage he presently finds himself. They are essential to his mental well-being. In speaking of the growth process in general we consider phases I and II as radically distinct from Phases III and IV.

Phases I and II are primarily what have been regarded by psychologists as minimal requirements for mental health. The primary values typical of those phases are the values necessary for a person's growth as a mentally healthy individual in society.

Phases III and IV also have important values, but they are primarily those values needed by a person who seeks to become self actualized (in Maslow's terminology) and have only recently achieved prominence in psychological literature.

Meaning Systems

The primary values at any phase are the ones that constitute the core of meaning for an individual at that stage. For example a person at Phase I will give priority to the values of self-preservation, self-delight and security.The acquisition of these values will satisfy his need for meaning. In other words he achieves meaning through security, self-delight and self-preservation. At Phase IV a person would seek meaning by organizing his life in such a way as to experience harmony with other humans and with the universe at large. Thus meaning results from orienting one's life out of his own phase of consciousness and behaving in such a way that he secures those values that are primary at that particular stage of development.

The Enhancement of Man

In order for man to be able to grow creatively or for the individual to maximize his potential in this world he has to experience and internalize the primary values. Traditionally psychology has emphasized those primary values characteristic of the first two phases as being essential for mental health. Yet in recent years there has been an increasing emphasis on those values coming from Phases III and IV as values necessary for growth. Let us try to look at this picture a little more closely. (See Diagram 16.)

Moving Through the Levels

In the diagram we have the four phases of consciousness on the left and the eight stages of value development with the designated primary value for each stage at the right.

In addition to this we have the context by which each pair of primary values is identified. For example the primary values at Phase I—self-preservation and self-delight—are to be understood as physical. That is to say self-preservation is primarily a consciousness about the need to protect my physical being. Self-delight is a sensory pleasure and refers here to a primarily physical experience.

The values at Phase II are social in their nature. A person concerned about self-worth is a person who is primarily worried about peer and family relationships, which can give him a sense of his own worth.

It is not until we get to Phase III that a person begins for the first time to choose primarily out of an independence of spirit and thereby becomes self-directed. The values are self-chosen and not selected primarily due to outside influence as at the first two phases. At the fourth phase the primary context is interdependence which requires not only self-direction but also a knowledge, understanding and deep trust of other people.

The reason we have divided the phases in the diagrams so prominently is to emphasize the fact that when a person moves from one phase of consciousness to another there is a radical reorganization of the manner in which he chooses values and of the criteria by which he makes those choices. Consequently the movement from one phase to another is often traumatic for an individual. The most traumatic experience comes when a person moves from Phase II to Phase III. The reason for this is illustrated in the following Diagram 17:

DIAGRAM 17

I.
  WORLD AS MYSTERY
	A. SELF PRESERVATION
	                                    PHYSICAL
	B. SELF DELIGHT

II.
  WORLD AS PROBLEM
	A. SELF WORTH
	                                    SOCIAL
	B. SELF COMPETENCE

"NO MAN'S LAND"	**AMBIVALENT IN VALUE** **PRIORITIES AND NEEDS**

III.
  WORLD AS PROJECT
  & INVENTION
	A. INDEPENDENCE
	                          SELF CHOSEN
	                          (CONSCIENCE)
	B. BEING SELF

IV.
  WORLD AS MYSTERY
  CARED FOR
	A. HARMONY
	                          INTERDEPENDENT
	B. SYNERGY

Authority

Phases I and II designate the earliest stages of a person's development. They are distinct in that for this period of time the person sees authority as being external to the self.

At Phases III and IV there is a change in consciousness where the person takes authority into himself. He has a sense of his own internal power and of his ability to choose in a competent manner. Authority is now internal.

No Man's Land

So when a person is moving from one phase to another and particularly from Phase II to Phase III, there is a tremendous reorganization inside the individual. "No Man's Land" in the diagram. The person who is between any two stages sees the practicality and need for values out of both stages and as such can become tremendously ambivalent. In our own work we have found that psychological testing of persons moving from one stage to another often leads to a negative diagnosis because they are so ambivalent. Educators should be made aware of this.

So we see that a person's life develops, and his ability to become himself and make his own choices increases as he moves from Phase I through Phases III and IV. There is a movement from being totally dependent on the environment through to a *final* consciousness of one's own authority where one takes charge of the environment itself both in a personal and technological manner at Phase IV.

WHAT MAKES PEOPLE GROW?

The growth process is fostered by reinforcing the environment of the individual at the stage of his present experiences and also of the next stage to which he aspires.

Environmental reinforcement enables the person to experience those conditions that permit him to internalize the primary values proper to his growth stage.

Internal Development

(The reader who wants detailed studies on how a person internalizes and gets these basic values reinforced, should consult the works of such people as Erik Erikson, Sullivan and Piaget. Also more detailed treatment of this process can be gained through reading *Value Clarification as Learning Process: A Source Book* by Brian Hall.)

In simple terms a newborn child in order to grow must first of all experience an environment that allows him to preserve his physical existence without threat. Once that child has received the love and kindness and care from the mother that make him feel that he is being physically protected then self-preservation will no longer be a predominant need for him even though it will always be a primary value in his life. However as a primary value all through his life, even in a crisis situation, it will not require constant attention and worry if he has experienced that environment early in his life which allowed him to internalize a sufficient "basic trust." The internalization of "basic trust" neutralizes anxiety about self-preservation. This is a term used by Erikson and dealt with by him in detail in *Identity and the Life Cycle*.

> The first component of a healthy personality I nominate a sense of basic trust, which I think is an attitude towards

one's self and the world derived from the experiences of the first year of life. By "trust" I mean what is commonly implied as a reasonable trustfulness, trustfulness as far as others are concerned in a simple sense of trustworthiness as far as one's self is concerned. When I say "basic," I mean that neither this component nor any of those that follow are, either in *child or adulthood*, especially conscious. In fact, all of these criteria when developed in childhood and when integrated in adulthood blend into the total personalities."

Self-Delight

Erikson's basic trust relates to the primary values at the first stages and includes self-delight as well as self-preservation. By self-delight we mean the physical feeling of pleasure that a child gains through the senses. This includes all of the senses. It covers the feeling of comfort and security gained from being cuddled and the feeling of awe and delight in a pretty object, flower or animal seen for the first time.

Reinforcing Phase I

In other words the basic environmental condition for the reinforcing of values at this level is the experience of love from others and the experience of an external environment that is not frightening but rather reinforcing. It is difficult to imagine how a small child brought up in a war as in Vietnam could ever grow beyond a certain level of development, having experienced so much fear and disruption at such an early period in his life. Anxiety about self-preservation would probably be constant because he has had no experience of reality as being trustworthy.

As we pointed out in the previous chapter under "meaning" one must reinforce the next stage of development if a child is going to grow and leave the delights of the first phase in order to pursue the adventure of the second phase. A child moves from Phase I to II because he has internalized the values of the primary stages and thus no longer experiences a need for them and therefore is driven to look elsewhere for meaningful experiences. Simple physical delight is not now sufficient, although originally it was what gave him meaning.

Phase II: Self-Worth and Competence

What gives him meaning now is belonging to the social world. He turns to his peers, to his friends, begins to socialize. Because his consciousness has changed he requires new skills, and he starts the process of internalizing new values. If he is to go through the second phase he must eventually internalize the feelings of self-worth and self-competence. Before we move on we should define these values.

Self-Worth

This means the internalization of the conviction that one is of value to others as well as to himself. It is the feeling that one is intrinsically good. Within religious experience—particularly the Christian and Jewish tradition—it is the affirmation that finally and ultimately God sees man as good and that creation itself is good. We may act badly at times, but still we are intrinsically good. To understand this and to adhere to this belief is to have internalized a sense of self-worth.

Self-Competence

This is an extension of self-worth and means that one knows that one is competent as an individual and has sufficient instrumental and professional skills to be of use to others and to oneself within society. It is a sense of adequacy. It is the opposite of the feeling of failure. It is one's awareness that one can begin and finish a job well.

Values and Schools

The two values that we have just defined should emerge from the school experience of a child. The purpose of education as we know it is to prepare him to have a sense of his own value, his own identity on the one hand and to be competent to go out and earn a living and make a contribution to the world and society on the other.

The reinforcing environment necessary for these values to be internalized is an environment that affirms an individual and teaches him in such a way that he grows up with a sense of his own ability rather than a feeling of disability or inferiority in the world in which he lives.

The values considered so far are external in their origin. Self-preservation, self-delight as well as self-worth and self-competence are given from the outside. They are consequences of an external environment that has supported the individual and allowed him to internalize these values. They are the social foundation of the development of every individual. They are the core of all developmental processes.

Making Values Conscious

It is the job of education through all the grade levels, to make these values a conscious reality for the child. The job of the teacher is to make the child aware of these values as soon as possible so that he can internalize them for himself and can be trained to set-up environments which contribute to other people realizing these values. A child who has a sense of his own self-worth must be taught how to behave so as to affirm the self-worth of others.

BELIEVING OURSELVES

At the end of the adolescent period a radical change takes place as a person has the opportunity to move from Phase II to Phase III. The reinforcing environment that allowed a person to internalize values at this level must be one that encourages independence and responsibility.

These are need-values in the sense that once a person has experienced sufficient self-worth or self-competence the striving after these values and their derivatives, such as success or prestige, gives little meaning any more. Once a person has internalized these sufficiently he begins to seek other primary values that become needs for him. These are the values of independence and being self.

B-Cognition Values

They are needs in the sense that the person needs them in order to find meaning in his life. This is why they have been called growth values or what Maslow terms B-Cognition values. The first four values that we mentioned are values that psychologists generally feel are absolutely necessary for physical and mental health. Almost all social work and counseling practice is directed towards the building of those values in an individual in order that he may function happily and productively in the society in which he lives. Maslow called these D-Cognition Values. Let us now define independence and being self.

Independence

The condition or quality of being independent; the fact of not depending on another (with various shades of meaning); exemption from external control or support; freedom from subjection or from the influence of others; individual liberty of thought or action. (This definition is from the *Oxford Unabridged Dictionary*.)

Being Self

This is the quality of being oneself and actualizing being in others. It is the experience of having been independent sufficiently to move to the point where I can create more and more experiences in the world that reinforce environments that allow others to become themselves also. Being self is different from independence in that it has the added quality of making one's presence felt in society.

Reinforcing Phase III

The reinforcing environment for this kind of development comes primarily from the individual. We are simply stating that this stage of dependence on the external environment has become a secondary rather than an essential priority unlike the first two phases. It is necessary therefore that a person be in an external environment that permits him to be independent in the first place.

That environment is one that is reinforced by persons who have actualized the value of being self. In other words the environment is one of freedom that permits a person to make mistakes and grow in his responsibility. He learns from those mistakes as much as from doing things correctly all the time, something that would upset a person emphasizing self-competence.

Harmony

Finally let us define the Phase IV values of harmony and synergy. Harmony: (*Oxford Unabridged Dictionary*) Combination or adaptation of parts, elements or related things, so as to form a consistent and orderly whole agreement, accord, congruity.

It is that value that stresses the natural flow of things. A man's body is a harmonious whole in the same way that a large piece of music is a harmonious whole even though it is made up of a tremendous amount of parts, processes and variations of the parts. Harmony makes reference therefore to persons, systems, and the over-all reality of the created world.

Synergy

Traditionally the value of harmony has related very much to the development of the human individual and his maximum potential. It is evident today that the harmony of the universe itself and the need for people to understand harmony rather than equilibrium as a basis for ecological development is important. 1. The whole unpredicted by the parts. 2. The ability of the individual to make meaning out of opposites. 3. The harmonious working of the various parts to form a new and transcendent whole.

The value of synergy is much used in the technological sphere. It is that value whereby many parts come together to form a new whole. Four people may come together with different ideas and in doing so they produce a new idea that was originally unknown by any of them. Harmony and synergy are very closely related because the whole that is produced synergetically operates harmoniously.

Being Natural

The environment that reinforces the development of these values is the natural environment itself. It is therefore a highly developed state of reality for individuals who operate together interdependently in community with a lifestyle that allows them to act in a harmonious manner with the total environment in such a way that they reinforce it and one another.

This reflects the whole difficulty that we might have as

individuals in understanding this phase of consciousness. While it envisages a high order of things still these values become need values for the individuals operating at the third phase and moving toward the last phase. Because it is a value that becomes an imagined value in the third phase it is something with which many people are familiar.

ENHANCING THE PERSON

In the last part of our original definition of value we noted that a value gives a person meaning and enhances human life. So it is that a part of the enhancement process is providing reinforcing environments both for the person who is doing the valuing and for the person who is trying to encourage values in another.

Value as Enhancing the Person

To enhance life is to develop primary values at each stage of a person's development in order that his life may be meaningful. For the first two phases the primary values are essential to the enhancement and development of a man, especially in relation to his physical and mental well-being. A person cannot develop mental health and cannot go beyond himself and reach out to others in a creative manner unless those original primary values of self-preservation, self-delight, self-worth and competence are developed.

Minimal Values

Enhancement of man beyond that point has to do with fostering those other primary values we have listed, such as independence. Basically then and minimally the educator must without compromise see to it that whatever else an educational system does it should ensure that these primary values are developed in the individual.

Need and Vision: Values for Reinforcement

We must stress values at the stage where the person presently finds himself and give him an opportunity to begin to envision for himself those primary values at the next stage of development. This is essential if people are going to grow in a creative manner. In the first stage then enhancement of man has to do with him being able to develop the need-values. However even if the person does acquire these values it does not make it certain that he is going to act in a moral way. Then what about morality and the enhancement process of man?

The point here is that once a person has acquired these minimal primary values he has the opportunity and the potential for making those moral choices that maximize the creative development of man. We will deal in more detail with the specific reality of moral choice and the skill needed for moral judgement related to the concept of enhancement later on.

It comes clear then at this point that all the parts of the original definition of a value such as the self, its environment, meaning making and enhancement of man, are components which will continue as a part of our discussion through this book.

THE CORE VALUES

We are now ready to look at the core values. These values are at the center of the value theory both in dealing with the value development and in terms of originating value-related educational strategies.

Thus far we have talked about phases of consciousness as being the world views of particular people at a particular stage of their development. We have talked about primary values as being the values that assume prominence as a result of those world views.

The core values, like the primary values, are those values that generally become priorities for a person at a particular stage of his development and are the choices that constitute meaning and contribute to the self-enhancement of an individual at a precise moment in his life. Of course the choices may not always be by an individual; they can be by a group or organization.

"I" Values

First we must explain more fully what we mean by core values. What kinds of things are they? Basically we are talking about "I" values. That is to say, we are talking about those values chosen by individual human beings in a given situation.

Later on we will talk specifically about institutional values. Before we proceed any further let us look at a set of "I" values that can serve as a basis for discussion.

DIAGRAM 18
"I" VALUES

1. Self-Worth	21. Sex (experience)	41. Power/Honesty
2. Community (personalist)	22. Instrumentality	42. Wholeness
3. Food/Warmth	23. Self-Control	43. Affection (physical)
4. Harmony	24. Friendship	44. Education (certification)
5. Intimacy	25. Social Affirmation	45. Interdependence
6. Recreation	26. Empathy	46. Community (supportive)
7. Self-Preservation	27. Discovery	47. Celebration/Limitation
8. Work/Labor	28. Congruence	48. Service
9. Relaxation	29. Equity/Rights	49. Cooperation
10. Solitude	30. Law (guide)	50. Presence (of other)
11. Ownership	31. Knowledge/Insight	51. Learning/Insight
12. Prestige	32. Self-Assertion	52. Simplicity/Play
13. Truth	33. Self-Delight (sensory)	53. Equilibrium
14. Being Liked/Appreciated	34. Wonder (curiosity)	54. Word
15. Achievement/Success	35. Health (personal)	55. Ecority
16. Transcendence	36. Creativity/Ideation	56. Convival Tools/Technology
17. Justice	37. Security	57. Human Dignity
18. Competence/Confidence	38. Construction/Order	58. Family
19. Self-Centered	39. Synergy	59. Beauty/Arts
20. Self-Directedness	40. Being Self	60. Leisure

This list of sixty core values is a set of values that we have worked with in our own educational strategies. They represent the value foundation or basis for human behavior. The idea is that these values-words are fundamental. They are bottom line items and do not point to any other underlying values.

"I" Values

The point is then that in value clarification techniques we are generally looking at a person's behavior and from that behavior we try to pull out underlying values. Or we may be looking at a particular event or a piece of literature out of which we can draw underlying values. We pull out the underlying values by discovering the different core values suggested to us by the value indicators. A value indicator is a piece of the total individual behavior that is not itself a core value but rather points to an underlying core value. This is why the technique of value clarification is so revealing. People are familiar with their own value indicators but may not grasp the values underlying their behavior. Let us examine the value indicator "money" as an example.

Money

The word "money" is not itself a core value but rather a value indicator. If you ask a person, what is the most important thing to him and he replies "Money" you can safely conclude that the money itself probably is not the value. A person is unlikely to value dollar bills or copper coins. The only person who would value money in this way would be a coin collector. So I suppose one could say that it is possible to value money in its own right but in that case it would be as an art object.

If one asked a person why he values money he might say something like "It can give me security;" "I would be able to buy a new house for my wife;" "I would be able to buy the kind of car I want." The point is that the money operates as an indicator of that person's core values, which are the basis for this quest. In value clarification methods the facilitator or the educator must be familiar with a set of values such as those on the list above and be able to pull them out of a given action. Let us continue with the example of money. What kinds of values can we pull out from the word money? Let us start with some values from the Diagram 18.

Examples: Self-worth, food and warmth, self-preservation, ownership, prestige, achievement and success, education, health, security.

Values Underlying Behavior

All of these could be the core values indicated by a person's statement that money is the most important thing to him. Of course a person might ask, "How do we know which of those values would be indicated by money as a value indicator?" Perhaps it could be any one of these or even something else that is not on the list. Another question to be considered is, "Do not different persons define all those values differently?"

Some people may look at a security one way and others

look at security another. The answer to this question is affirmative, but that will be clear as the process continues.

This points to the fact that value development as well as value clarification is basically a method whereby the value clarifier is continually investigating with others a particular situation in order to discover its underlying values. So let's continue with the process.

THE PROCESS: THE EDUCATIONAL METHOD

Once one has listed the above values the individual would be asked if there were any other core values he would derive from the idea of money or whether those values would cover the experience. Let us suppose that our individual decides that the above list just about covers it except that he would add the value of leisure. Having settled on these values the individual would then be asked to choose three or four of those values that are the most important to him and to rank them in order of priority.

Stance as Values Ranked

The reason for this procedure is that behavior, the stance of the self to the environment, is always a matter of values ranked in a particular priority. It is never one given value. In helping people analyze an experience I usually suggest that they choose four underlying values and then rank them. Perhaps our subject in this case might choose the following value ranking from the indicators; money:
  1. Prestige
  2. Success
  3. Ownership
  4. Leisure

Priority and Consciousness

One can see that his ranking will lead to a certain kind of behavior. The person who places prestige and success first is going to behave quite differently from a person who puts leisure and ownership first. For one thing a person who puts leisure first is operating out of a different stage of consciousness than a person who puts prestige and success first.

The next task regarding the person who chose money as

a value indicator would be to check out with other persons (this is best done in a group) whether or not this person's value-ranking reflects the kind of person he is behaviorily on a day-to-day basis.

Once this has been established one still has to answer the question "Does this individual define prestige and success and these values in the same way that other people do?" Various individuals might understand these values in a different manner. Because of this we have not yet completed our investigative process.

The final part of the process is to take the four values starting with prestige and ask the individual to define each of them out of his own experience.

In group discussions or in classroom educational settings we usually ask the students to form groups of four, to brainstorm on various experiences they have had of the value, in this case prestige, and out of that come to a consensus definition of what they mean by the term.

As part of the consensus definition we ask the persons to check with certain reference books, such as dictionaries, particularly the *Oxford Unabridged Dictionary*. In this way they begin to make the value of prestige something that they own themselves. The value thereby is brought to their consciousness.

Clarification

Often people will find their definitions are different from the definitions in the dictionaries, in which case they are asked to choose a more appropriate word. This is a clarification of a value for them. For example a person who put prestige first might eventually find that he really meant achievement or self-competence.

In trying to be honest a person will often state that he chose prestige because he wanted to be admired for doing well at college. He might say, "My parents always wanted me to be an engineer." But when questioned more closely he might admit that the most important thing was really his sense of personal accomplishment: self-competence and achievement. The objective in such a method is to help the person clarify what "is." What core values are really operative? The final process of defining the value would make this clear.

Process Defined
1. Examine a particular piece of behavior or event
2. Pull out the underlying core values
3. Get a person to choose several of those values and rank them (e.g., four values)
4. Have the individual then take each of those values and define them in terms of his own experience and then line-up his definition with some given authority
5. Finally have him look over his new definitions and in light of his revised understanding rerank the values if he deems it appropriate.

This process is an ongoing evaluative experience. A person may then choose to rerank the values in terms of the kind of behavior he wishes to have rather than the kind of behavior he does have. This last step moves the exercise beyond value clarification to a value development exercise.

VALUES AND VALUE-RANKING

The above list will make no sense unless each of those values becomes your own by defining it in terms of your own experience.

In training sessions we have people define these values so that they understand what each one of them means. Then we train them in pulling out these underlying values from value indicators or constellation experiences (experience involving a cluster of values). These experiences may be from the classroom where a teacher pulls out the values and then spontaneously makes up strategies with the children without ever discussing the underlying values. Trained counselors can pull out these values from a given situation to check where an individual is in the counseling process. From all of this two things should be clear:

The Value Defined
I. A value, any value, changes its definition at each stage of consciousness. Take the value of work as an example. Work would be defined differently at each stage of consciousness.

One way to understand work is that it is the way in which man modifies his environment for specific purposes. For example we imagine a cave man wearing no clothes standing looking at the trees. Suddenly an animal growls at him and he runs frightened into the cave to get away from the animal. He then barricades the front of the cave in order to prevent the animal from coming in. We would say that he modified his environment in order to protect himself from the animal. Work is always modification of environment, for example killing an animal in order to make a coat to protect oneself from the weather. Given this definition of work—modification of the environment—we may now look at what the definition of work would be at each of the four different phases:

PHASE I—   Work here might be defined as follows: Modification of the environment for the purpose of survival.

PHASE II—   Work here would be defined as modification of the environment for the purpose of success and prestige among my fellow man, such as "I want to become manager of the TV station."

PHASE III—   Work here is the modification of the environment for the purpose of serving mankind.

PHASE IV—   Work now is the modification of the environment for the enhancement of the environment itself, such as working for legislation to change pollution laws.

The point is then that any value changes its definition depending on the stage of consciousness of the definer. However there is a core understanding of what work means that is constant even though a person's perception and understanding of what work is will change at every phase. Another good example of this is the way in which people perceive education. For a small child at Phase I education is simply going to school because one's mother told one to go. One goes because one loves one's mother. At Phase II education is often primarily identified with certification. Education is something one does at school in order to obtain grades. But for many people at Phase II education is identified with grading because grading is identified with getting a job and becoming successful in the world. At Phase III a person may see education for the first time as learning for its own sake. At the fourth phase education might be simply intuitive insight.

Again there is a common something that runs through education. It is always a question of learning, it is always a question of the pursuit of knowledge and it is always a question of an individual gaining something that will enable him to know more. However granted all this the definition still changes depending on the phase of consciousness. Indeed an individual value will change its definition not only in terms of the over-all phase of consciousness but also in terms of each individual stage of value development.

The Value Prioritized

II. Second, the priority ranking of any particular value changes depending on the phase of consciousness. At Phase I work is the modification of the environment for the purpose of survival. An example might be spending ten hours a day putting beer caps on beer bottles in a plant that has an inside temperature of 100°. Even though one recognizes a grave need to get money for his family, don't expect him to like the work he does! In fact there might be a lot of things that are much more important than work even though it is very high on one's need schedule. One may work every day in order to get out of the work situation, get home and have a bottle of beer in front of a TV set. Leisure may be of value and a much higher priority than work. One's family and all that they give may be much higher in value than work. So regarding the value of work at Phase I a ranking may be as follows:

1. Family
2. Leisure
3. Work

In fact if one is working in a Phase I environment it is unlikely that work is going to be very high on the priority list. But now let us take a look at a person at Phase II. Here image and prestige as related to self-competence are very high on the value needs. At Phase II work as it relates to self-competence is very important. And therefore although one works very hard for one's family one really doesn't have a lot of time for leisure. Behaviorally one finds himself working a 90-hour week because one needs to succeed. So in terms of personal behavior one finds the following ranking is true:

1. Work
2. Family
3. Leisure

At Phases III and IV the value ranking will probably change again. At Phase III, where work tends to be vocational, it can rank high on a priority list. Often we find people at this phase working with their wives, for example a clergyman. In my experience clergy don't have their wives going to work with them but often they do a lot of entertaining and she works very much with him playing a role in many parish groups. The point is that at this third phase the family and work may eventually occupy parallel places often initially causing a person difficulties and conflicts.

From this we can arrive at two conclusions:

1. Any value changes its definition according to the stage of consciousness at which the person is operating. However, every value also has a core meaning that is maintained through all the phases of consciousness.
2. Any given value changes its place of priority in the way it is ranked in relation to other values at each level of consciousness.

As a consequence of these two facts we can now come to a third conclusion that we have discovered in our own research:

3. Certain values appear as priorities at each phase of consciousness and at each stage of development.

These values continue to be a necessary part of the human being's development both before and after that phase of consciousness, but they take a lesser place on an individual's priority scale.

STAGES OF VALUE DEVELOPMENT

There are four phases of consciousness that break down into eight stages. Value development then constitutes eight stages. At each stage of development there is a set of core values that tend to become priorities at that stage. They are designated and described in the following chart:

DIAGRAM 19
VALUE DEVELOPMENT GUIDE

LEVELS	STAGES—CORE VALUES

I. World as Mystery
   Self as Center
	A. Self as Center. *Self-Preservation.
	   Survival. Warmth Food.

Physical / Existence Innocence	B. *Self-Delight. Wonder—Sensory Pleasure. Sex. Affection. *Security. Discovery.

II. World as Problem
   Self as Belonging
	A. *Self-Worth. Appreciation. Being liked
	   Friendship. Belonging. Family.

Social / Interaction
          (Doing)
 	
Work
	B. *Self-Competence. Work as Labor
	   Instrumentality. Success. Achievement. Prestige.
	   Law. Control. Ownership. Education as certification.

III. World as Project and
   Invention.
   Self as Independent.
	A. Self-Action. Self-Assertion. Power
	   *Independence. Self-Directedness.
	   Equity/Rights. Honesty. Learning
	   as insight. Equilibrium. Empathy.

Conscience / Acting
 	
Maintenance
	B. *Being Self. Creating. Ideation
	   Service. Order. Justice. Relaxation.
	   Health. Recreation. Cooperation. Community,
	   (Supportive) Construction. Human Dignity. Leisure.

IV. World as Mystery Cared
   For.
   Selves as Life Giver
	A. Congruence. *Intimacy and (waiting)
	   Solitude as Unitive. *Interdependence.
	   *Harmony. Community (Personalist)
	   Celebration/Limitation. Wisdom.

Interdependence / Being
 	
Freesence
	B. *Synergy. *Truth and knowledge as intuitive
	   insight. Presence (Of Other) Simplicity/Play.
	   Trancedence. Word. Ecority. Convivial tools
	   and technology.

*Indicates the "Primary Values."

Reflections

The above diagram takes sixty "I" values and places them in the order of priority in which they tend to appear for the eight stages of value development.

The reader must remember that anyone of these values would be defined differently at a different stage. We are simply stating these words symbolize certain values that appear as priorities at these stages. Of course a person would not be able to make these conscious for himself until he reached a later stage. At the first two phases a parent or a teacher should be especially cognizant of the appropriate values that are necessary for holistic human development. A child should learn to internalize these on the one hand and on the other hand have skills to foster them in others.

For example the value of self-competence may be resident in a teenager who does well in a particular subject. However it is also necessary that the system of education enhance education as a value in itself by teaching that young man or young lady that the very nature of competence itself is to be sought after as a value. Another clear example involves success and achievement. These are to be enjoyed at the second phase, but the teacher should be aware that they need to be made conscious and conscious in a way that maintains a balanced perspective. To stress success or achievement through a grading system and to make this the only priority can be destructive. It is my opinion that grading should be eliminated for the most part, because it stresses success, achievement and prestige but does so often to the detriment of education itself as a value and to the detriment of some of the other values such as instrumentality and self-competence.

We should keep in mind also that all the values are potentially present in an individual from the beginning. They simply rise up as priorities at a particular stage. It is our opinion, as we shall illustrate later, that all sixty values should be a part of the educational system from the first grade. It is simply that the higher values appear in a different form at the earlier stages. For example the value of intimacy and solitude would appear in Phase I as affection and patience. The value of harmony can be spoken to through the subject of esthetics in such activities as a dance or music.

In order to use these values and to be able to draw them out of given situations or circumstances or pieces of literature an individual needs to make these values his own. One should take each value, brainstorm on one's own experiences of that value, try to come to a definition and check it against some authority such as the *Oxford Unabridged Dictionary*.

SOME OTHER DEFINITIONS

Earlier we defined all the major primary values from self-preservation to synergy. Most of the values are self-evident in terms of their basic meaning and can be checked against a dictionary. However the meaning of some of the values might escape one, so we might define a few of them at this time. These are taken from the value-development guide.

Sex Stage I—B

Sex at the first level is primarily physical (see first column). It would be defined here as the need for physical touch and care in the child and in the adult the need for sexual intercourse without the concommitant responsibilities that would be typical of a higher level.

Instrumentality Stage II—B

This refers to the pure skills developed by an individual, like reading, writing or arithmetic. This also includes professional skills at a later level.

Education as Certification Stage II—B

The implication here is not that education is certification only. A person gets a great deal of education for its own sake and this should be stressed. It would be the teacher's way of stressing education at the third phase, however it must be stressed that a person at this stage needs to be rewarded, needs to be reassured that he is accomplishing something and that he is successful. Hence an individual at this stage tends to stress education as certification. If the environment is not well guarded a person could conclude that that is all education is.

Construction Stage III—B

This is a third-level value and the assumption is that the individual has a great deal of independence. Construction therefore designates a person building his own world. It refers to a person building his own business and constructing his own ideas but moving from his own individuality constructively into society. It is the technological side of personal and independent action. It is moving out into society beyond oneself in a creative act.

Intimacy Stage IV—A

Intimacy is the ability to share one's deepest hopes, aspirations, fears and anxieties with one significant other repeatedly and in such a way that he/she is free to do likewise. This definition could include more than one individual, but that is rare. Intimacy as such is a very deep process and is the ideal of many religious organizations concerning what they think a marriage should be. It requires a great deal of pain-tolerance and other skills and so is a Phase IV value. Attached to the value of intimacy is the value of solitude. We have written in the value chart "Intimacy and Waiting Solitude as Unitive." Intimacy here is related to the act of solitude that is the disciplined process of contemplation traditional in the East and the West. It is the ability to sit and reflect in such a manner that one's life comes together in a meaningful way so that a person participates in the act of intimacy with the Other. This is not restricted to any particular religious tradition but rather is a firm reality of all religious traditions and therefore has a place in this value chart. The reader might refer to the works of Zen or the mystical writings of the West.

Ecority Stage IV—B

This is a value that refers to the technological application of harmony as ecology, a man's authority and caring for the whole earth. It is a planetary concern that is technically manifested as a concern for nature and creation.

Conivivial Tools and Technology Stage IV—B

Related to the previous value are convivial tools. (The reader is referred to the work of Ivan Illich.) A convivial tool is any tool, machine or technology that should be controllable in the hands of the individual. We should only make cars for example that can be maintained by individuals who would be trained to do so by their schooling. As such this is a futuristic value but one that is applicable to our present day world with its crises of famine and energy.

(The above notes are added to the previous material to help the reader come to grips independently with these values and their definitions.)

Stages A and B

It becomes evident then as we study the value development guide, with the eight stages divided into Stage A and B for each phase, that it has a particular pattern running through it. Stage A of each phase tends to be more subjective and personal, whereas Stage B tends to be that dimension that moves an individual out into the world. In the later phases Stage B becomes the technical side of a person's reality.

For example at Phase III, Stage A the emphasis is on independence and therefore a personal honesty and integrity. It is personality development at its best. Stage B is the manifestation of this in the corporate society. Individual honesty is now manifested as human justice leading to construction that would be the corporate act of individuals moving into society to do something about their own independence and to relate it to the reality of invention. They are moving beyond personal independence to societal invention. Invention has to do here with creating new things.

Phase IV, Stage A is personal and the values tend to reflect those values that have been current in the great traditions of religious mysticism. Stage B is beyond this and is the technological manifestation of this personal view in values such as conviviality. The value of synergy itself is technological. It is a value that is very much a part of the life process. It requires the corporate acts of men, and much of our technology is in fact synergistic.

The examination of the value guide is something that requires the individual's own practice and attention. A book such as this is limited in what it can do. For this reason we have found that to have students examine a piece of literature where most of the levels and stages of value development are manifested is very instructive. The purpose would be to have the reader understand value development by an analysis for example of Charles Dickens' *David Copperfield*, using the eight stages of development.

CONCLUSION

In this chapter we have dealt with value development and have related how the four phases—the four world views—move us to an understanding of how values develop at eight different stages. Just as importantly we have related this to a specific educational method, an approach to clarifying and developing values.

This of course leaves us with a number of unanswered questions. Are there not other kinds of values besides "I" values? What about the great values of honor and respect? The core values introduce us to the subject matter and begin to provide us with a method—an anthropological method—a way of observing behavior. It is only a beginning. Much research has to be done beyond the scope of this writing. However we will look at institutional values more specifically in a later chapter.

Another question: Are people not at different phases and stages at different times? Is this a heirarchy? How does development occur—can we help it?

The questions about development have to do with the acquisition of skills. Values and priorities are behaviorial and are therefore related to skills. Life is learning, and learning has to do with skill building. This is the subject of the next chapter. Hopefully it will also begin to answer more questions.

CHAPTER V

TOOLS FOR GROWTH— SKILL BUILDING

ONAZCO, The Working Class Painting—16. Mexican National Tourist Council.

The test of the validity of new understandings in the search for human perfection is whether they "work" as a means of making people, individually and collectively, more able to "grow up"—that is, better related to each other, more at peace with themselves, more able to adjust to events, in fact "happier" in a wider sense than that of immediate satisfaction.

Rosemary Haughton

INTRODUCTION

Familiarity with the stages of value development and with the values appropriate to each stage does not of itself ensure growth. Such knowledge merely helps a person realize where he is developmentally and indicates to him what values have to become operative for him to reach the next stage of development. To this a person must add some awareness of the functional consequences of the distinction between underlying values and value indicators and of the relative influence on his behavior of personal and institutional values. But even all that fails to make growth inevitable. Growth in values and the concomitant expansion of consciousness is dependent on the acquisition of certain skills.

Growth and Its Cause

Skill building is an integral part of personal development. The various schemata of development by people like Erikson, Piaget and Kohlberg are of little educational use unless the educator has some idea of how to help a person move through the various stages described. At present, especially with regard to Kohlberg's stages, there seems to be a presumption by some teachers that a student merely has to be convinced that the next stage offers a sounder base of moral judgment than he is currently using for him to move to it. That may motivate him to grow and give him some concrete and immediate growth goals, but of itself it cannot produce growth. In a recent exchange with Simon, Kohlberg himself indicated that he was still working on the problem of how his stages could be utilized by teachers to promote growth.

Our contention, based on clinical observation, is that a number of skills have to come together in a holistic fashion for growth to occur. An educator interested in promoting the growth of his students must be trained not only to recognize the stages of development but also must become a skill builder.

The areas where skills are needed and the fact that development depends on skills is illustrated by the following story about Chug the caveman.

A STORY

Many years ago in a distant land there lived a caveman named Chug. He gave the appearance of being a mass of hair with two eyes peering out. Chug spent his days wandering naively about the world, picking berries and gawking curiously at the universe. His was the simple life. He ate when he was hungry. He slept out under the stars. He needed no clothes or fire because winter had not yet come.

Then one day as he was out walking a cold wind suddenly came up. He seemed surrounded by thunder claps and jagged streaks of lightning and a chilling rain began to drench him. He spied a cave on a hill and ran for cover. To warm himself he started a fire. As he sat enjoying the warmth and getting dry he studied the storm. All at once it dawned on him that by cutting down some trees he could build himself a permanent shelter like a cave.

So Chug designed and began to build a house. At first due to his lack of skill he banged his thumb often with his stone hammer, which prompted him to create some new words. But' by the time his house was finished he was a skilled carpenter. One day after he had completed the finishing touches on his house Chug was sitting smugly on his porch confidently dreaming up some new projects when a group of fierce-looking club-wielding primitives appeared in his front yard and eyed him ominously. They told him most indelicately that they wanted him to vacate his house.

Ever the fast thinker Chug meekly told them the house was theirs, but warned them that it wouldn't be too long before other men with superior weapons would take the house from them. War with its accompanying atrocities would be unavoidable. Chug suggested that their futures would be all brighter if they joined hands and forged ahead together. He offered to help each of them build his own house, adding that a well-placed and fortified wall would discourage unwelcome visitors with ignoble intentions.

And so they founded the first city and called it Chugsville. Because of his lively imagination and exceptional organizational talents Chug was appointed mayor. Initially city life was fairly simple. Chug distributed the work loads according to individual inclinations and community needs; some people were assigned to develop skills in raising crops, some in caring for the flocks, others in making clothes, still others in the construction business.

But eventually because of considerable population expansion a need arose for more elaborate tools and more complex human social institutions. A group of lawmakers were selected, both police and judicial systems had to be established, and Chug insisted that they set up an environmental protection agency.

THE FOUR SKILLS

Thus in a matter of few years Chug and his friends had come a long way. From a group of primitive cavemen they had become more or less sophisticated city dwellers. In the process they had acquired many new skills, skills upon which all human development is contingent. These skills fall into four general areas:

1. Skills in coping with systems
2. Instrumental skills
3. Interpersonal skills
4. Imaginal skills

As we explore each of these areas in some detail it will become apparent that there is some overlap from one area to another. The lines of division are not all that clear cut, but there is something distinctive about each skill area that prevents this fourfold arrangement from being completely arbitrary.

1. Coping With Systems

There seem to be three basic kinds of systems with which a man must learn to cope:

1. His own body
2. The family
3. Social institutions

To get on in life and develop his potential a man must acquire skills in dealing with each of these areas.

Unless a person possesses skills in managing his own body, effort expended in gaining other systems skills will be largely wasted. The body is a complicated and powerful system whose demands are delivered without any prior consultation and only rarely with prior warning. To ignore or to lack the skills to respond appropriately to those demands is to risk and even to encourage being controlled by the body. No existing form of governing devised by man operates as autocratically as the human body.

Body as System

Early in life the child must learn to form suitable replies to the body's cries for attention or else be prepared to surrender to the body a major portion of control of his life. So a person interested in his own growth must develop skills in caring for his own body (health), skills in bringing the various members of the body together into cooperative efforts for the purposes and intentions of the self (control).

Thus there are three generic types of skills that equip a person to manage his body so as to help rather than hinder human development.

1. Chug's ability to complete the many projects to which he devoted his energy was clearly dependent on his bodily health. Had he not headed for the cave to escape the chilling rain he might quite possibly have died from pneumonia. (Health)
2. Coordinating the specific functions of his eyes, arms and legs enabled Chug to build his house without seriously injuring himself. (Coordination)
3. Chug's capacity to use his imagination in dreaming up new projects and in solving as yet unencountered problems relied on his skill in ignoring the many insistent and distracting demands for attention that originated in his bodily needs. (Control)

The objective of health, physical coordination and bodily control in a developmental framework is the harmonious cooperation of mind and body in the pursuit of growth goals. Without harmony the various elements of man's makeup can go their independent ways and lead a man imperiously to conflicting courses of action. This fragments a man's efforts and renders him ineffective. Sickness and pain restrict a man's imaginative endeavors, a case where the lack of health makes control extremely difficult.

A holistic approach to the body pays attention to all three elements: health, coordination and control.

Being Your Own Doctor

The child must learn early in life that the primary responsibility for his health care belongs to him. Far too many people see their health as in the hands of their doctor! This is not to imply that there are not cases where the special expertise of physicians is needed, but only that a person should not abdicate his primary responsibility in this area. The role of the physician is to assist a person in the exercise of that responsibility.

The more knowledge and skill the individual acquires qualifying him to handle his own health needs the less often will a doctor's assistance be required. A person must learn to listen to his body's demands and use discretion in judging what is consistent with over-all harmony. Obviously not every demand for food, drink or pleasure merits satisfaction. One must learn how much exercise and what kinds of drink and food are conducive to health. One ought to gain some diagnostic skills either at home or at school so that one can himself treat some of the less severe ailments. This ability to cope with the body's health is the first and most basic systems skill needed by any man.

Coordination

The body is like a complex tool or machine that has many moving parts. If the parts do not work together much energy is wasted and the desired end result is not achieved. In this respect the body is not unlike a large organization that functions smoothly only as long as the individual members perform their appointed tasks with a view to reaching a common objective.

Coordination is the skill that transforms an awkward energy-wasting body into an orderly, organized and efficient instrument. Failure to develop this skill closes many doors and misspends much effort that can be channelled productively elsewhere. Clearly not everyone's potential is the same in this particular area, but a certain minimal dexterity is within everybody's reach.

Today, educational toys that challenge and intrigue the child are available in abundance while at the same time they train him to use his body in a coordinated way. In school, besides physical education courses, activities such as dance, drama and roleplaying can help the child develop coordination.

Besides contributing to this sense of self-worth this skill equips a person for those tasks that require physical coordination and once achieved frees him from much frustration and from feelings of inadequacy while at the same time supplying him with extra available energy.

Control

Control is something that increases with an individual's maturity or development. It advances on two fronts: 1) inner control and development of moral conscience, and 2) control as it relates to external expectations of the natural and social environment.

1) Inner control is a part of the natural process of development of every healthy individual. It is of course impossible to separate completely the physical and emotional components of a person. Clearly the physical attributes of an individual are related to one's personal value structure. Persons with excessive weight problems more often than not have difficulties with a sense of their own self-worth. Therefore specific skills such as physical exercise, dieting and the harmonious interrelating of work, rest and leisure are essential to value development.

Being in Control

Inner control is necessary at all levels of development. At the first two phases this control and skill training should be provided externally through home and school environments. By internalizing these skills the mature individual at either of the other two phases of development is able to control autonomously through his adult life the harmonious running of his own body. This internal environment replaces the external one of the earlier stages in reinforcing the core values of security, self-esteem, competence and self-directedness.

2) External control factors. Man being the social animal he is has to limit the negative effects of the social environment on his body. We work to provide the minimum necessities of life and shelter from wind and rain. The kind of clothes we wear, the kind of hours we live and the kind of transportation we use reflects our values. These are all control factors affecting the body.

More concretely the abundant and confusing alternatives, and the pressures of our present human societies cause unusual emotional and consequent physical strain. The relationship between anxiety, alcholism, overeating and heart disease is well documented. Men need to acquire the ability to develop skills to control not only internal consumption but also bodily tension.

Body Skill Training

Basic skills to be called on here would be the confronting of overconsuming life styles through life goal-setting, financial planning and work and leisure rhythms. Also helpful would be training in basic relaxation techniques such as those commonly used in the East through Yoga and Zen schools or some Western methods like autogenic training (Wolfgang Luthe) and the disidentification method of Robert Assagioli. Such methods teach bodily relaxation and help a person control his body and shield him from the problems and expectations of the world around him.

For development at the higher levels advanced training in solitude and meditation should not be reserved for a religious ghetto but ought to be a part of every man's educational journey.

Dealing with Personal Emotions

At the Center for the Exploration of Values and Meaning dealing with the body as system is a part of teacher training. Take for example the problems of anger, anxiety and tension, the last a major cause of heart problems.

For leadership at a Phase III period of development being self is a primary value. This means one has to be a physical and interpersonal self as well as being able to express oneself by being a leader.

People in management positions are often moved by external pressure to produce and perform and by internal pressure to keep the machine, so to speak, running well. This often causes anxiety and anger. The body has to be in good shape, and the *value* of health is stressed.

Autogenic Training

Quite specifically we talk about diet and physical exercise. We teach a number of relaxation methods, relying on the work of Johannes Schultz and Wolfgang Luthe. They have the following to say:

> Autogenic Training is the basic therapeutic method of a group of psychophysiologically oriented autogenic approaches which constitute 'Autogenic Therapy.' In contrast to other medically or psychologically orientated forms of treatment, the methods of autogenic therapy approach and involve mental and bodily functions simultaneously.

Put simply it is a relaxation method, used outside of therapy to help persons relax and reduce tension.

Physical Exercise

However this is only part of the program, relaxation does not always help very energetic and creative people. Rigorous physical exercise such as the Canadian 5 BX (10 BX for women) or a program at the local YMCA is also necessary.

Conflict Resolution

Finally strategies in the creative management of anger and conflict resolution are necessary skills in body and of course in interpersonal management. For example rules for expression of anger in one-to-one relationships in management systems might be the following:

1) Do not let your anger go unexpressed for a long period of time
2) Confront the reason you are angry with another in private and always start from the "I" position. Do not begin with direct attack unless you are ready for war
3) Be specific in your grievances, expressing your hurt, not disregarding the other parties

4) Learn to confront spontaneously before the anger boils up inside. Confrontation means making the other person hear what you say—that is your responsibility

5) Be clear as to what your responsibilities are. Let the other person be responsible for his and for the consequences.

These kinds of rules plus many others, of which these are a partial example, are some of the skills needed for body management. Conflict management in families, between large groups and in a polarized setting would constitute continuation of training in over-all systems skill. Clearly the last example overlaps into the following areas also.

The Family

The first system outside of his own body with which a child must learn to cope is his family. The child is so constituted that as he moves from a comfortable intrauterine existence where his needs for nourishment and warmth have been automatically met he is forced to direct his attention outward to the external environment in order to discover new sources for and new ways of satisfying his basic needs. This produces the first major expansion of consciousness and like all later development is need-related. In this new environment mother is the key figure.

While in the process of familiarizing himself with his new world the child acquires the ability to manipulate mother so as to have her take care of his needs for food and warmth and physical comfort. He learns that crying, whether in anger or discomfort, frequently evokes the desired response from his mother. He is learning to cope with a system, for mother is also wife!

Family as System

Because it never loses its utility perhaps the most basic skill the child can profitably acquire is doing a read-out of the family system. Any effort the child expends in this direction will ultimately more than pay for itself in appreciable returns. Only such a skill enables the child to situate himself realistically in his world.

An essential element of this coming to grips with his world is developing a sort of internal Geiger counter that measures expectations: the expectations that his mother has of him; then his father, brothers and sisters and even an occasional aunt or two. Soon he learns to read his unique family system.

The language of reward and punishment is the only one he can understand. That same language enables him to discover what he can expect of others. Only repeated experimentation allows him to settle on a more or less consistent approach to the family, a process that takes years.

It is within the family environment that the child gains the conviction that he has a place in the world and that the world is safe and fairly predictable. Such a conviction provides the child with an embryonic sense of belonging that must eventually deepen if he is ever to mature.

In this regard, speaking of disadvantaged families, the authors of *Families of the Slums* write:

> One essential feature of the family and home environment is its impermanence and unpredictability. These characteristics make it difficult for the growing child to define himself in relation to his world. In home visits we encountered a world in which objects and events have a transient quality. For example, a bed shared by two or more children can be turned over to a different child or to a semi-permanent visitor while its original occupants are crowded into a section of another bed. The geography of the home and its arrangements impede the development of a sense that "I have my place in the world."

In such an environment it is difficult to imagine how a child's basic needs for security, pleasure, belonging and self-worth can be satisfied. Such a child will inevitably learn the skills to meet these basic human demands. His world views will tend to remain at an earlier phase because of his physical environment and the way he has to adapt to that environment, given his limited experience and lack of resourcefulness. A person trying to help such a child must use as much effort in attempting to create a more healthy environment as he does in ministering to the psychic needs of the child. The two elements are interrelated.

Virginia Satir mentions the following skill-related lessons that parents must give their children if healthy growth is to take place.

1. To teach "roles" or socially accepted ways to act with others in different social situations. (These roles vary according to the age and sex of the child.)
2. To teach the child to cope with the inanimate environment.
3. To teach the child how to communicate; how to use words and gestures so that they will have a generally accepted meaning for others.
4. To teach how and when to express emotions, generally guiding the child's emotional reactivity. (The family teaches the child by appealing to his love and to his fear, communicating to him verbally, nonverbally and by example.)

These are merely some of the skills with which the child must equip himself if he is to deal effectively with his family and later with the larger human community. In terms of learning to cope with that larger world out there Satir maintains that it is especially important that the child within the family develop esteem for himself both as a masterful person and as a sexual person. The parents have the responsibility for providing the type of family environment that reinforces values such as self-esteem, womanhood or manhood.

Families as Systems
The key however is in understanding the uniqueness of families as systems. In the same way as parts of the body are unique and dependent on each other yet work as a harmonious system, so it is with the family.

As the family counselor has learned long ago, individual treatment of an emotionally unwell child in a family may be totally fruitless. For the family is a system and he may be sick as a consequence of total-system sickness. For example if the mother and father are continually fighting because the father is not home half the time then a child may not get the attention he needs. His sickness would be then his adaptation to that system. He would have learned a systems skill. The problem is of course that the systems skill he has learned, which is very healthy in *his* system, gets him in serious trouble when he enters another system such as a school.

A Strategy

An interesting strategy is to draw two family-system diagrams. One of when you were between five and seven years of age and a recent one (what would constitute family for you now). You must first remember a specific event when all the family were present—a conflict usually works well—then diagram as follows, using circles for people. The distance between the circles is the emotional distance in the event. The size of the circle is its importance.

DIAGRAM 19

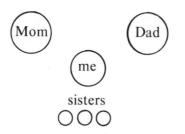

In the diagram I was caught between Mom and Dad over a bad school report card and they did not agree on what to do about it. My three sisters were backing me up. I felt small.

Now the point is to compare this with a recent situation and see if you can see some system similarities. Compare:

1. Similar or dissimilar diagrams
2. Similar or opposite feelings
3. Similar or opposite roles
4. Role reversals (behaving like someone in a previous event) and skills learned.

We have found this useful in helping people view the family as a system rather than a group of individuals.

Social Institutions of Varying Complexity

As a person grows through the phases of consciousness his world expands and he finds himself confronted with the problem of coping with more and more systems. The child grows up and has to go to school where he must deal with schoolmates, teachers and administrators. Eventually he goes to work where he must meet the expectations of a boss and of his coworkers. The systems get more complicated and demand more ingenuity from a person than the family ever did.

Chug demonstrated development in this area when he organized his cohorts into a city and distributed various responsibilities among the citizenry. He had the foresight to recognize what needs might arise in the newly founded city, and he also possessed the executive ability to assign people to jobs that would meet those needs.

Revolution and History

A particular area worthy of examination in this regard is the history of revolutions. A successful revolutionary must have fantastic systems skills. He must be able to read the expectations of the masses (Hitler was a master at this). He needs to be in touch with the mood of the times. He must have a sense of timing and an ability to foresee obstacles. And of course without the gifts to excite the imagination of his followers he could never get the revolution off the ground. Throughout the whole revolutionary process he must organize people, distribute tasks and adapt to the unexpected. Lenin, Castro and Chairman Mao have all exhibited these qualities.

Ancient Sparta provides an excellent example of a people, in fact a whole culture, who devoted all their energies to becoming a militaristic nation with exceptional fighting skills. But because they lacked the more sophisticated systems skills after they conquered Athens they were unable to rule her effectively.

Richard Nixon

Any attempt to assess accurately the rise and fall of Richard Nixon would entail an evaluation of his systems skills. The fact that in spite of his apparent political demise in the early Sixties he obtained the backing of the GOP and was elected to the presidency twice. This indicates that his talents in this area were considerable. He also manifested imagination and originality in his foreign policy. But at some point in time (pardon the expression) he lost touch with the mood of the

American people by isolating himself behind a relatively small number of appointed officials. Leaving aside any moral judgments one can safely say that he lacked the ability to foresee and forestall the complications that eventually forced him to resign.

The examples used and the observations made thus far might lead a person to conclude that these skills are to be cultivated only by the leaders of an organization. But anyone who is affected by a system must learn to cope with it. Just as the child has to learn to define his role within the family and live with it so must any individual define his role in the more complex systems in which he involves himself. This is not to assert that he should not forge a new role for himself as he learns to deal with the system. That too is a needed skill.

Integration as Skill

The following model may help us to see the units of body, family and larger institutions as systems.

DIAGRAM 20

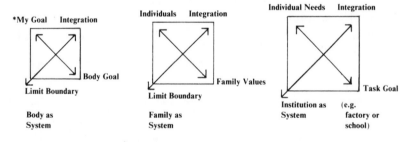

*Adapted from the works of Talcott Parsons

All three systems are similar. As system they *all* have similar tensions:

1) N—T. The tension between the individual's needs and the system's own goals, values or tasks. In the body as system an individual may want to work all night to get the job done, *but* the body as a system might not be able to take it—it has its own peculiar rules and limits. An

individual in a family might want everyone to go out to a picnic on Sunday, but the family may have prior commitments to visit relatives—as a whole family.

In the last diagram, reducing the tension between personal needs and the task of the institution is the perennial job of the manager and leader. The task might be profit versus minimal security for the employee. In a school the task might be to enable 1500 students to learn minimal skills to be able to work in society. But you only have 100 teachers. The tension is how to keep them happy, how to satisfy their needs as teachers in a very limited situation.

2) The second tension then is the integration of task versus personal needs within the boundaries or the limits given. Everyone has a body with different needs. Some persons have to live with handicaps. They have to face it and integrate it into a life style. A child who has no father in the home has limits that many others do not have and has to adapt to that system.

Finally every leader or administrator has a different set of limits and things he must integrate if tensions between people-needs and getting the job done is to be accomplished. Take a teacher in a classroom. The school may have expectations of what they expect her/him to accomplish with these children; but the teacher needs to be told he/she is doing a good job:

Teacher's N ———————————————— T School's

Needs   Expectations

This is individualistic. To see this as systems we would need to ask how can these be integrated? We might say that the school principal would arrange for team discussion one hour a week to give peer support. Also a limit boundary might be set by the school: maximum class load 35 students. Then our system diagram would look like this:

DIAGRAM 21

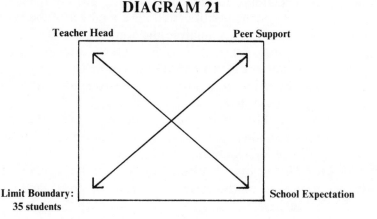

The last example is of course limited, but serves to illustrate how systems skills are distinct from such skills as communication. Clearly a future direction in education must be to teach students and teachers systems skills: how to understand and deal with difficult situations, to get inside an irritable principal or teacher and cope with the system.

Some System Skills

It is difficult, if not impossible, to formulate a complete breakdown of the skills needed to cope with complex systems. But certainly some of the more important skills needed are the following:

1. The ability to read the present and future expectations of the system as represented by the leadership or the membership
2. The ability to discover or shape a personal role in the fulfillment of those expectations by making sure the system wants and needs me
3. The ability to foresee and handle obstacles and opposition
4. The ability to read the signs of the time as they are significant for both the individual and the system

5. The ability to motivate others to achieve the goals of the system and of oneself as a member of the system
6. The ability to analyze the components of a task and to make sure that each is taken care of, assigning specific responsibilities in the process
7. The ability to assess both the strong and weak points of the system
8. The ability to decide on realistic goals for the system
9. The ability to enhance personal meaning from the institutional source
10. The ability to distinguish between the myth and the reality of the system, to separate propaganda from reality.

Systems Skills and Development

An added point to bear in mind is that what is a skill at one stage of a person's development might become an impediment to growth at a later stage. For example as a child moves out beyond the family into society he initially needs to learn to fit himself into that society and its systems. But if his basic concern as he involves himself in these systems is only to conform or always fit himself in then growth to Phase III will be prevented by his unwillingness to become self-directed. What was a valuable skill and a means for achieving a sense of belonging at one time has now become a liability. Passive responses should eventually give way to creative initiative and active responsibility.

In the same vein unless manipulative behavior that is normal and necessary in the young child is replaced by an ability to evoke free and genuine responses from other people maturity will remain permanently out of reach. Recently I have been seeing a twenty-three-year-old male who has an aversion to getting a job. Married and father of a son he has thus far managed to get by through manipulating others—his mother, his wife and his in-laws—so that they meet his financial responsibilities. Manipulation has worked for him so well for so long that it seems never to have occurred to him that other approaches might ultimately be more satisfying. His systems skills are destructive rather than creative towards others.

The problem that he has recently encountered is that

complex systems like finance companies and those typical of the working world do not respond favorably to his manipulative efforts which are actually directed at avoiding responsibility and its hardships.

So skills appropriate to one stage of development need to be discarded and replaced by others more consistent with the next stage of development. Normally a person integrates his behavior to fit the results he desires. As he develops to later phases his skills are geared to cooperative accomplishment rather than needs only.

Leadership

The leadership in any system has to have the maturity to recognize that their responsibility is to do more than keep order or make people comfortable. They must not confuse care for the members of the system with refusal to cause confrontation and conflict where that is necessary. They are integrators of tension within limits. They must have real vision if they are to move people to higher levels of maturity. In this and other areas of systems behavior moral issues become prominent.

A moral issue arises because systems have a way of accentuating and reinforcing the powerlessness of individuals. Systems sometimes tend to crush the individual and take control of his life. This not only inhibits growth but it destroys a person's individuality. Every system needs people with vision skilled in integrative or change processes who can bring such abuses to consciousness and pave the way for reform.

Morality is also involved when the leadership tolerates all manner of corruption and abuses of responsibility that poison the whole system. Again there is a need to build into the system strong communication networks, which is its own watchdog. The point we are making is that some portion of the membership of any system ought to be skilled in and responsible for protecting the system from disintegration. A well conceived limited design criterion as described in the next chapter is one instrument that can serve this function.

These are merely some of the systems skills that are essential to growth. At present there seems to be very little thought or energy devoted to the development of these kinds of skills in our educational institutions. The same thing cannot be said of the next category of skills—instrumental skills—because a major portion of the effort of most schools is aimed in this direction.

2. Instrumental Skills

Chug exhibited instrumental skills in starting a fire and building his house, not to mention in his ability to verbalize.

Recently a pilot film for a planned series entitled *Movin' On* appeared on TV. The story revolves around the adventures of two truck drivers with sharply contrasting approaches to life. The one is a beefy, highly physical character in his late forties or early fifties. He first appears smacking his lips over a cup of coffee at a truck stop while waiting for a waitress to finish her work so he can "spend" an hour or so with her. The other driver is a young graduate of an Eastern law school who opposed the war in Vietnam and is driving trucks while he tries to find himself.

At one point in the story they have contracted for a job that includes a $100 bonus upon safe delivery of the cargo. When they fulfill their end of the bargain and arrive safely at their destination they are informed that no bonus will be given. The inclination of the older "physical driver" is to beat the $100 out of the welcher. But the younger more cerebral driver intervenes and obtains the $100 by threatening court action in highly technical legal language.

Each driver has a different set of instrumental skills (coming from distinct phases of consciousness) on which to rely in this conflict situation. In this instance moral force proved more effective than physical force. But both the ability to fight and the ability to analyze the business transaction in legal terms are instrumental skills.

Instrumental skills are task oriented. They encompass all those abilities an individual can rely on to get jobs done. They cover the very general skills needed by nearly everyone in a given culture, like reading and writing in the United States or hunting and food gathering in some primitive societies. Highly professional or specialized skills like truck driving, using a pippet in chemistry or performing brain surgery are also instrumental skills. Both the designing and using of tools are instrumental skills. This presents us with the following break down of instrumental skills:

I. General Skills—such as reading
II. Professional Skills—such as practicing law
III. The design and use of tools.

Of course these skills can be divided in other ways, as for example bodily and mental skills. We have selected this particular division because it is so serviceable within a developmental framework.

General Skills

Unless a person masters those general skills expected of members of a particular society and culture he cannot be said to fully belong. Indeed without those basic skills his achievement of a sense of self-worth will suffer a severe setback. These general skills represent the minimum expectations a society built into its culture. This is made visibly explicit in the puberty rites of some primitive societies, ceremonies that are the ritual certifications that the initiates are qualified skillwise to function as adult members of the tribe.

Certification by a school or successfully passing through an apprenticeship serves much the same function in technological societies, though without the religious overtones of primitive ritual.

Professional or Specialized Skills

A sense of belonging and self-worth also derive from the acquisition of these more specialized skills. A professor of history belongs to a very select group and can be confident that his peculiar specialty is not typical of the general populace. The same can be said of a plumber.

But professional skills also empower a person to be more independent than others who must cope with life without these less widely distributed skills. The competence such a person has attained frequently frees him from the worries and concerns typical of someone whose basic aim in life is to meet the expectations of others. The same thing is not true of skills like reading and writing, which are maintenance skills. All we are asserting here is that all other skill development being equal the special competence that accompanies the acquisition of professional skills opens the door to Phase III and IV existence in a way that is not true of the more general instrumental skills.

The Design and Use of Tools

The skill to use tools can be a simple or a highly sophisticated art as Ivan Illich indicates:

> I use the term "tool" broadly enough to include not only simple hardware such as drills, pots, syringes, brooms, building elements or motors and not just large machines like cars or power stations. I also include among tools productive institutions such as factories, which produce tangible commodities such as cars and electric current, and production systems for intangible commodities such as these produce, "education," "sick care," "conflict resolutions" or which "make" decisions. I use the term "tool" for lack of any other which would be equally general and simple.

Not everyone is equally qualified to use all the tools described by Illich. A Phase IV person must have the ability to design and use tools that meet the needs for the construction of the ideal world as he perceives it in his vision of the future. This is beyond the reach of a person whose capabilities are strained by using a hammer or screw driver or merely reading. It is especially in the designing of human institutions which promote the values typical of Phases III and IV that highly skilled people are required.

Thus these three categories of instrumental skills are all developmental. Nearly everyone may have the ability to verbalize, but no one would claim that every verbalizer has equal ability. The same can be said of any instrumental skill. They all admit of degrees and are always open to further development.

Tools, Skills and Consciousness

Instrumental skills, the key to modern education, for centuries have emphasized ideas and the natural side of man as being the key to what is human. Man's growth in cognitive abilities, his application of thought to the manufacturing of tools and the expansion of his varied personal skills constitute the history of the development of civilization.

An instrumental skill is no more than the manner by which man utilizes his tools. At one level an individual has skill in using the hammer. His hands and brain coordinate the maximum use of "the instrument called hammer." Skill then is a coordinating function.

At a more sophisticated level a director of a hospital uses "skills" and coordinates the use of the tool "medicine." He has to organize laboratory, doctor, radiology, nursing and many other parts into a single efficient instrument. Here we are still referring to "instrumental skills" as the use of tools.

Minessence and Tool Making

Let us look a little more deeply into a process we will call *Minessence*. It consists of three interchangeable processes as follows:

1. Miniaturization
2. Objectification
3. Consciousization

It is through this basic process that tools have always come into being. Let's take Chug as an example to see how it works.

Our caveman is standing in the forest admiring the scenery. Suddenly the sun disappears behind a cloud and it rains and is windy. Chug is cold. After this has happened several times, and after weeks of reflection, he has a terrific idea. "I will cut down some trees and build a house to protect me from the elements and keep me warm."

Getting serious about the problem let us assume that our caveman has never seen a house before. Where did the idea come from?

Briefly, I am suggesting that having assimilated a lot of data that was reflected on over a period of time Chug "miniaturized" all that data through an intuitive act into the one new "idea"—house.

What separates man from the animals is this intuitive factor, what we might call reflective intellect where he is able to collect data, fantasize, think (reflect) and synergetically come up with new ideas. When any mass of data is assimilated into a *new* integrated whole such as an idea we call that process "miniaturization."

But man the tool maker has always had the capacity to objectify this miniaturized form into the environment. Chug built the house. He took the idea inside of him and made a tool, "house," in the external environment. This is "objectification."

All tools, whether they are hammer and saws, houses and office complexes, or social organization like medicine, law or schools, are all objectifications of man's ideas projected into the environment in the form of "tool." Paolo Soleri speaks of the process as follows:

> "The brain has compressed (miniaturized) the "universe" in a few pounds-inches of space-matter-energy. Only by way of this miraculous contraction of performances (information, communication, etc.) is the brain a concrete (willful?) process presiding over the other miniaturized "universe" of the body." (The Arcology of Paolo Soleri, p. 23.)

This then is a life process. But concretely in the social history of man complexity is reduced (miniaturized) to ideas in our inner world and shaped into tools in our external world.

Man is a social animal; he cooperates and exchanges these ideas across generations and history and culture. In this he is unique again. Two people with a set of mundane ideas can come up with a third and brilliant thought. Social complexity is miniaturized. Ideas are put together with new data to form an hypothesis that is tested with new data and made into a scientific law.

Through discovering and utilizing laws of science and social organization man creates inventions and governs societies. My point: miniaturization, objectification, indeed "tool-making" changes consciousness.

The artist receives data through his senses about the world. A Rubens or a Michaelangelo sees something different. He takes that complexity and miniaturizes (reduces) it and objectifies it as a painting that he hopes will help us to be more conscious of the beauty of the world around them.

Miniaturization is an implosion making complexity small. This is fashioned outwardly as a tool that in turn causes an explosion of consciousness causing even greater complexity, that someone will miniaturize again. This is the developmental process of tool-making.

Tools are also expressions of the moral development of man, because they can provide security and love in a house and thus contribute to human development, or they can foster fear and mistrust when they are fashioned into tools of war and death. Moral choice is an instrumental skill itself as Kohlberg has already elaborated.

Moral Choice: An Instrumental Skill

The ability to arrive at and apply criteria for measuring the morality of a person's behavior takes cognitive skills that are basically instrumental even though such activity calls for some imaginal capabilities. As Kohlberg has demonstrated clearly, the use of such a skill is developmental, the criteria changing as the person develops. Such development follows inevitably as a person's world view and consciousness expand. Any cognitive skill that deals with values necessarily adjusts itself to the needs that assume prominence in the subject's current world view.

So from our perspective the following schema of moral development by Lawrence Kohlberg constitutes a graph of an expanding cognitive instrumental skill that at any stage expresses one aspect of the person's world view or value stance. Each stage is a spinoff from the cluster of needs that constitute the central point in consciousness of a person at that point in his development.

Kohlberg's work is the key to the decision-making process; he describes how people choose what is right, the "ought," at different stages of their maturity as follows:

Definition of Moral Stages

I. Preconventional Level

At this level the child is responsive to cultural rules and labels of good and bad, right or wrong, but interprets these labels in terms of either the physical or the hedonistic consequences of action (punishment, reward, exchange of favors) or in terms of the physical power of those who enunciate the rules and labels. The level is divided into the following two stages:

Stage 1: The punishment and obedience orientation.
The physical consequences of action determine its goodness or badness regardless of the human meaning or value of these consequences. Avoidance of punishment and unquestioning difference to power are valued in their own right not in terms of respect for an underlying moral order supported by punishment and authority (the latter being stage four).

Stage 2: The instrumental relativist orientation.
Right action consists of that which instrumentally satisfies one's own needs and occasionally the needs of others. Human relations are viewed in terms like those of the market place. Elements of fairness, of reciprocity and of equal sharing are present, but they are always interpreted in a physical pragmatic way. Reciprocity is a matter of "You scratch my back and I'll scratch yours," not of loyalty, gratitude or justice.

II. Conventional Level

At this level, maintaining the expectations of the individual's family, group or nation is perceived as valuable in its own right, regardless of immediate and obvious consequences. The attitude is not only one of *conformity* to personal expectations and social order but of loyalty to it, of actively *maintaining*, supporting and justifying the order and of identifying with the persons or group involved in it. At this level there are the following two stages:

Stage 3: The interpersonal concordance or "good boy—nice girl" orientation.
Good behavior is that which pleases or helps others and is approved by them. There is much conformity to sterotypical images of what is majority or "natural" behavior. Behavior is frequently judged by intention—"He means well" becomes important for the first time. One earns approval by being "nice."

Stage 4: The "law and order" orientation.
There is orientation toward authority, fixed rules and the maintenance of the social order. Right behavior consists of doing one's duty, showing respect for authority and maintaining the given social order for it's own sake.

III. Postconventional, Autonomous or Principled Level.

At this level, there is a clear effort to define moral values and principles that have validity and application apart from the authority of the group or persons holding these principles and apart from the individual's own identification with these groups. This level again has two stages:

Stage 5: The social-contract legalistic orientation, generally with utilitarian overtones. Right action tends to be defined in terms of general individual rights and standards that have been critically examined and agreed upon by the whole society. There is a clear awareness of the relativism of personal values and opinions and a corresponding emphasis upon procedural rules for reaching consensus. Aside from what is constitutionally and democratically agreed upon the right is a matter of personal "values" and "opinion." The result of an emphasis upon the "legal point of view" but with an emphasis upon the possibility of changing law in terms of rational considerations of social utility (rather than freezing it in terms of stage four "law and order"). Outside the legal realm free agreement and contract is the binding element of obligation. This is the "official" morality of the American government and Constitution.

Stage 6: The universal ethical principle orientation.
Right is defined by the decision of conscience in accord with self-chosen ethical principles appealing to logical comprehensiveness, universality and consistency. These principles are abstract and ethical (the Golden Rule, the categorical imperative); they are not concrete moral rules like the Ten Commandments. At heart they are universal principles of justice, of the reciprocity and equality of human rights and of respect for the dignity of human beings as individual persons.*

The schema carries an individual into our Phase III, after which a new moral criterion begins to operate—the individual's vision of a new world.
Moral Education, edited by C. M. Beck, B.S. Crittenden, E. V. Sullivan University of Toronto Press, Toronto, 1971.

Level IV—Morality and Phase IV Consciousness

Beyond Kohlberg's sixth stage traditional concepts of justice give way to a vision of the future that, while structured by justice's demands, makes the not yet existing world, the ideal, the new norm of morality. The imaginative resources of the individual and values like harmony, synergy and inter-dependence become the sources of moral imperatives through the development of constructive tools. The demands of justice that emerge from the already existing world cede their norma-tive role to the basic requirements for the construction of a not-yet-existing human community characterized by the values typ-ical of Phase IV.

In other words, the dominant note of the moral norm of this new level of consciousness is a vision of the future based on human harmony and convivial tools. This vision accepts the norms of universal justice of the previous level but redirects them toward the establishment of a new and more just world.

Some might assert that Kohlberg's final stage includes all this. If so it needs to be made more explicit. Certainly uni-versal norms of justice demand changes in the world as it is presently constituted and to move people to devote energy to creating a new, more just world. But it seems to us that a per-son using justice as a norm is not necessarily going to envision a human future characterized by the Phase IV values of con-gruence, harmony, intimacy, synergy, convivial technology and interdependence.

By his own admission Kohlberg's schema deals with a cognitive skill that we have classified as instrumental while the main point of this chapter is to suggest that for people to grow other kinds of skills are indispensable, not the least important of which are interpersonal skills.

Interpersonal Skills

Human growth is evidently dependent on the cultivation of interpersonal skills that equip a person to enter into deeply satisfying human relationships. There is a noticeable correla-tion between a person's expansion of consciousness and a wid-ening of his social relationships. The person who remains isolated or habitually cuts himself off from others thereby ef-fectively stunts his own growth. In order to increase the radius of his social sphere and also to intensify and deepen already ex-isting relationships a person must acquire special kinds of skills. The following diagram of Erikson can serve to illustrate this:

DIAGRAM 22

Worksheet

	A Psychosocial Crises	B Radius of Significant Relations	C Related Elements of Social Order	D Psychosocial Modalities	E Psychosexual Stages
I	Trust vs. Mistrust	Maternal Person	Cosmic Order	To get To give in return	Oral-Respiratory, Sensory-Kinesthetic (Incorporative Modes)
II	Autonomy vs. Shame, Doubt	Parental Persons	"Law and Order"	To hold (on) To let (go)	Anal-Urethral, Muscular (Retentive-Eliminative)
III	Initiative vs. Guilt	Basic Family	Ideal Prototypes	To make (= going after) To "make like" (= playing)	Infantile-Genital, Locomotor (Instrusive, Inclusive)
IV	Industry vs. Inferiority	"Neighborhood," School	Technological Elements	To make things (= completing) To make things together	"Latency"
V	Identity and Repudiation vs. Identity Diffusion	Peer Groups and Outgroups; Models of Leadership	Ideological Perspectives	To be oneself (or not to be) To share being oneself	Puberty
VI	Intimacy and Solidarity vs. Isolation	Partners in friendship, sex, competition, cooperation	Patterns of Cooperation and Competition	To lose and find oneself in another	Genitality
VII	Generativity vs. Self-Absorption	Divided labor and shared household	Currents of Education and Tradition	To make be To take care of	
VIII	Integrity vs. Despair	"Mankind" "My Kind"	Wisdom	To be, through having been To face not being	

(Identity and the Life Cycle, Selected Paper by Erik H. Erikson, page 166)

Columns B, C and D are particularly appropriate to our present discussion. Column B describes the sphere of significant relationships that gradually widens as the person grows from the "Maternal Person" at stage one to "Mankind" at stage eight. The movement goes out from the mother, to the family, to the neighborhood, to school and work until it reaches all mankind. At stage six words like "partners in friendship" and "cooperation" suggest the development of more intense relationships.

Column C contains key words that represent concomitant development or as Erikson puts it "related elements of social order." As the child relates to these expanding spheres of interpersonal complexity his mind expands and he familiarizes himself with an ever-widening range of social issues. For example at stage two as he experiences his relationship to parental persons as providers of guidance and direction he is furnished with an experiential base for understanding law and order.

Column D relates more directly to our present subject of skills, even though some of them listed by Erikson are instrumental or imaginal rather than interpersonal, like "to make things" or "to make like." Still "to make things together," "to be oneself," "to share being oneself," "to lose and find oneself in another" and "to take care of" are all interpersonal skills some of which will be enlarged upon below. For the moment suffice it to say that Erikson sees these skills as developmental and necessary for growth. Some of these skills like "to share being myself" apply to most human relationships while others like "to lose and find oneself in another" are reserved for only the most intimate kind of relationships.

The ultimate in one dimension of the interpersonal is the capacity to see the whole human race as one's "in group." To make this a behavioral reality takes incredible skills and represents a gigantic expansion of consciousness that contrasts sharply with the awareness stage of the young child who sees himself as the center of the universe.

The ultimate in another dimension of the interpersonal is the capacity to enter into intimate human relationships where the "I" of consciousness becomes a "we."

The following diagram spells this out:

DIAGRAM 23

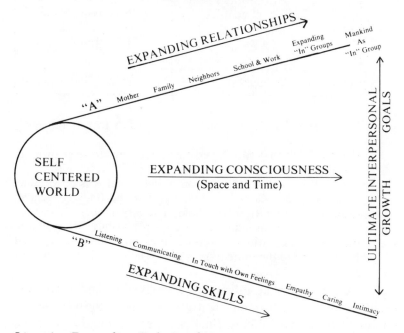

Line A—Expanding Relationships

The top line of the diagram represents the enlarging of significant relationships that normally accompanies personal growth. It describes a person's in-groups, a term that Allport suggests *resists precise definition.*

> "It is difficult to define an in-group precisely. Perhaps the best that can be done is to say that members of an in-group all use the term *we* with the same essential significance."

This "we" includes more and more people as a person grows.

The way a person views his in-groups identifies his basic loyalties. These loyalties quite literally permit us to see where "he's at" because they clarify his identity by bringing into focus where he sees himself belonging. In this regard Allport writes:

> Thus the sense of belonging is a highly personal matter. Even two members of the same actual in-group may view its composition in widely divergent ways. Take for instance

native white Protestant gentiles	native white Protestant gentiles, Negroes, Catholics, Jews, Immigrants etc.
as seen by individual A	as seen by individual B

Fig. 1. The national in-group as perceived by two Americans.

the definition that two Americans might give to their own national in-group.

The narrowed perception of individual A is the product of an arbitrary categorization, one that he finds convenient (functionally significant) to hold. The larger range of perception on the part of individual B creates a wholly different conception of the national in-group. It is misleading to say that both belong to the same in-group. Psychologically they do not.

A strategy that might yield interesting and surprising results is to have a person identify and define the various in-groups to which he belongs. Such an exercise could expose the narrower world view that inhibits the mental and behavioral expansion envisioned on line A.

Normally an in-group implies an outgroup, hostility towards which tends to increase one's in-group loyalties. But this need not be so. A person reaching Phase IV sees mankind as his in-group, leaving nobody on the outside. Admittedly when a person accepts such an all-encompassing in-group, intense and warm loyalty is difficult to generate. It calls for attaining the kind of lofty ideals that typify visionaries like Jesus (love your enemies) a behavioral reality.

But to label a thing difficult is not to acknowledge its impossibility. In a section devoted explicitly to this matter of humanity as an in-group Allport maintains that such loyalty lies within the realm of the possible.

"Narrow circles can, without conflict, be supplemented by larger circles of loyalty. This happy condition is not often achieved, but it remains from the psychological point of view a hopeful possibility."

This is the sort of ideal to which educators interested in promoting the growth of their students must dedicate themselves. Specifically in the area of social studies crosscultural lessons with a values orientation can pave the way for this kind of mental expansion. But such an expansion becomes a real possibility only if there is a concomitant increase in interpersonal skills.

Line B—Expanding Skills

Line B in Diagram 23 lists some of the skills that must be acquired if relating to any in-group is to be meaning-enhancing. In this regard the intimate relationship can function as a prism that breaks down and makes possible the identification of the various skills that enter into the developing and sustaining of human relationships.

An intimate relationship is one in which I share my innermost being, my hopes and fears, anxieties and aspirations, my thoughts and emotions with another human being in such a way that I encourage him or her to feel free to do likewise.

Obviously such a relationship is beyond the grasp of any person who can neither attentively listen to another nor accurately communicate his own thoughts and feelings. These skills basic to any human relationship must be fostered at home and early in a child's school experience. Both attentive listening and accurate communication can be promoted by some strategy similar to the following:

1. Have two students discuss a topic that is likely to elicit an interested and emotional reaction from them. Before one student can respond to the other he must paraphrase the first student's remarks in a manner that is acceptable to the original speaker. Such an exercise can awaken students to the problems involved in accurately understanding the words of another and to the corresponding need for clarity in expressing one's own thoughts and feelings.

2. Have two students discuss a past experience. One person starts by telling of a significant event in his life that has some emotional impact. Then the other student must parallel share by giving a similar experience so that the original student feels he was understood. An evaluation of such an experience

can help students see how much they can share, trust (how much emotional detail they gave) and empathize (understanding through sharing).

3. Have two students share their talents and limitations with another. Then repeat accurately what they heard. Again this gets at basic communication skills of sharing sufficient information and the ability to listen sensitively.

A most essential interpersonal skill and yet one often neglected is the ability to get in touch with one's own feelings. Most people learn to express what they think about something, for example about their mistreatment by somebody. But how many people in the face of mistreatment are able to sort out and deal maturely with how they feel about such an experience? Until a person can do this he really is not master of himself, in fact he does not really even know himself in his innermost being and therefore cannot share that inner self with another.

Empathy is the ability to get in touch with the feelings of another. As Thomas Oden says in *Game Free*:

> Empathy is capacity for one person to enter imaginatively into the sphere of consciousness of another, to feel the specific contours of another's experience, to allow one's imagination to risk entering the inner experiencing process (initmus) of another.

Persons who develop this skill can sustain many friendships, without it intimacy is impossible. Both empathy and the ability to get in touch with one's feelings can be fostered by an imaginative use of roleplaying exercises. For example a story dealing with a conflict situation appropriate to the age group involved can be described and then roleplayed by several different sets of students, followed by a shared class analysis of the situation.

Oden builds his discussion of intimacy around six antitheses that he finally breaks down into the following negatively stated points:

1. Intimate relationships do not grow if not given time
2. Intimate bonding is less palpable if it never has ways of becoming intensified into ecstatic moments of intimate sharing

3. If relationships lack contractual clarity or if the contracts are easily terminable, then to that degree the relationship is less intimate-capable
4. If within the framework of sustained accountability the relationship is not able to be renegotiated in the light of specific new demands and occasions then it is less likely to be intimate
5. If partners are unable to empathize with each other's feelings intimacy is inhibited
6. If partners are unable to feel their own feelings clearly and fully then the empathy that intimacy requires is constricted
7. If emotive warmth is absent consistently one is not likely to call the relation intimate
8. Relationships that are unable to face conflicts are less likely to develop intimacy
9. Insofar as partners need to resort to deceptive and manipulative behaviors or lack honest self-disclosure the relationship is to that degree probably less intimate
10. To the extent that the relationship requires the constant monitoring of one party and thus inhibits the self-direction of the other intimacy is decreased
11. Insofar as the relationship is not recognized as finite and therefore vulnerable to death it is less likely to achieve genuine intimacy because it will be prone to idolize the partner.
12. And yet intimates know that when they are most together they are most aware of that which transcends their togetherness, echoing the abysmal capacity given and with reality itself for communion. It is this experience that energizes the hope that intimacy in some mysterious way not fully explainable at this time transcends death.

Described in that rather extended quote are the kinds of interpersonal skills that must be acquired if the growth goal of intimacy is to become a real possibility.

Following are two diagrams that further clarify this area of interpersonal relationships. The first diagram, 24, is simply an elabortion of line A from Diagram 23 that attempts to spell out how a person at each phase would decide who is a member of his in-group and who must be consigned to his out-group. The middle column merely indicates the bonds that might unite people of each phase of consciousness. Diagram 25 presents a breakdown of the six skills found on line B of Diagram 23 indicating some of the necessary components of each skill and obstacles that stand in the way of the acquisition of that skill.

DIAGRAM 24

A DEVELOPMENTAL VIEW OF SIGNIFICANT OTHERS

	IN—GROUP	BOND	OUT—GROUP
P H A S E I	— I — I AND THOSE ON MY SIDE, WHO HELP ME GET MY WAY	— TYRANNY OF MY EGO — MY SELF-CENTERED NEEDS AND INTERESTS	— MY COMPETITORS FOR SECURITY AND PLEASURE — THOSE WHO OPPOSE ME IN MY EFFORTS TO GET MY OWN WAY
P H A S E II	— I AND THE "THEY" WHO COUNT—FAMILY, PEERS — THE ESTABLISHMENT AND ITS SUPPORTERS	— ATTRACTION TO THOSE LIKE MYSELF — MY NEED FOR APPROVAL — STRONG RELIANCE ON AUTHORITY CONCEIVED AUTOCRATICALLY	— THOSE WHO DO NOT COUNT OR OPPOSE THOSE WHO DO — THOSE WHO OPPOSE THE ESTABLISHMENT
P H A S E III	— I AND THOSE WHO SHARE MY CAUSES — I AND OTHERS WHO ARE EVALUATING THE ESTABLISHMENT	— IDEALS AND OBJECTIVES OF MY CAUSES — COMMON CONCERN ABOUT OPPONENTS AND THE ESTABLISHMENT — DEMOCRATIC TYPE OF AUTHORITY	— OPPONENTS OF MY CAUSES — CONFORMISTS — RIGID INSTITUTIONALISM
P H A S E IV	— WE WHO ARE BUILDING A NEW WORLD — HUMANITY — THE CREATED ORDER	— VISION OF NEW WORLD — RELATEDNESS BASED ON INTERDEPENDENCE — AUTHORITY—SHARED RESPONSIBILITY	— OPPONENTS OF HARMONY — NO OUT-GROUP

DIAGRAM 25
SOME INTERPERSONAL SKILLS

SKILL	SOME COMPONENTS	SOME OBSTACLES
General Communication	Ability to verbalize Sense of self-worth—confidence Imagination Spontaneity Enjoyment of others Accuracy and precision	Lack of verbal skills Self-consciousness—lack of confidence Lack of trust of others Lack of imagination Fear of disapproval
Listening	Attentiveness to another Curiosity Expanding interests Ability to concentrate	Excessive preoccupation with self Indifference to others Physical orientation—too body conscious Lack of self control
In Touch With My Own Feelings	Ability to listen to emotions Appreciation of emotions as valuable sources of information and as life enrichers Ability to constructively use emotions as judgment faculty	Suppression of emotions Ignoring emotions Fearing emotions Inability to use emotions constructively Inaccurate Interpretations of one's feelings
Empathy	Sensitivity to feelings of another Ability to identify with another Lively imagination Objective mental attitude Intuition	Indifference toward others Preoccupation with "D" needs Overly subjective mental attitude Lack of imagination
Caring	Openness and availability Empathy Happy with self Willingness to let others be themselves Pain tolerance	"D" need orientation Need to control others Too busy with self Lack of empathy
Intimacy	Tolerance for self-disclosure Willing to be accountable for another Conflict capability Emotional Warmth Consistency	Secretive about self Inconsistency or fickleness Intolerant of demands of others Intolerant of Conflict

Imaginal Skills

In actuality a fertile imagination is an indispensible element in the acquisition and exercise of all the skills already considered. It takes imagination to cope effectively with systems, to design tools or to relate creatively to other persons. Still we have not yet explicitly investigated the structure and role of man's imagination.

Chug serves as an excellent model of a man with great imaginative resources. When the natural environment with its cold and its rain turned on Chug he did not passively submit to its power but by creative use of his imagination he mastered the environment. He figured out how to start a fire and discovered a new use for trees as he designed his house.

When faced with the predatory intentions of his neighbors Chug did not despair but used his imagination and powers of persuasion to come up with an alternative to the seemingly inevitable loss of his house. This is the use of the imagination to create hopeful alternatives.

His responsibilities as mayor of Chugsville repeatedly taxed Chug's imaginative resources. In the face of numerous new and challenging problems confronting him as the man charged with running a complex human organization Chug had to originate human institutions that would appropriately answer those challenges. This was the use of the imagination to create tools that would modify man. In this instance Chug benefited from the assistance of other citizens of Chugsville, making this a communal as well as a personal use of the imagination.

The Structure of the Imagination

What we mean by the imagination is the synergetic interaction between the fantasy, the emotions and the reflective intellect of man. This process of interaction results in a product, the idea, which is a miniaturization of the data gathered from the person's environment, having first been evaluated, organized and reflected on constructively. What does all this mean?

First of all one must recognize that the imagination is not three things but an integrated whole here divided into three components only for the purpose of clearly identifying three different aspects of the imaginations activity.

Fantasy

1. *The fantasy* refers to the operation of the imagination that uses psychic energy to convert data received from either the external or internal (the memory or the unconscious) environment into images consisting of colors, shapes, sounds, movement. This image-making ability while natural to all men is more developed in some people than in others. For example accomplished artists are capable of elaborating complex images that they in turn imprint on canvas, stone or wood. Children at home or in school can receive encouragement to improve their ability to fantasize by various exercises by being asked to convert all sorts of ideas into visual images.

As he contemplated the problem of how to protect himself from hostile weather Chug was able to create an internal image of a house that he later externalized (objectified). His internal process of considering the many elements of his problem, such as protecting himself from the weather, issued in a product, first the idea and later the house itself. The complex data was simplified or miniaturized into a single idea-house. But we are getting a bit ahead of ourselves. There are other aspects of this process.

Emotions

2. *The emotions* in this context designate a person's feeling-response to the data picked up from the environment. The emotions evaluate the date, perceiving it as helpful or harmful, desirable or to be avoided. We have good and bad feelings about things. It is rare that this data is neutral. Shapes and colors and sounds may in themselves be neutral, but normally they are present in images as qualifiers of something else that does have emotional significance. Sometimes images from a person's unconscious even enter consciousness with emotional overtones that are not comprehended.

DIAGRAM 26

THE DATA	THE PROCESS	THE PROCESS
ENVIRONMENTAL DATA	FANTASY	THE IDEA Chug's Internal Response— An Idea of A House
COLD AND RAIN	IMAGE OF COLD AND RAIN . . .	
	LATER OF WARM HOUSE	
	EMOTIONS— Uncomfortable and Anxious,	
	Later happy with House	
	REFLECTIVE INTELLECT— Considering How to deal with weather, i.e. alternatives	EXTERNALIZED INTO
CHUG IN RAIN AND COLD	CHUG IN CAVE USING IMAGINATION	CHUG'S HOUSE

So there is interaction between the fantasy and the emotions. The emotions evaluate and pass judgement on the images created by the fantasy. Chug's internal image of cold and rain and physical discomfort was evaluated by the emotions as unpleasant. It was the activity of the reflective intellect that supplied the fantasy with new data leading to the formation of new images such as a house, which in turn called for new evaluations—the house as pleasant and warm.

Reflective Intellect

3. *The reflective intellect* examines and organizes the data picked up from the environment (as depicted by the fantasy and judged by the emotions) with a view to simplifying the data and constructing an idea (miniaturization). One of the key activities of the reflective intellect so typical of creative people is to conjure up and consider alternative ways of dealing with data. This explains why the imagination is so often described as the faculty that enables a man to see alternatives to reality as presently constituted.

It was this kind of activity that allowed Chug to construct the idea of a house. A less imaginative person than Chug, when faced with a band of hostile cavemen, might have felt trapped or doomed. But Chug not only originated a creative alternative for himself, but convinced his would-be foes that this alternative could also benefit them. That took imagination.

So these are the three operations that characterize the activity of the active imagination. But the imagination does more than produce simple ideas. It also combines several ideas so as to form a hypothesis and then uses the hypothesis to examine new data to form a theory. Eventually after sufficient testing of the theory it may formulate a law like Newton's law of gravity. These various activities of the imagination are depicted in the following diagram.

DIAGRAM 27

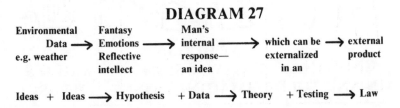

Miniaturization

Miniaturization is operative in all the activities contained in the above diagram. All are examples of complexity being simplified or, to use a special term, compressed. The idea is a miniaturization of external data. The hypothesis is the miniaturization of several ideas; the hypothesis and new data result in a theory that with the test of time may become a law. This internal process of miniaturization is described in the section called "Instrumental Skills." To quote Soleri again:

> To understand this one must see clearly the essential chain that connects matter to mind. The chain is knowledge, that imponderable but formidable stuff working by way of information (data), communication (Transmission), retention (memory), manipulation (coordination), thinking (invention-creation) that grows out of the energy of matter by feeding on packages of energy more and more selected and concentrated (complexity and miniaturization).

Through the imaginal skills man modifies his external environment by applying his ideas there in creative rather than destructive tool-making. This applies equally to tools that modify the physical environment (Chug's house), tools that modify man (the human institutions that regulated life in Chugsville) and tools that enhance life (works of fine art).

Imagination and Self-actualization

In any one of the three operations of the imagination discussed above a person may either hinder or promote his own development. Stated another way how a person uses his imagination plays a large role in determining where he is developmentally.

As a person interacts with his environment it is his imagination that determines whether he will be a responder or a creator.

For whatever reasons if a person adopts a generally passive attitude towards his environment he will not demonstrate the creativity characteristic of an imaginative person. Such an individual is responsive rather than original, content to let others take the initiative and then to shape his own activity into a reply to the demands originating in an environment largely controlled by others.

Educators and Imaginal Skills

In order for the imagination to be stimulated, basic needs (Phase I and II needs) like security, approval and a sense of personal adequacy and worth have to be minimally satisfied. At this point a person can begin to explore alternatives to his present lifestyle. But his imagination must be stimulated by teachers, educators, leaders—those he looks up to. He must find vision and honest self-expression in those he admires.

Stunting Imaginal Growth

It is not difficult to imagine the kind of home and school environment that might foster the behavioral characteristics just described. Following is a list of some possible environmental factors that would inhibit the development of the imagination:

1. Presence of the style of authority that creates dependency and reliance on authority.

2. Initiative discouraged and even punished.

3. Fatalistic approach to life—"whatever will be will be."

4. Members of family not given challenges that stretch their resources.

5. Success so stressed that fear of failure is strong and initiative and experimentation discouraged.

6. An absence of a creative use of leisure like fairy tales, family dreaming, travel, knowledge of other cultures.

Fostering Imaginal Growth

Contrast this to the following type of environment:

1. Authority is democratic in style, encouraging initiative.

2. There is enough consistency in daily life to support security, but pliability and variety have their place.

3. Members given challenges that stretch their resources but in a supportive fashion that is not too demanding.

4. Resourcefulness and experimentation even if they lead to failure are rewarded.

5. Creative use of leisure, family reading, travel, varied vacation patterns, familiarity with other cultures, past and present.

6. Group problem solving (brainstorming) is typical.

7. Honest self-expression and independence are valued.

Imaginal Skills as Integration

The imaginal skills have to do with the interpretation in an individual of all the other skills. It has the synergetic quality of allowing the person to see aspects of himself in relationship to the whole, for it is only as we have a sense of the total picture that we can have vision.

Valuing as a process is itself an imaginal skill. For it is only possible for one to choose from alternatives after considering the consequences to the extent that one has an active imagination. However imaginal activity that is not based soundly on limitations—indeed the conscious limitations of my entire reality—is an unreal and nonproductive exercise in dreaming.

In short imaginal skills must cover a range of skills if they are to be balanced and healthy:

1) The ability to fantasize and create new alternatives
2) The ability to see another's reality and see its alternatives
3) The ability to be able to see the consequences of the alternatives (negative as well as positive) and to prioritize the more productive ones
4) The ability to criticize and evaluate situations and read their potential and limitations
5) The ability to be able to project concrete practical (constructive) suggestions from the imagined alternatives (tool making).

Quite concretely imaginal skills relate to all the other skills in the following ways:

DIAGRAM 28

THE FOUR SKILLS: HOW THEY RELATE
"EXAMPLES"

Imaginal	Instrumental	Interpersonal	Systems
Fantasy Creating New Alternatives	New Abilities Widen alternatives e.g. Driving: Travel/ New People, etc.	Meeting New People: widens one's possbilities (man is a social animal)	Systems Make Transcendent Alternatives possible through human cooperation
Seeing Another's Alternatives	1. All Cognitive Learning increases alternatives through increased ideas. 2. Professional Skills: give other opportunity e.g. medicine: new health	To the extent I see another's ideas and possibilities mine are so increased	Knowing systems make institutional renewal possible.
Seeing Consequences and Creatively Prioritizing	Technology can help us forsee outcomes: e.g. law. The Genetic Revolution	Experiences of Love and Intimacy, Trust and Sharing teach me the science of personal consequence.	Systems Modeling is a way of creating viable future and avoiding some negative conquences
Criticizing and Evaluating	Evaluation and statistical analysis are developed Instrumental Tools; both in science and social science	Viewing my limitations through healthy criticism evaluates me in my potential and keeps my imagination healthy.	Evaluating Systems is freeing individuals and freeing the imaginal to work.
Making Concrete Suggestions (Tools)	Tool making is an instrumental skill; of bioengineers, civil engineers, organization development	The human tool is the construction of all our axiological institutions.	A system in a human tool.

Skill and Development

We now need to take a look at some concrete examples
of the relationship between the development of values and the

acquisition of the four skills. As an over-all review the following diagram might be helpful.

We will use the diagram as a reference point as we discuss the following examples. First let us look at Case 1.

A Hospital Administrator

Rosemary was an administrator of a 1500-bed hospital in a large city. She was experiencing loneliness and doubts about her self-worth. due to the fact that she was approaching retirement and had very few friends. She also felt that her role as administrator in the hospital being one of authority did not permit her to get to know people in her work situation very well. During a consultation session we asked Rosemary, utilizing pictures from magazines, to construct a collage on how she saw herself and her life vocation.

To make the story brief once she had described her picture we were able to pull out underlying values that she said were representative of her own behavioral priorities. She listed them as follows: 1) self-competence, 2) achievement, 3) independence, 4) self-worth. As she described this ranking she noted that self-worth was very important to her and was low on her list because of her sense of loneliness even though she had gained a great deal of self-worth through her ability to achieve and through her recognized competence in the medical field. However she also said that a high priority for her was independence, but it was third on the list because running the hospital, which was the most important thing to her, made independent action difficult. When she was asked now she would like these values to be prioritized in her behavior, she ranked them as follows: 1) self-worth, 2) independence, 3) self-competence and 4) achievement. Interestingly she described independence as being able to do some creative things on her own and to get to know new people.

DIAGRAM 29

VALUE AND MORAL DEVELOPMENT

	WORLD VIEW	CORE VALUES	MORAL DEVELOPMENT	VALUES AND PRIORITIES
P H A S E I	World as Mystery (Preconventional—Physical) Self as Center	Security Survival Pleasure Wonder	*Survival: Avoidance of Pain Self-Happiness	Eg. Work: Survival ——— ——— Work
P H A S E II	World as Problem (Conventional—Social) Self as Belonging	Belonging Work Self Competence Self Worth	*Peer Image: "Good Boy Orientation" Authority is right by virtue of office	Work: Self-Worth Work ——— ———
P H A S E III	World as Project and Invention (Post Conventional—Conscience) Self as Independent	Independence Equity Rights Service Creation	*Law Order Orientation— Evaluated and change within Innate Intuitive Conscience, Justice	Work: Enhances Creative Development of Man ——— ——— Work
P H A S E IV	World as Mystery Cared For (Contemventual—Congruent) Selves as Life Giver	"Convivial Tools" Harmony Interdependence Intimacy Synergy	Orientation Towards Interdependence, Wholeness and Intimacy Orientation Towards action based on a convivial awareness— whole system orientation	Work: Creative Act ——— ——— Work

The Four Skills Needed For Integrated Development:

(1) Systems Skills　　(2) Interpersonal Skills　　(3) Instrumental Skills　　(4) Imaginal Skills

*Work of L. Kohlberg

She felt that self-worth meant much to her because she was lonely and would like to have something in her life other than work. As we began looking at the situation we recognized that in her initial ranking that described her behavior the first two values are from the second phase of consciousness and the third one is at the third phase. When she described how she would like to be the value that came from the third phase of consciousness moved to first place. Reflecting on this situation we might conclude that we have here a description of a person growing from one phase of development to another.

As she described herself she noted that she had a high sense of competence and was in fact able to achieve and deal with the system of the hospital effectively. One would therefore assume that she would naturally move into that third phase of development. But as she herself noted there was something that stopped her. An obvious conclusion was that it might have something to do with self worth.

It is at this point that we recognize that a confluent theory of values does not help at all if it only helps us to describe the values that are present. That is the role of value clarification, which only describes "what is" and does not help a person to move anywhere but only takes, so to speak, a photographic shot of a moment, helping people see where they are.

In order to see the developmental picture more clearly we need to look at the four sets of skills. When Rosemary described her four skills she noted that she had done very well in both systems and instrumental skills but felt that she was not a very creative person and often had difficulty in relating to people. This made it evident that a lack of interpersonal skills contributed to her diminished sense of self-worth. A program of development for her would have to help her structure her personal relationships or obtain assistance in relating better to people so that her self-worth could be enhanced, and this would in fact allow her to grow into another phase of development. In short she needed to develop interpersonal skills.

As we looked into her history we discovered that here was a lady who really knew a great deal about the workings of the hospital and had no difficulty in talking to persons in authority, was able to raise money and get things done efficiently. In short she had good instrumental and systems skills. Then as often is the case the system responded to her systems skills and made her administrator of the hospital. But leadership that is independent and holistic requries more than instrumental and systems skills.

For example without imaginal skills a leader would not be able to move the system along but would simply end by maintaining what had been. It is imagination that enables the leader to have vision. As we investigated we found that this was the case with Rosemary. Then too because of her lack of interpersonal skills she tended to move the system along with a blatant disregard for the people involved. She did not dislike people; on the contrary she simply lacked sufficient interpersonal skills.

Leadership

The last example points to the minimal requirements that are necessary for a person in a leadership position. Obviously if a person is placed in a position of being the head of an organization he can no longer be dependent on others but rather has to lead the others. In terms of phases of development this must mean that they are *minimally* at the third phase of consciousness with the needed *concomitant* skills. Contemporary society requires at least that much.

The televised Watergate hearings presented many instances of leaders who had not achieved an ability to make independent judgments consistent with the third phase. The classic example was when ex-Attorney General Mitchell was questioned by the Watergate committee as to "Why was it that he had not recognized that he had done anything wrong?" Mitchell replied, "I put my trust in the role of the president." Looking back to Diagram 29 we note that Mitchell's response was at the second phase of development, the image orientation that views external authority as right by virtue of its office. The Watergate committee however came at him from a law-and-order orientation where innate intuitive judgments of conscience were expected of him as a minimal leadership requirement. As Kohlberg's research has indicated when persons are separated by a level or more there is little communication. If any of you watched the hearings you would recognize that Mitchell and the Watergate committee passed like ships in the night—there was no communication.

The goal of effective leadership training should at least be the third phase. To return to Rosemary we simply are asserting that in order to be holistically present at that phase as a leader one has to have all four skills operating in one's behavior at that phase. The person must be able to move the organization with vision (systems and imaginal skills) and yet be able to deal with individuals in a caring manner (interpersonal skills). At the same time he must be able to deal with the system and must have the professional skills to pull it off (instrumental and systems skills).

Rosemary's difficulty was that she only had two of the skills at a sufficiently high phase. This presented problems not only because she could not manage the organization in a comfortable way, but also because her own individual development as a human being was being frustrated. So it is necessary for leadership to have all these skills, indeed if it is necessary for an institution to insist that leadership have all these skills, for in doing so environments are reinforced that will help individuals grow rather than lock them into a static level of moral development. Institutions need to encourage the kind of leadership that is integrated, holistic and moral in its development.

Clearly then a confluent theory of values must take into consideration the four skills as well as the total developmental process.

Interpersonal Skills Revisited

Another short example can serve to make us aware of the need for acquiring all four skills. Recently there has been a great emphasis in psychological literature on interpersonal skills as being essential to integrated development. However it seems to us a mistake to assume in an unqualified way that the interpersonal skills are the most important. This has more to do with the fact that persons holding this opinion are often at the beginning of that third phase of development and therefore stress honesty and communication as if little else mattered. In fact interpersonal skills would probably be ranked first among the four skills for a person at that third phase of development. Our opinion is that different skills assume priority depending on the stage of development of the individual even within a particular phase of consciousness.

For example we have come across many cases where an individual like Rosemary has excellent imaginal, instrumental and interpersonal skills. Often such a person has gone a long way in an organization as a consequence of this and has been promoted into a leadership position on the basis of his ability to get along so well with people.

What happens however is that a person will then be promoted to a position of leadership that is reinforcing him or her to be at that third phase of consciousness at a time when he does not have sufficient systems skills.

As a consequence the person then approaches systems interpersonally because it is the only skill available for dealing with people. The consequence of this is that such a person is more often than not seen as a manipulator of others. Such a person will get into a business meeting and play on emotions to obtain the desired results from the meeting. This of course causes alienation and inhibits personal growth.

The point here is that in helping such a person in leadership training one would not simply brand the person as a manipulator but rather would point out that the problem is a lack of integration and highlight the need for more systems skills. Such systems skills can be acquired through management courses. The point is that at each level a person needs a new set of skills.

Imagine a person becoming a leader for the first time. It is unlikely that he is going to have all the skills he needs immediately. There is a need for more sophisticated leadership training courses that will help new leaders see where their weaknesses lie so they can get appropriate training or even receive cooperative assistance within their own organization so that they will not falter as they start new roles.

A lot has been done recently on peer-pairing relationships for new executives. A new executive will immediately be paired off with a peer with more experience so that the one who has had more experience can help the new person move into his new role with a minimum of difficulty by helping him to supplement his skill needs. By creating such a pair relationship using peer or retired leaders these four skills can be supplemented until such time as the new leader has sufficient experience.

Questions To Be Addressed

The over-all model of course raises many questions. We do not claim in this book to have the answers. In fact one of our aims is to raise questions. A great deal of research and investigation will have to be done in many of these areas. A major issue that is often raised however is: Is this schemata hierarchical? Is it not like Maslow's hierarchy of needs suggesting that the fourth phase is better than the others?

Phases, Skills and Evolution

This is a difficult question that cannot be addressed fully here. I would like to speak to it briefly however in order to get the four skills of the confluent theory in perspective. The model is not basically hierarchical as much as it is developmental. People grow at a natural rate and learn through the processes of selecting the alternatives available to them.

It is a process of evolution, a process that happens gradually. Such a process can be retarded or perhaps speeded up a little. The main factor however is the environment and the manner in which it reinforces development. If existence at one phase is being naturally reinforced and the next stage is also being reinforced I would claim a person will move naturally and smoothly through those developmental stages.

History and Its Role

The fact is that institutions (family, school, business) reinforce individual development. And in turn a civilization as a whole reinforces the institutions of any particular society. That is to say a particular point in history will in fact be reinforcing persons at a particular developmental level. Excluding the very exceptional and unusual persons, such as Buddha or Christ or Socrates who somehow symbolize man's future potential the majority of people like ourselves can only grow to that phase of development that is openly reinforced by our society. To reinforce a phase means of course to reinforce through education all the skills necessary to make it behaviorally possible.

The point then is that values that precipitate out of the phase of development where we are are not so much hierarchical but are the limits imposed by the conditions of history itself. Simply put the fourth phase of development as spelled out in this essay is as far as we can see at this point, as far as our present history and imaginal skills allow us to see. In this respect I am talking about the present authors and their limited vision; maybe other persons who read this can see further than that phase.

An Example in Guatemala

I am reminded of working in a rural area in Guatemala a number of years ago where the malnutrition rate was more than fifty percent, the unemployment high and the skill ability of the local population to make a reasonable living for itself depressingly low. Disease was often rampant and the life expectancy was in the early thirties.

A leader was required for a local episcopal mission. One of our tasks was to go to that area and give some counseling to two individuals who were working with the person who was running the mission. The mission included a local clinic, a school and an agricultural plantation. Being somewhat naive at that time I considered the individual who was in charge of the mission to be an insensitive person who lacked many of the skills that one would obviously expect of a middle-class Anglo-Saxon.

However as I reviewed the situation over a period of years I became convinced that the so-called "sensitive Anglo-Saxon" would never survive in such a situation. His level of development would be inhibiting to the people—would be wholly unhelpful in fact and would probably cause him and his family to get physically ill.

The developmental state of that particular area required leadership that would understand it and that could deal with it. The persons living in this particular area, Guatemala, were at best at the first phase of development and would have to be understood by a person no more than one stage above where they were otherwise there would have been little communication. In short a person who could survive with those people, understand their problems and live with them in a caring manner could not be too far removed from their stage of development.

The Survival Climate

To speak as I often did with this man about values like

honesty, trust, construction, relaxation and leisure for a new world was simply ludicrous. There was no communication. He was living in a world of violence and of history; the natural environment itself was reinforcing a survival existence. The humanizing process required a person who could reinforce people where they were and assist them in moving to a new stage of development. A new level of development has to be merely one stage ahead of where the people presently find themselves. It is not a question of hierarchy, it is a question of value development within the limits and context of history. People are where they are concretely in a particular society.

The Genetic Revolution

To be entirely fair I suppose one could talk about the hierarchy if one talked about the development of civilization itself. I do believe that civilization is progressing in its phases of consciousness; I do not however see this as hierarchy in the sense of one stage being superior to the other, but rather that it is something that will come about through time. Briefly I see it as a part of the genetic revolutionary process or the evolution of man himself.

The Separation of Skills and the Integrated Person

Another question that is raised continually is are we not all at different stages on the values scale at various times? And are not our skills at different phases? Briefly the answer to these questions is that the degree to which the values reflected in a person's behavior are separated from those reflected in his imagination determines how "spaced out" a person is going to be. This is also true with the skills.

The Integrated Person

An integrated person is one whose behavior reflects his values at one phase and who has all the skills needed to express those values with his imagination being at least a stage ahead of that point. However this does not speak to the question of whether or not we can move down the scale as well as up it. And can this upward and downward movement happen on a day-to-day or week-to-week basis?

Changes in the Environment

Generally speaking I think a person usually stays where he is and moves forward very slowly in the developmental process. But environment can change and a person can temporarily drop into a much lower phase of development. This of course has confusing consequences because the imagination is not totally reduced even though the behavior might suddenly be, in which case momentary confusing behavior is manifested. I can give an example from my own experience.

Shock

A year ago I was giving a workshop on the developmental theory. In the middle of the workshop while I was having coffee I met an old friend. While I was talking to him I discovered that a couple I had known many years previously and with whom I had lost contact three months earlier had both been killed in an accident. It seems that the husband had been accidentally killed by a gun shot that led his wife to turn the gun on herself. After the coffee break I went back to the podium and was almost unable to complete the workshop. In fact the only way I was able to finish was by telling the people about what had happened.

Self-Preservation

The following night I had nightmares of being chased by someone who was trying to kill me and all sorts of old fears emerged that I thought I had forgotten. As I reflected on this I recognized that the shock of the death of my friend and the grief that I was feeling had literally moved me back to a survival phase of existence where I was beginning to feel all the old feelings of anxiety about self-preservation and insecurity that I had experienced earlier in my life. I was at the same time trying to give a lecture on the third or fourth phase of development. The effect was ludicrous in that there was a gap between where I was and what I was trying to talk about.

In short situations can move us up and down the value scale. The loss of a job, the sudden declaration of war between one society and another, or even on the reverse scale, suddenly being given an award or receiving a degree or getting a new job can move a person forward on the scale with new responsibilities and a new vision of his hopes for the world in which he lives. These things do move us up and down the scale but I would claim that there is a steady core of development to which we can generally relate. And we do this in an educational setting by concentrating on the development of the values expressive of where we are and on the development of the appropriate skills so that we can develop in a holistic manner.

New Horizons

We need to be able to look at the world in a more integrated and holistic fashion. Far too often methods of teaching, styles of leadership and even ways of healing people have been too narrowly confined to one set of skills to the neglect of the others or to one set of values to the neglect of the others.

Holistic Education

For example often people in counseling have stressed the need for interpersonal skills and for values like honesty and trust. These things are doubtlessly essential to the development of an individual's mental health. But they are only a part of a whole. Others values and skills are needed. A counselor from a psychological background in order to be in touch with some other values like harmony or construction may need to learn about engineering and the arts as well as about psychology. This means that in the future methods of education are going to have to be more integrated. Inter-disciplinary curricula with a values orientation will be in demand.

Systems Skills

Not every teacher employs the same educational method. One may be very enthusiastic about behavior modification as a means of aiding students. Another may be devoted to cognitive development, trying to convey a great deal of information to the child. In the latter case the instrumental skills receive nearly exclusive attention, a tendency that has constituted the main thrust of traditional education. There has been little effort for example to acquaint teachers with the kinds of skills they might gainfully use in dealing with the educational system itself. Teachers need to confront themselves with questions like: "Do I use this educational method because I'm convinced it is the best or does it merely reflect where I am developmentally? What new skills do I need?"

Leadership Training

We may see the implications of this as we begin to look at the field of leadership training. I have often found myself in management courses where I have been told that certain kinds of management that are paternalistic or certain kinds of bureaucracy that are primarily set for efficiency are simply the consequence of the needs of the organization. Very little has been done in research to see whether or not the styles of leadership reflect much more the level of consciousness of the leader than the needs of the group.

Social Agencies

In this respect it is very interesting to view the history of social agencies, particularly in social work in Europe where in the 19th century many of the social institutions developed. In England many such agencies were started by good people who had money or were at least supported by wealthy persons who gave money to well-meaning people who in turn set up an agency to care for orphan children or unwed mothers.

As time moved on these institutions were structured so that the original founders were replaced by boards of trustees whose job it was to raise money for the institution and to be guardians of the agencies' aims and goals. As a consequence the values of power and influence have become the criteria for selection of members for the board of directors of a modern agency. The only problem is that the board of directors of the modern agency are often selected simply because of their power and influence and they lack the tremendous care and concern that those original founders had when their agencies were formed in the 19th century.

Consequently we have many agencies now where the board of directors has absolutely no concern about what the agency was set up for in the first place. Often a poor social work director with ulcers spends most of his time trying to please the board or even obtaining a quorum where the board does meet and trying to get them to raise money to keep his agency going. Such an agency is reinforcing a level of moral development in the director that insures that creative leadership and integrated development are impossible—the very reverse of what most of these agencies were historically set up for in the first place.

Institutions of the future will have to consider new ways of doing things. One might recommend:

1. That human organizations create designs based on specific values and then organize in such a way as to allow those values to emerge.

2. That boards of directors be chosen based on those values not on means values like power and influence.

3. That judgments regarding what leadership is and what good personnel are be based on the candidates phase of consciousness and holistic skill development.

4. That education and service in the future consider all the skills in any subject matter and at any phase.

5. That a scientist be considered a good scientist not simply because he understands the system of nature but that he also have the necessary interpersonal skills and the imagination to see things that he might not ordinarily see.

Do we really believe that President Nixon failed in 1974 because of lack of faith of the people? Was it simply because he lacked certain skills? Or was it really because his phase of consciousness did not permit him to operate at that level which the people of America understand as necessary for integrated moral leadership?

An awareness of the four skills and of their relationship to values can help us to see things more holistically. We have all the skills we need in the present world. All the values that we speak of are operative. They simply need to be brought into harmony and integrated into the individual man and into the institutions of his society.

Conclusion

In this chapter we have dealt with skill development and the fact that skills need to develop in an integrated way at each phase of development.

So far in this book when we have talked about values they have been listed for the most part as personal values. We also designated a list of sixty such values. There are of course many ways of categorizing values—how do other people do this? We shall take a look at this in the next chapter.

The treatment of the skills, especially systems skills, raises the question of institutional values. Are not some values posited for us objectively in society through law and our institutions that we are pressured to accept? When I grew up (London) the values of God, King and Country were very serious values having objective norms that I was expected to follow. This question will be the subject matter of this next chapter.

Clearly then we are saying that in man's over-all development the bridge between his own personal being and the development of that complex social system we call civilization is the tool—the man and his skills. It is the process J. Bronowski calls The Ascent of Man.

> Among the multitude of animals which scamper, fly, burrow and swim around us, man is the only one who is not locked into his environment. His imagination, his reason, his emotional subtlety and toughness, make it possible for him not to accept the environment but change it. And that series of inventions, by which man from age to age has remade his environment, is a different kind of evolution—not biological, but cultural evolution. I call that brilliant sequence of cultural peaks The Ascent of Man.

CHAPTER VI

INSTITUTIONAL VALUES:
OUR OBJECTIVE SELVES

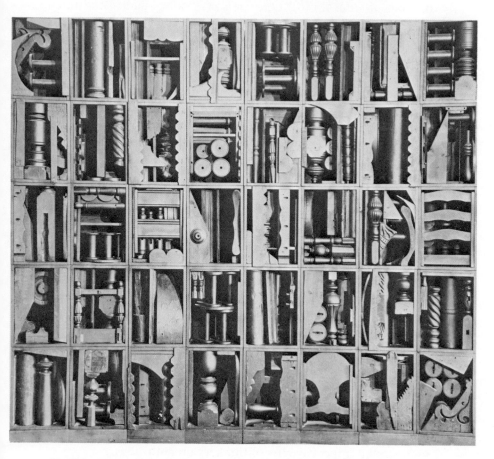

NEVELSON, Tide I Tide 1963, 108" x 144", Black Painted Wood, The Pace Gallery, New York.

Few of us would claim that the social changes we forecast arise out of the blue or come solely from men's imaginative design. Even when they emerge first as ideas they have to be embodied in institutions; and to chart social change is to chart the changes in the character of axial institutions.

Daniel Bell

INTRODUCTION

As we suggested at the end of the preceding chapter our division of values into "I" or personal values and institutional values is only one way of classifying values. That type of classification suits our purpose in terms of constructing a clinical base for value exercises and developing an educational methodology. But there are other ways of approaching values as this chapter will indicate by examining the views of several contemporary authors. In this connection we intend first of all to take a closer and more exacting look at the subjective-objective argument regarding values than we did in the second chapter. Finally we will explain in some detail what we mean by institutional values and how they can be utilized in educational practice.

The Subjective-Objective Dilemma

The issue of whether values are subjective or objective cuts through the whole history of the philosophy of values. No other problem regarding values has received nearly as much attention as this one. Risieri Frondizi in a book entitled *What is Value?*, which is principally an examination of this problem, formulates it as follows: "Are things valuable because we desire them, or do we desire them because they are valuable?"

Subject or Object? History and Philosophy

In other words do objects exist as values independent of a valuing subject or is it the activity of the subject that makes the object valuable? A roll call from the history of philosophy produces an impressive list of thinkers on both sides.

Thinkers like Hume, Spinoza and Hobbes cast their votes on the subjectivist side, denying that values exist in objects. They have their modern counterparts in people like Perry, Carnap and Bertrand Russell.

In the camp of the objectivists can be found Aristotle, Thomas Aquinas and the Scholastics, down to a modern like Max Scheler. For a thorough and readable treatment of this question the reader can study the Frondizi book.

He asserts as we did briefly in the second chapter that the solution to the problem lies exclusively in neither extreme;

rather elements of both positions need to be combined into an answer that builds on insights derived from both sides and attempts to answer objections that have been leveled against each viewpoint.

The following is particularly appropriate in this regard:

> Subjectivism is right in asserting that value cannot be entirely divorced from valuation, but it errs when it tries to reduce value to valuation. If values were nothing more than a projection of the pleasure, desire or interest of the subject, there would be axiological chaos, since desires and interests vary from one country to another and from one individual to another. And it is true that complete agreement does not exist; yet it is no less true that agreement is much greater than disagreement.
>
> On the other hand if values were created by the subject, without taking into consideration any element which might transcend the subject himself, the behavior norm would be reduced to personal caprice and all possibility of establishing any stable form of esthetic appreciation would disappear . . . . To the psychological act of valuation, certainly very important, it is necessary to add the axiological element in order to know whether what we desire in fact is worthy of being desired. Subjectivism is not enough. Its contribution consists in pointing out an important element in the axiological relation, namely, the subject who evaluates, but it falls short when it leaves aside, unconsciously or deliberately, the other aspect of the relation.

Frondizi concludes that value resides exclusively neither in the object nor in the subject but in the synthesis of the two.

"In brief, value is a Gestalt quality, the synthesis of objective and subjective contributions, and which exists and has meaning only in concrete human situations."

Not Either/Or

One of the consequences of the either/or approach to this question is that it tends to restrict the attention of the thinker to the abstract with the result that individual elements of the concrete are ignored. The entire complex situation of the act of valuing must be brought under scrutiny. Both the subject and the object and their dynamic relationship are situated concretely in a specific place, a specific time, a specific culture. Each circumstance of the act of valuing may make some contribution to the unique reality of the act.

It is precisely at this point that the phase of consciousness of the valuer plays such an important role. A bystander cannot adequately appreciate or fully understand another's act of valuing unless he has some familiarity with the valuer's world view or phase of consciousness. However this does not mean that valuing is therefore totally subjective but only that the subjective plays its part in the over-all process.

Seeing the Whole Value

Suppose that I am observing someone working ninety hours a week. It is easy for me to conclude that he considers work a value. But I fail to grasp the complexity of the dynamic relationship between the man and his work unless I am familiar with his mental world. By extensive conversation with him I may discover that he gets paid by the hour and that he has a very sick son whose medical bills are astronomical. He is working long hours to increase his income to meet those bills because he loves his son. The work and the long hours may be distasteful to him. The work is a value because it brings in extra money, which in turn is a value because it can pay the medical bills for the son, his love for whom is the basic value underlying the whole operation.

I might observe another person who is also working ninety hours a week but out of a totally different mind-set. Conversation with him might reveal that he works such long hours because he sees this as a gateway to success, prestige and social advancement. He might be a "workaholic" or devoted to public service.

These two examples serve to emphasize that both the subject and the object in any act of valuing are situated concretely and therefore cannot be adequately scrutinized in an abstract fashion. In both instances the specific act of valuing makes sense only when seen in relation to the real psychological needs of the subject. On the other hand the object—work in both cases—has certain characteristics that enable it to be seen by each of the subjects as something responding to his needs. In these examples it is the need-satisfying capability of the object work that moves the subjects to act and enter into dynamic relationship with the object. The relationship is complex because in neither case is work prized simply for its own sake. Work is chosen because of the values that are seen as connected to it: money and helping a son in one case, prestige, success and social advancement in the other.

All the examples we have discussed earlier in the book yield similar conclusions. The act of valuing is a complex reality; thus any attempt to locate the value in either the subject or the object is an oversimplification of the whole process. It does seem to us that the introduction of the levels of consciousness into the discussion of the subject-object dilemma especially contributes to an over-all clarification of the issue. Then add to that the realization that every act of valuing involves at least implicitly a complex process of value-ranking and it becomes evident that the object itself is never a simple reality.

Ranking

As we indicated above, values usually appeal to a subject not in isolation but in clusters like success, prestige, competence. The reason for this becomes clear when we realize that these value clusters or constellations relate to a specific world view or phase of consciousness. And it is principally the need-area of consciousness that seeks satisfaction in these value clusters. In this respect the need for meaning is most demanding of the subject's attention.

Needs and Subject

At the same time one must realize that needs arise in human consciousness sometimes as a result of the general human condition and sometimes as a consequence of activity by the subject himself. When needs such as those for security, belonging and self-worth dominate consciousness we are permitted to conclude that they are universal human needs and therefore objective because they are found in all men. The only thing that varies from subject to subject is the precise time when these needs make their presence felt. That of course depends on factors specific to each individual like environment, particular stage of development and the specific circumstances of daily life. While these last conditions are all subjective the need for security, belonging and self-worth are objectively rooted in human nature itself.

Value Moments

But some needs arise as a result of deliberate activity on the part of the subject. I was once interrupted by a friend who was experiencing some frustration. The source of the frustration was a number of demands from friends for some of the time she had mentally set aside for a vacation. She needed some solitude—she wanted to be away from people for awhile.

Normally she is gregarious and enjoys contact with others regardless of whether it is of a professional or social nature. By a free decision on her part she had conditioned herself to count on a period of solitary leisure. This had become an especially strong value for her at this particular moment in her life. This value was rooted not in the general human condition but in her own self-induced subjective need.

The point of this is simply that values people prize may arise from either the objective or subjective order. To locate all values in either one or the other realm is to oversimplify. Even my friend's need for solitude, while subjective in origin at this specific moment, is rooted in a general human need for being alone from time to time. On the other hand the conditions that cause those basic human needs like security and belonging to surface in consciousness at a specific time are frequently subjective in origin.

Wolfgang Kohler

In *The Selected Papers Of Wolfgang Kohler* an entire chapter is devoted to this problem. As a scientist he was deeply interested in convincing other scientists that values have an objective base in reality. At the same time he realized and clearly stated that any adequate theory of values must also recognize the influence of subjective elements in the valuing process.

He spoke consistently of the demand character of a value resident in the object inviting the subject to enter into a dynamic relationship with the object, as in the following passage:

It shall not be denied that the demand which issues from a value object is mostly, though perhaps not necessarily, directed toward the self, and that as a consequence the self is likely to become active toward or away from, that object. In this case, it may rightly be said, vectors actually arise of which the self is the center. But as a rule this happens because, in the first place, there is a positive or negative demand in the object.

This passage clearly puts Kohler in the camp of those whose maintain that both the subject and the object make a real contribution to the constitution of a value as a value.

Nicholas Rescher

Support for this position can also be found in Nicholas Rescher in his *Introduction to Value Theory*. While he gives the subjective-objective question only brief consideration, he does conclude that an adequate value theory must combine elements from each position. The following quotation summarizes his view:

Value has, therefore, an objective basis and can be assessed by impersonal standards or criteria that can be taught to an evaluator through training. Value—in this conception—is relational (in viewing the value of an object as something that arises from the nature of its interactions with people, or perhaps intelligent beings generally) but objective (since evaluation is, in general, based on objectively establishable and interpersonally operative standards).

He goes on to say that some values are primarily subjective, others objective, but his basic position is that values are relational.

Abraham Maslow

Maslow nowhere treats the objective-subjective question explicitly. But a careful reading indicates that he too takes elements from both positions. Some values are chosen in response to needs that are essentially rooted in human nature and are therefore fundamentally objective. Other values are created by the subject valuers. This is indicated by the following brief passage:

Values are partly discovered by us within ourselves as I have said. But, they are also partly created or chosen by the person himself. It is rare that self-search discovers something strictly univocal, a finger pointing in one direction only, a need satisfiable in only one way.

This rapid survey of contemporary authors readily lends itself to the conclusion to which we adhere, that values, while generally rooted in the objective order, also receive something real when they enter into a dynamic relationship with the valuing subject.

Various Ways of Classifying Values

Our classification of values into "I" or personal values and institutional values, while based on clinical experience, is at the same time arbitrary in the sense that there are many other ways to categorize values.

Rescher

Rescher in his *Introduction To Value Theory* suggests a number of different ways to classify values. They can be grouped according to subscribership that results in classes like personal, professional, work, national and so on. Others can be placed together on the basis of the objects at issue such as thing values, environmental values, individual or personal values, group values, and societal values. The last mode of categorizing values relates closely to our "I" values and institutional values as we will point out in more detail. He also divides values in respect to the type of benefit at issue, of the purpose at stake, of the nature of the relationship between subscriber to the value and the beneficiary thereof. Finally he classifies values concerning how they relate to other values.

Rokeach

Values can also be separated into instrumental and terminal values. Rokeach has done much with this classification, conducting several sociological surveys, the results of which are found in *The Nature of Human Values*. Instrumental values are what philosophers have traditionally called means values, that is they are desired not so much for themselves as for what they can lead to. Terminal values are ends values and therefore are sought for their own sake. Values like ambition, courage, logic are instrumental values while equality, a comfortable life, pleasure and things of that sort are terminal values. The following chart gives his breakdown of these two types of values:

DIAGRAM 30

TABLE 2.1 TEST-RETEST RELIABILITIES OF 18 TERMINAL AND 18 INSTRUMENTAL VALUES, FORM D (N = 250)

Terminal Value	r	Instrumental Value	r
A comfortable life (a prosperous life)	.70	Ambitious (hard-working, aspiring)	.70
An exciting life (a stimulating, active life)	.73	Broadminded (open-minded)	.57
A sense of accomplishment (lasting contribution)	.51	Capable (competent, effective)	.51
A world at peace (free of war and conflict)	.67	Cheerful (lighthearted, joyful)	.65
A world of beauty (beauty of nature and the arts)	.66	Clean (neat, tidy)	.66
Equality (brotherhood, equal opportunity for all)	.71	Courageous (standing up for your beliefs)	.52
Family security (taking care of loved ones)	.64	Forgiving (willing to pardon others)	.62
Freedom (independence, free choice)	.61	Helpful (working for the welfare of others)	.66
Happiness (contentedness)	.62	Honest (sincere, truthful)	.62
Inner harmony (freedom from inner conflict)	.65	Imaginative (daring, creative)	.69
Mature love (Sexual and spiritual intimacy)	.68	Independent (self-reliant, self-sufficient)	.60
National security (protection from attack)	.67	Intellectual (intelligent, reflective)	.67
Pleasure (an enjoyable, leisurely life)	.57	Logical (consistent, rational)	.57
Salvation (saved, eternal life)	.88	Loving (affectionate, tender)	.65
Self-respect (self-esteem)	.58	Obedient (dutiful, respectful)	.53
Social recognition (respect, admiration)	.65	Polite (courteous, well-mannered)	.53
True friendship (close companionship)	.59	Responsible (dependable, reliable)	.45
Wisdom (a mature understanding of life)	.60	Self-controlled (restrained, self-disciplined)	.52

Maslow and B and D Cognition

Further study would be needed on this but a case can probably be made for claiming that many of Rokeach's instrumental values are what we call value indicators. For example a person is never ambitious or courageous except in relation to something else. Ambition or courage as values point beyond themselves to some more basic values; they might well *indicate* another underlying value.

Maslow's celebrated distinction between D cognition and B cognition readily adapts itself to a comparable distinction between D values and B values. The real foundation of this classification lies in the two kinds of needs that Maslow has observed in people.

> D needs that lead to D values have the following characteristics:
>
> a) The deprived person yearns for the gratification persistently
> b) Their deprivation makes the person sicken and wither
> c) Gratifying them is therapeutic, curing the deficiency-illness
> d) Steady supplies forestall these illnesses
> e) Healthy (gratified) people do not demonstrate these deficiencies

The values that correspond to these needs are generally those that are typical of our first two phases of consciousness, values like security, survival, belonging and self-worth.

On the other hand the B values correlate more or less with the values characteristic of a person at the third or fourth phase. Below is Maslow's list of B values:

> 1) wholeness (unity, integration, tendency to oneness, interconnectedness, simplicity, organization, structure, dichotomy-transcendence, order);
> 2) perfection (necessity, just-right-ness, just-so-ness, inevitability, suitability, justice, completeness, "oughtness");
> 3) completion (ending, finality, justice, "it's finished," fulfillment, finis and telos, destiny, fate);
> 4) justice (fairness, orderliness, lawfulness, "oughtness");

 5) aliveness (process, nondeadness, spontaneity, self-regula-
    tion, full-functioning);
 6) richness (differentiation, complexity, intricacy);
 7) simplicity (honesty, nakedness, essentiality, abstract, es-
    sential, skeletal structure);
 8) beauty (rightness, formal aliveness, simplicity, richness,
    wholeness, perfection, completion, uniqueness, hon-
    esty);
 9) goodness (rightness, desirability, oughtness, justice, be-
    nevolence. ¬onesty);
10) uniquene⸍s (idiosyncrasy, individuality, noncomparabil-
    ity, novelty);
11) effortlessness (ease, lack of strain, striving or difficulty,
    grace, perfect, beautiful functioning);
12) playfulness (fun, joy, amusement, gaiety, humor, exu-
    berance, effortlessness);
13) truth, honesty, reality (nakedness, simplicity, richness,
    oughtness, beauty, pure clean and unadulterated, com-
    pleteness, essentiality);
14) self-sufficiency (autonomy, independence, not-needing-
    other-than-itself-in-order-to-be-itself, self-determining,
    environment-transcendence, separateness, living by its
    own laws).

So in reality Maslow's division of values into D and B
is incorporated into our schema of the phase of consciousness.

Reflections on Methodology and Values

It is noteworthy that the approach to values and value
theory differs depending on whether one is functioning as a
clinician like Maslow or a sociologist like Rokeach. We make
an approach similar to Maslow where our evidence is
derived from working directly with individuals and groups
rather than basing our conclusions on a statistical approach.

Sociological and Psychological Methods

Surveys tend to treat people as objects of observation
and as such limit the alternatives necessary in a process or
developmental model. Only so much information can be obtained in this way and qualitatively that information tends
to be only a survey or prevailing opinion in society. Rokeach
for example takes a list of instrumental and terminal values

(as above) and asks people to rank them in order of preference. In our opinion this yields questionable results where
values are concerned because the value-ranking is not
derived from actual behavior; it is rather an opinion survey.
Further it is not clear whether this is a survey of real or ideal
values.

By real values I mean values that are rooted in behavior. Ideals would be rooted in the imagination, and as such
are thoughts and verbal responses only. These two pieces can
be seen in relationship to the four skills.

DIAGRAM 31

Concrete Behavior	Ideal
Example: Ambition 1) **Systems Skills: political mind set, studying** 2) **Interpersonal Skills: working in my own sense of power or authority. Getting skills in life with what I want to be** 3) **Instrumental Skills: Developing Professional Skills to suit ambition**	4) **Imaginal Skills: expression of vision of where I want to be**

The point is that a really healthy person will use his
vision to limit how he presently operates in order to prepare
for the vision he imagines. However most people will naturally confuse the value ambition with what they *want*
rather than what they *are*. For example in the diagram ambition is expressed in all four skills through concrete behavior, but most people believe that they value ambition even if
they are not working at it! It may indeed still be a value but
it would be very low on one's *behavioral* list. A survey can't
take this into account.

Georges Allo in his writing is convinced that in dealing with values people cannot be treated as objects of obser-

vation but must actively take part in the process, studying their own values as subjects. They must become active judges of their own behavior not just of their opinions.

Clarifying Behavior

If value-clarification exercises have taught us anything it is that people frequently do not know what values they adhere to behaviorally until they confront their values in a concrete behavioral situation. It is only when they are aided by a value counselor in analyzing their own behavior that they are led to see their real values. A list of values ranked on the basis of actual behavior might differ considerably from the ranking resulting from values thrown at them from a list such as that compiled by Rokeach. We have found, especially in analyzing guilt situations, that the values people actually have and the ones they wish to have are quite frequently different.

Rokeach found that blacks for example ranked equality much higher than whites. But nothing in his study indicated that blacks actually adhere in behavior to equality as a value. At most one could conclude that they were of the opinion that society ought to have equality as a high value. How they as individuals actually behave is not discovered by the survey. A survey always runs the risk of uncovering where people's imaginal skills are and not their total-behavior skills. As we have already indicated above we have found that most people's imaginations are ahead of their actual behavior.

The added problem in the survey approach is that people define values differently depending on their level of development. Even though Rokeach gave one or two word definitions in his list it is questionable whether that would significantly affect what people meant by the value words on the list. In value-clarification exercises people must be able to define their own words if one is to help them truly discover what their real values are.

INSTITUTIONAL VALUES

Our division of values into "I" or personal values and institutional values is practical in origin. In conducting value-clarification exercises with a variety of individuals and groups and drawing out the underlying values from specific instances of behavior we discover that the values that motivate people quite naturally fall into these two categories.

In preparing a value curriculum for public schools we researched the value expectations and goals of the offices of public instruction from various states and came to the conclusion that some were institutional and some were personal. The following excerpts from a statement by the Idaho Department of Education and the Idaho State Board of Education is a specific case in point:

> Thus, the primary concerns of public education are the cultivation in learners of:
>
> ● attitudes of self esteem, respect and compassion for others, and reasoned commitment to the general welfare of men.
>
> ● ability to enter into healthy relationships with others
>
> ● recognition of the need for an ecological balance between man and his natural environment.
>
> ● confidence in democratic procedures for social action and orderly change.
>
> ● respect for legitimate authority responsibly exercised.

These values have been rearranged by us, locating the personal values at the beginning and placing the two institutional values at the end. But this statement is fairly typical of those issued by other states. These kinds of state guidelines have been a factor in our dividing of values into personal and institutional ones.

Testing Objectives
Values as Symbol
Clearly what we mean by a value is a symbol that signifies a set of meanings, generally described by a word (for example security) in a dictionary (a minimum consensus is necessary) that has been objectified by a society's history and

tradition for the purpose of being a creative force for men to consider. It is also clear that in order for society to survive there are certain values men must have in common and agree upon. We call these values institutional values. In short if we consider a society the sum of its institutions there is bound to be a common set of values that are chosen institutionally, representing its goals and the quality of its existence. These values are prioritized and chosen differently by people depending on the institution they are representing in their actions.

At this point we need to separate the difference between institutional and personal values. First let us look at the following Diagram 32 as a representative set of institutional values:

DIAGRAM 32

MAJOR INSTITUTIONAL VALUES

1. Loyalty (Consistency, Respect, Responsibility)
2. Patriotism—Esteem (group)
3. Law (rules—Reason)
4. Control (Order—Discipline)
5. Interdependence
6. Cooperation
7. Life
8. Mission (Goals)
9. Security—Survival—Safety
10. Work/Labor
11. Productivity—Creativity (Consumption)
12. Justice (Rule)
13. Courtesy—Respect
14. Pioneerism (Innovation, Progress)
15. Distribution
16. Equality
17. Pluriformity
18. Education (Knowledge—Wisdom)
19. Unity—Solitary
20. Ecority—Beauty
21. Objectivity
22. Efficiency
23. Support
24. Service
25. Tradition
26. Family—Community
27. Research—Originality—Knowledge Creativity
28. Honesty
29. Communications
30. Function
31. Power (Authority)
32. Expressiveness—Freedom
33. Health
34. Economics
35. Administration
36. Management—Identity (Group)
37. Obedience
38. Duty—Obligation
39. Honor
40. Convivial Tools
41. Adaptability
42. Accountability—Responsibility
43. Property
44. Membership—Institution
45. Workmanship
46. Criteria—Rationality
47. Competition
48. Growth and Expansion
49. Harmony (System)
50. Ritual (Meaning)

Now it needs to be noted that any of the 'I' values from Chapter IV could also be institutional values. The value of security might be a personal value: One always behaves in such a way as to insure that one and one's family are cared for first for example. It could also be an institutional value and as such it would be the same value but with a *systems* character. Security here might be making sure the year's profit margin was up so everyone would be assured a job and that their medical and pension benefits could be increased.

The first rule then is that 'I' values and institutional values are interchangeable, the difference being 'I' values are defined in terms of the person from his vantage point, and institutional values are defined always in terms of the (institutional) system from a systems vantage point.

Diagram 32 is a fairly comprehensive set of institutional values pulled from state educational requirements.

Values: Personal and System

As with the personal "I" values in order for the educator or trainer to use these each one must be defined in relationship to one's personal experience and tested authority. Tested authority regarding institutional values is a little more complicated than are "I" values because by their very nature they are community values requiring a broad consensus. Therefore history and law must be consulted as well as the dictionary and personal experience. The defining of these values would be a curricular undertaking all its own.

Relationship of Personal to Institutional Values

One cannot understand the difference between a personal and institutional value without differentiating in each case between behavior and imagination. Any of the sixty "I" values or the fifty institutional values can be related to either behavior or imagination.

Behavior and imagination are both value indicators. Behavior tells us about the present state of actual consciousness of an individual or institution. Imagination points to the values that are part of the present vision, beliefs and aspirations.

The following diagram illustrates this:

DIAGRAM 33

BEHAVIOR AND VISION

THE PERSON		THE INSTITUTION		THE SOCIETY	
Level of Consciousness	Vision	Level of Consciousness	Vision	Level of Consciousness	Vision
Core values expressed by an individual's behavior	Core values expressed in an individual's imagination & hopes (Imaginal Skills)	Values expressed by man's tools	Limited design or limits placed on structures to enhance autonomy and interdependence	Its law governance and customs	Natural law and enhancement of created order

Values Reflecting Behavior

Some thoughts and reflections:

The Person

The level of consciousness and of value development (see the previous chapter) of any individual is expressed by his actual behavior. This is discovered by the process we call value clarification. It clarifies one's behavior as it is. It is a contemplative act and should be regarded as a sacred task—one sees another as vulnerable and unprotected.

For example a wife is continually worried about obtaining sufficient life insurance for the family. The family is already well cared for, but she wants more and more protection. This is a pattern of behavior for her. What might the underlying values be and how are they ranked? They could be security, health, self-worth, family.

Of course only the wife could actually decide on the correct ranking. Family might deserve to be at the top of the list. Affection might even be a value operative in this situation. She might see the increased life insurance as a sign of love on the part of her husband. The point here is that *behavior is the true indicator of underlying core values and consequently of the phase of consciousness.*

The next point is that a human being's hopes and aspirations, his vision of the future, is an indicator of the values and phase of consciousness appropriate to the stage of development to which he aspires. Thus the imagination reveals the values he strives for.

In the healthy individual not suffering from excessive anxiety the vision will reflect values majoritively typical of the next phase of consciousness.

Peter was a student of mine who worked very hard. Not only was he carrying a full load at college but he also ran a program at a law agency for the economically deprived. Because he was concerned about what people thought of him he enjoyed having the image of student and worker.

He admitted to and was happy with the following values:

1. Family
2. Work
3. Education
4. Prestige

These are values from the upper end of the second phase of consciousness, Phase II-B. When we addressed the question of vision and hopes for the future to him he spoke about being an agency administrator who would really deal with the problem of poverty in the city. He was determined to change things. His hopes were expressed in the following value ranking:

1. Self-directedness
2. Justice
3. Family
4. Construction

Peter talked about being of service as an administrator by becoming "my own man," "directing the show and really accomplishing something." Justice was important to him but so was family. He wanted to reconstruct society. All these ideals relate to Phase III, A and B values.

So in the healthy person the vision is always realistic, within sight, a real possibility. The vision looks to an environment that will reinforce growth. Good imaginal skills contain not only vision but a critical looking at one's own limits as well.

Forebodings

It was Tolkien who maintained that even the fairy tale that is not sufficiently grounded in reality is empty and maybe indicative of psychosis. The more that imagination and vision become separated from day-to-day behavior the more the individual experiences anxiety. Very bright people often have a vision far beyond their behavioral level of consciousness. This can be damaging to the personality.

1. *When a person's verbal messages are identified with his vision rather than with his behavior mental ill-health is beginning to operate.*

2. *When there is an exaggerated distance between vision (imagination) and behavior (separated by more than one value level) and that vision is consistent with that person's public verbal statements but inconsistent with his over-all behavior then more serious mental health and adjustment problems will occur.*

The painter, Van Gogh, was expressing a Phase IV consciousness in his art continuously. Yet his personal life was at a survival stage, he had an overpowering need for affection typical of the first and second phases of consciousness. In the end he cut off his ear, burned his hands and finally committed suicide. Obviously this was an experience produced in one man by the gap in phases of consciousness. Such a gap involves a gigantic conflict in values that the human organism cannot tolerate. This is why it is so important for all persons involved in the process of educating to insist on an holistic interpretation of all four skills.

Educator's Response

The educator needs to take care not to provide environments or learning situations beyond the consciousness and skill level of the individual. He at the same time must beware of the difference between exaggerated behavior that is natural to development and the kind just described.

The Institution

A tool is an objectified entity, a modification of the environment, that enables man to cope with and enhance the created order. I mean by this that the tool is external to the person—it is objectified, made into an extramental object. A man wants to kill an animal. He needs a spear with which to do the job. He gets an idea—a pointed stick that he could throw fifty feet and kill the deer. The idea, internal to the man, is externalized or objectified. He turns the internal image into a concrete object by modifying the environment. He cuts a branch off a tree and converts it into a spear. He has made a tool. Here the words of Ivan Illich are relevant.

> Tools are intrinsic to social relationships. An individual relates himself in action to his society through the use of tools, he actively masters, or by which he is passively acted upon. The degree that he masters his tools, he can invest the world with his meaning: to the degree that he is mastered by his tools, the shape of his tool determines his own self image. Convivial tools are those which owe each person who uses them the greatest opportunity to enrich the environment with the fruits of his or her vision.

Institutions are made up of persons. Thus once we understand the personal, the institutional comes more easily. The stage of consciousness that an institution reinforces in its people is apparent in its overt behavior. *Institutional behavior is the manufacture of and the organization of tools.* Richard Wagner points out in his *Environment and Man* that:

> The consistent use of tools is of great significance in the effect of environment on man's evolution. For the first time an animal could use its brain to meet the challenges of its environment, instead of having to make gross structural adaptations. This is why further changes in outward appearances of man have been small. When man first started living in the arctic, he did not have to grow fur, he wore clothes; when he first flew he did not have to develop wings by mutation, he used a tool. With culturation, that is, the achievement of culture, man was freed from most of the direct selective effects of his environment.

Tools and institutions are thus intertwined. In fact, in a real sense, an institution itself is a tool. What is a tool?

Tools Expanded

Tools are therefore concrete objects that relate directly to man's social development. They are modifications of the environment. We transform trees into planks of wood and clay into bricks in order to build houses that will protect us from the weather that is part of the natural environment. By living in houses, which are tools of community living, we enhance and promote our social relationships.

Paolo Soleri

Paolo Soleri speaks of the physical structure of society and the concreteness of life in *Matter Becoming Spirit*. He refers such ideas to the development of the city of the future.

> The physical structure for the society of man will be wrapped, by force of the concreteness of life, around vectors and will form 'city miniatures' of three congruous dimensions connected to major 'river cities' ribbing the continents and not suffocating them under asphalt, cement and pollution.

Tools then are more than hand or power tools, they are buildings and cities themselves. In fact tools include other modifications of the environment. Our laws, the rules and organizations that structure our lives, even our institutions are tools. The following diagram clarifies this:

DIAGRAM 34

TOOLS TO MODIFY THE ENVIRONMENT	TOOLS THAT MODIFY MEN	TOOLS TO ENHANCE LIFE (SOCIETY)
Hammer	Laws	Art
Tractor	Politics	Music
Oil Refineries	Business	Social Interest
Paint	Organizations	
	Institutions—e.g.,	
	Medical Profession	

Institutions for the Person

Tools are expressions of behavior that indicate the underlying values of the institution that employs them. They also point to the underlying values of the person or institution using them. Ultimately they always point to personal values because institutions exist for the service of man.

This is a gigantic subject and is presented here only as an introduction that forms a part of an over-all confluent approach to values. We hope some of the ideas found here will encourage others to do more extensive research on values as they relate to institutions.

Institutional Vision

An institution is designed to serve the people. The ideal institution would therefore be a convivial tool. There is of course a great range of institutional styles. From the perspective of values they run from those that enhance the freedom and autonomy of the individual through those that restrict freedom and impose rigid sets of values.

Institution and Vision

As we saw earlier in the chapter on skills systems always exist with two major potentials or tensions:

1) Individual goals and needs versus institutional (in systems) goals and needs.
2) The integration of those needs versus the limits the over-all environment sets.

DIAGRAM 35

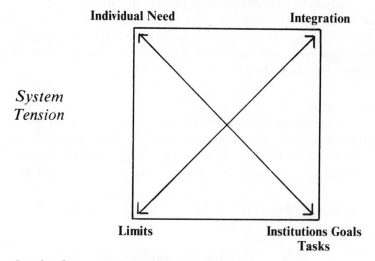

Individual Need   **Integration**

*System
Tension*

Limits   **Institutions Goals
Tasks**

Leadership or Value Indicators

Every institution has these tensions: *But the nature and purpose of its structure as reflected in the original leadership will set its boundary limits.*

The leadership and the way it administrates through the structure reflects a series of core values that will indicate 1) boundary limits, 2) institutional and individual tension.

A Value Analysis of An Institution

Having helped administrators come to a consensus on systems values we have found the following graph to be helpful. At the center where I work the following institutional values were chosen as priorities.

1. Personal development (Phase III)
2. Limitations
3. Consequence
4. Interdependence
5. Construction

Immediately values one and five highlight the tension between individual needs and institutional requirements. In each case an administration would have to define these values we set. This is basically a professional adult education consultation firm.

Personal Growth as Value
    Personal development was seen to mean that a person should be encouraged to get all the skills he needed, to be critical in his own right, to be able to share and confront others on the professional staff spontaneously, and to have an area of knowledge that he was expert in.

Construction as Value
    Construction was defined by us as the ability to work interdependently as a professional staff member, in order to build the firm up and bring in a minimal amount of the budget in hard money each year through personal initiative and contacts.
    Originally the graph was as follows:

DIAGRAM 36

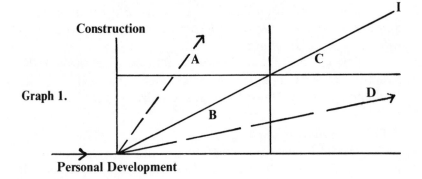

Institution and Tension
    The graphs portray the tension between the vertical axis, construction, *versus* the horizontal, personal development. The ideal administration would have attempted the integration of the two poles through B and C above (I).
    However it did not work out that way. This was an organization with a number of psychologists and educators trained in human relations. As such they tended to be overly oriented to personal development and not attentive enough to getting the job done (construction).

DIAGRAM 37

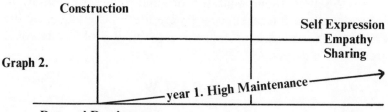

Graph 2.

Construction

Self Expression
Empathy
Sharing

year 1. High Maintenance

Personal Development

Maintenance in Institutions

As a consequence (Graph 2) the year was spent in long hours of staff maintenance. The analyzed values were:
1) Self expression as honesty and confrontation
2) Empathy as caring and listening
3) Sharing of information and feeling.

The catch was that anxiety also went up because an organization cannot spend too much time in self-maintenance as good as these values are without going out of business! In such a situation once the leadership is aware of it there is a tendency to swing the other way:

DIAGRAM 38

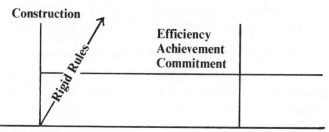

Construction

Rigid Rules

Efficiency
Achievement
Commitment

Personal Development

Here we see a high rating on construction and very little on personal development. Immediately the values stressed were:
1) Efficiency
2) Achievement: a direct relationship between work and its utility to the institution in terms of profit

3) Commitment to the value of construction as the most important priority.

We then found that the original values of limitation, congruence and interdependence were ideals. Consequently the graph begins to look as follows as a picture of institutional growth:

DIAGRAM 39

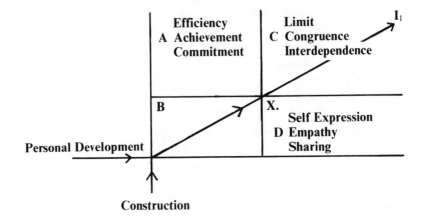

Integration

Limitation meant individuals facing their own time and energy limits. Congruence was understood as a person being in touch with his skills and societal needs so as to be able to work out constructive educational suggestions that would be acted on. And finally interdependence meant working in closer cooperation, evaluating the skill deficiencies of the staff and delegating authority better.

Interim Values

What was fascinating was that in a period of a year and a half a new set of interim values appeared—point X on the graph. They were:

1. Health. This meant individuals watching their own physical and energy limits more *and* the staff doing

more cooperative long-term planning and evaluation.
2. Cooperation. Learning to be more constructive and build the team more so that interdependence might become possible.
3. Service. Examining more closely the work that was done and planning more realistic limits on it through continuing evaluation. The next graph is as follows:

DIAGRAM 40

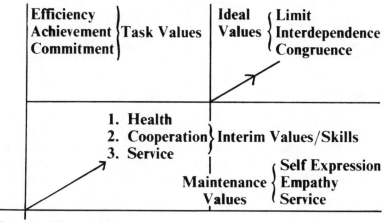

Personal Development

↑**Construction**

Building a Vision

There is much research to be done in values and organizational development. The latter is a very brief introduction out of our own research. Its importance lies in the premium it puts on realistic *vision* and direction for an institution while not neglecting *tensions*. The interim values are concrete indicators of skills to be developed in a particular setting. Health and cooperation pointed to systems skills both personal and institutional. Cooperation and service demands imagination, instrumentation and the interpersonal skills.

As a simple strategy reflect on this graph of a small for-profit organization and see if you can envisage some of the situations portrayed by the values.

DIAGRAM 41

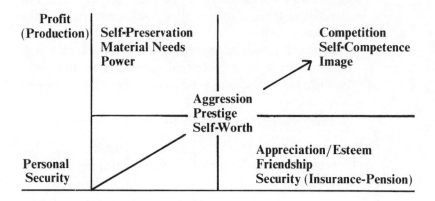

Profit (Production)

Self-Preservation
Material Needs
Power

Competition
Self-Competence
Image

Aggression
Prestige
Self-Worth

Personal Security

Appreciation/Esteem
Friendship
Security (Insurance-Pension)

1. *Institutions as Questions.*

This is the ideal to which institutions aspire. It is the institution that is designed to enhance the liberty of individuals in an interdependent and cooperative manner. Its minimal goal is the development of Phase III consciousness and the fostering of the values appropriate to that phase: self-direction, independence, being self, service to others and construction of a better world.

This means that the minimal leadership requirement is for people who are comfortable at Phase III with a vision of Phase IV. This may seem a bit idealistic, but to us it seems to be the minimum that should be required of leaders in our time. What we are saying is that to the normal skill requirements of any leader we are adding the following two:

1. The leader must have achieved a Phase III consciousness.
2. The leader must have a vision for the future that is a Phase III B or IV A.

This would be a minimal design limit for any major adult institution.

2. *Institutions Imposing Values.*

This happens whenever the core values of the founder of the institution are rigidly institutionalized. Let us take a simple educational example. An adult education institution of fine arts is set up to teach. Mr. Jones, the founder of the school, gathers together great artists from the community to teach art to whomever wants to receive instruction.

As the years go by the original artists leave and new ones are hired. Someone on the board suggests that all new employees must have the minimal educational requirement of a high school diploma. Sometime later a minimum of a master's degree is introduced as a condition of employment.

Fifty years later a newly elected chairman of the board proudly asserts in a television interview: "We do not consider a person who graduates from our school to be an artist unless he attended all the classes (a three-year program) and received at least a B in all courses. Further we do not consider a person to be an art teacher unless he is licensed by the state and has a master's degree."

The day after the television interview a world-famous poet is refused a job at the school because she has no master's degree. What went wrong?

The original core values of a group of artists became institutionalized. Because it lacked proper leadership the institution started to control rather than serve its members. The institution was no longer convivial. Referring to our graphs there would be little integration with a stress on institutional task and a lack of attention given to individual needs.

This is the opposite of "Institution as Question" because the institution both asked the question and provided the answer. It did not ask with an open mind as did the founder: "What is an artist?" Rather it said: "An artist is anyone who has met our criteria." Institutions that do not allow new and viable questions to threaten their structure ensure a Phase II consciousness and prevent growth.

Limited Design as Vision

Well thought out and well-formulated restrictions on institutions protect the autonomy of the individuals who constitute the membership. This is the only way the vision can be safeguarded because the vision originates not with the institution as such but with individuals. The core institutional values and the particular way they are prioritized in a given instance place limits on what the institution can do. These values are off limits to the institution in the sense that they cannot be tampered with, unless the individuals decide to reprioritize their values. This is what we mean by a "limited design criteria" (an expression I first heard from Ivan Illich). These limits defend and in a sense constitute the vision of the institution.

Ultimately the deepest values are the "I" values that form each individual as he or she contributes to institutions and society. Value clarification helps us to go beyond institutional questions to the core of the matter. But consideration of the institutional dimension is absolutely essential and often the starting place for clarifying an individual's values. For the limited design criteria to be operative certain questions must be addressed to the institution, examples of which follow:

Questions

Example I. Institutional questions related to the value of education:

What is education?
What is a school?
What is a teacher?

Primary value questions that must control the activity of the institution by limiting it:

How does Johnny learn?
Who is it that teaches?
Example II. Institutional questions related to medicine:
What is a doctor?
What is a hospital?
What is health care?

Primary Value Questions

Primary value questions that must control medical activity:

What is healing?
Who heals?
What is pain (For example, what is death and where does one have the right to it? Must a person in pain live as long as he can?)
Example III. Institutional questions related to religion:
What is a church?

What is the ministry of the minister?

What is a layman?

Primary value questions that must limit a church's activity.

Does God exist? Does he make any difference?

What makes life meaningful?

When an institution raises only the first sets of questions and neglects to foster among its members discussion of the primary value questions it is destructive in that it limits both vision and the development of consciousness.

Limited design criteria then limit institutional rules— lives or structures that prevent people from asking and getting answers to these primary questions.

A society reveals its corporate consciousness by its behavior as expressed in its laws, customs and style of governance. Society is the institution writ large. Values to be studied here would be the same as for other institutions as they relate to personal values. The difference would lie within the precise subject matter studied. For example a high-school teacher who wanted the class to study the values of society rather than of institutions would design a curriculum around that society's government, law, culture, customs, history and tradition.

The vision of a society is normally expressed in the great statements of its tradition. It comes to us of a later age through works of art and literature and through laws.

History of Ideas

No less important and often more seminal than these factors is the history of ideas themselves. In a curriculum this could be taken up in the study of metaethics or of ideas as they relate to personal, institutional and societal behavior in the development of civilization.

This subject matter is gigantic and cannot be given extensive treatment here. In our opinion the clue to creative societal development is in the organization of its axiological (value) institutions and in the way in which they are limited. A science of limits needs to be developed if human consciousness is to grow. (In this regard the reader might go to Daniel Callahan's *The Tyranny of Survival* where this subject is treated at some length.)

Denis Goulet

Denis Goulet writing in the *Harvard Educational Review* on societal development states this limit as follows:

> Authentic development aims at the full realization of human capabilities: men and women become makers of their own histories, personal and societal. They free themselves from every servitude imposed by nature or by oppressive systems, they achieve wisdom in their mastery over nature and over their own wants, they create new webs of solidarity based not on domination but reciprocities among themselves, they achieve a rich symbiosis between contemplation and transforming action, between efficiency and free expression. This total concept of development can perhaps best be expressed as the "human ascent"—the ascent of all men in their integral humanity, including the economic, biological, psychological, social, cultural, ideological, spiritual, mystical, and transcendental dimensions.

Significative Values and Normative Values

Denis Goulet distinguished between significative and normative values. Significative values have to do with a meaning system that confers significance to existence. Normative values belong to a large category of operational values, but themselves are intended to guide people and control behavior in the interest of the core values of a group.

Declaration of Independence

The coming to be of the United States as a distinct body politic can serve as a model that reveals the functional role of the various kinds of institutional values. In the Declaration of Independence, Jefferson verbalized the core values around which the nation was to be institutionalized. This document came not only from Jefferson's imagination but from the living experience of the colonists and the vision of their leaders as well. Their common treatment as victims of tyranny and their lack of freedom was the source of energy that powered the movement towards independence. Their common experience of mistreatment and of an inability to control their own destiny crystalized in a shared need for independence.

The declaration as a document operated within the whole process much as does a religious creed. Both express values and beliefs that are considered vital to a high-quality and meaningful existence. Both affirm the core values of the institution in question. Both are symbols of a shared stance towards life. The expressions contained in each document do not discover or constitute the core values of the institution involved; they merely verbalize values and beliefs that are derived from a common life experience.

Core Values and Meaning

The values expressed in the Declaration of Independence are both core values and significative values. Life, liberty and the pursuit of happiness were perceived as the natural rights of all men by a group of men who found their current experience in life intolerable because they were being deprived of those rights. These values functioned as core values in that they were at the heart of the new nation that was being established. They were the values the new nation was organized to obtain and defend.

They were also significative values in that they signified (symbolized as in a creed or symbol) what the new nation stood for. Doubtlessly they were closely tied to the meaning system of many of the colonists, a frequent function of a significative value.

Constitution

The Constitution of the United States was a later attempt to structure an institution that was suited to provide all its members with the opportunity for obtaining these core values. In its detailed prescriptions the Constitution dealt with normative values that were seen as essential for the protection of those core values such as dividing the various powers of government into the three branches to make it impossible for power to be centered in the hands of any one individual or group. The distribution of power was a normative value that legislated a system of government consistent with the demands of liberty and destructive of tyranny.

Bill of Rights

The Bill of Rights was an ingenious device later added to the Constitution invented to limit the powers of government in certain areas considered essential to the liberty of individual citizens. These first ten amendments functioned then as a limited design criteria, expressing normative values and operating in the interest of the core values that were behind the entire Constitution. They stated what the government could not do in terms related to the core values, limited design criteria always put negative limits on behavior in the service of positive values. After all the basic function of the Constitution is to structure a body politic devoted to the core values expressed in the Declaration of Independence.

The organization of institutions in general follows a similar pattern. It can be outlined as follows:

1. The vision giving rise to the institution
2. The symbolic expression of the vision
3. The constitution of the institution—the institutionalizing of the vision
4. The laws governing the institutionalized vision

Points one and two deal with core or significative values, three and four cover normative and instrumental values that are ideally designed to promote the core values.

This schema easily applies to religious institutions. Take Moses and the organization of Judaism. The vision of Moses focused on a people free to enjoy intimacy with God. The core values present in the vision had to do with freedom and intimacy. These values eventually came to be expressed symbolically or creedally in passages like the following:

> For you are a people holy in the Lord your God: the Lord your God has chosen you to be a people for his own possession out of all the peoples that are on the face of the earth. It was not because you were more in number than any other people that the Lord set his love upon you and chose you, for you were the fewest of all peoples; but it is because the Lord loves you and is keeping the oath he swore to your Fathers, that the Lord has brought you out with a mighty hand, and redeemed you from the house of bondage from the hand of Pharoah king of Egypt. (Dt. 7:6, Revised Standard Version)

This passage is a sort of creed or symbol, a declaration of the core values of the institution. Portions of the books Leviticus, Numbers and Deuteronomy give the basic constitution of Israel as a nation and religious body and also formulate in laws the normative values that were to characterize Israel. In later periods when normative values became ends in themselves and began to obscure the core values prophets arose to turn Israel around.

Vision and Change Prophets

From time to time every institution needs prophets to vitalize the original vision, if indeed the original vision still has viability. Institutions need reformers when either normative values cloud the original vision that inspired them or when core values need reformulation in a new vision. Core values lose their dynamism not because they cease to be values but because they lose their priority status. Other values assume new urgency for the members of the group.

Because man is a being who develops it is to be expected that not all values have the same urgency for him at all times. Another way of saying this is that an institution that is meaningful to a man at one stage of his development may at a later stage seem to him unworthy of his interest. A man who has been a dedicated worker for the optimists in his thirties might in his forties redirect that energy to a group instituted to promote ecology. A new vision replaces an old one because new values have attained priority in his life. So the institutions a man joins and for which he works are one index of his value priorities and a measure of his personal development.

Behavior True Indicator

Thus far we have restricted our considerations of institutional values to the official documents of those institutions like the statements of goals and purposes, constitutions and laws. But as in the case of personal values the ultimate criterion of an institution's values is behavior. Normally of course an institution's behavior is shaped by these officially stated value stances. If the institution in question has a legislative organ then the laws it enacts from time to time are behavioral expressions of values. But there are other behavioral value indicators of an institution. The day to day administrative decisions of the managers of the institution and even their style of operating reveal that institution's values. So too do the activities of the members when they are acting in their capacity as members. Thus to find the actual values of an institution these behavioral factors have to be examined. Only such an examination enables a person to discover if the institution's present behavior matches its original purposes.

Another clue to the operative values of an institution is contained in its self-legitimatizing statements. As Peter Berger clearly suggested in *The Sacred Canopy* every society has its legitimizations expressed in materials designed to perpetuate the society and defend it against attacks on its validity. These constitute a body of practical wisdom available for use by those interested in maintaining the institution in question. Usually this wisdom is pretheoretical in nature—it is not deduced from a well-worked out theoretical rationale of the institution. In fact it resists theoretical examination. White supremacists, a loosely organized institution, dole out such wisdom in statements like: "All blacks are alike." "Blacks are oversexed." "Blacks are intellectually inferior to whites." And the clincher: "Would you want your daughter to marry one?" These are legitimizations of institutionalized racism and reveal the values of those who issue or subscribe to such statements. Nearly every institution has a similar body of practical wisdom that reveals its values and is intended to socialize men to accept its viewpoints.

Reciprocal Relationship

This leads us to a consideration of the dynamic interaction that characterizes the relationship between an individual and his institutions. There is a reciprocal relationship between man as an individual and the human institution that surrounds him. They are after all part of his environment. Institutions are produced by men but at the same time men are shaped by institutions. The following diagram illustrates this phenomenon:

DIAGRAM 42

INSTITUTION

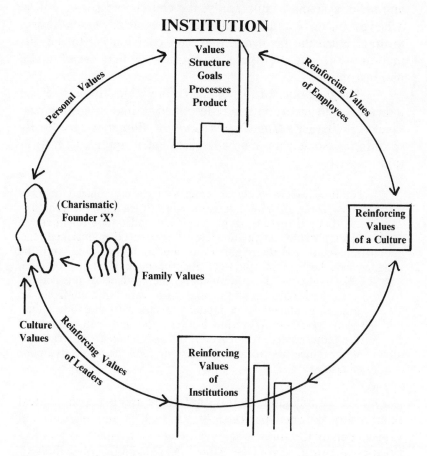

It is a curious but readily understandable fact that a person assessing a particular value stance of any individual will discover that institutions have played a large part in situating him in his values even though institutions ultimately trace the origin of their values to individual men. An individual in turn can be a force for reshaping the values of the institutions he encounters. It is for this reason that all arrows in the diagram point in both directions, thus stressing the reciprocity of the relationships.

Individual X in the diagram is influenced by the values and belief systems of his family, the church and society. If he achieves maturity and is a self-directed creative person he will in time return the favor and make his contribution to the formation of the values of these institutions. He may even found a new institution.

The dynamics of this dialectical relationship between an individual and institutions are described brilliantly in this passage from Berger's *The Sacred Canopy*. Berger is specifically speaking of society in a broad sense, but it applies to institutions as well:

> The fundamental dialectic process of society consists of three steps. These are externalization, objectivation, and internalization. Only if these three moments are understood together can an empirically adequate view of society be maintained. Externalization is the ongoing out pouring human being into the world, both in the physical and the mental activity of men. Objectivation is the attainment by the products of this activity (again both physical and mental) of a reality that confronts its original producers as a facticity external to and other than themselves. Internalization is the reappropriation by men of this same reality, transforming it once again from structures of the objective world into structures of the subjective consciousness.

We simply add to this that there is also a dialectical relationship between personal or "I" values and institutional values. Personal values that have been externalized and objectified in institutions are thereafter internalized by other individuals. For purposes of development and education it is important that the individual bring this whole process to consciousness. Otherwise he is in danger of being controlled by his institutional environment and of becoming, to use Freire's terms, object rather than subject.

Clarifying Instutional Values

Value clarification as a technique must aid an individual examine the influences of various institutions in shaping his values. It is a fact that some individuals internalize values under the influence of institutions unconsciously. Value clarification can help bring this to consciousness and empower people to decide freely to accept or reject those values.

But value-clarification techniques applied to institutions must be designed to distinguish between core values and instrumental or normative values. It can happen that a person discovers that he has a whole-hearted commitment to an institution's core values but finds its instrumental or normative values unsuitable. He may then decide to stay with the institution and to continue to work for its purposes while at the same time trying to create normative values that are more appropriate to those purposes.

A most obvious example of this occurs today in some religious communities. Many members find they have mixed and confused feelings about the communities' value stances, but some of the confusion can be eliminated if they distinguish between end values and means values. We have found after engaging in extended value-clarification strategies some religious have rediscovered hope in their order's future. They continue to share in the core values of the institution but are convinced that some normative values must be modified.

The following extended example provides us with the opportunity to analyze concretely the complex relationship that often exists between personal and institutional values. This incident took place at a workshop where the participants received instructions to diagram a recent situation that involved a conflict between personal and institutional values. They were to focus on a precise moment in the conflict and with the aid of a facilitator draw out the underlying values. They were told to diagram a personal institutional conflict. Rules for constructing the diagram were as follows:

1. Persons are symbolized by circles.
2. Institutions are represented by squares.
3. The size of the circle or square indicates how important the persons and institutions seemed at the time, for whatever reason.
4. The distance between the circles represents emotional distance between the persons.

Dave, the director of a counseling service, drew the following diagram:

DIAGRAM 43

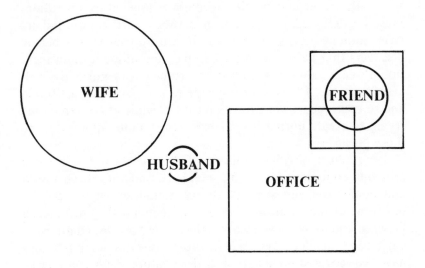

He explained the conflict depicted in the diagram as follows:

He and his wife had just returned from a delightful vacation. When he checked in at the office he discovered that a friend of his had applied for a job as a counselor while he was away. So even though he still had a day left on his vacation he invited the friend to his house for dinner. When he informed his wife of this she got angry because she resented the intrusions of work into the home even before the vacation was over. He lamely justified his action by explaining that the fellow was a friend, but both he and his wife knew the reason for the invitation was job-related.

A group brainstorming session then attempted to discover the values underlying Dave's behavior with a view to isolating the values principally operative in the conflict. The brainstorming produced this list of value words:

Family
Security
Work
Productivity

Image/Prestige
Being Self
Self-worth
Power
Duty/Obligation
Accountability/Responsibility
Friendship
Honesty
Self-directedness
Construction

It is important to realize that these words describe the values that the husband saw operating in his behavior and in his reactions to the conflict. The wife would undoubtedly have come up with a very different list. Dave was next asked to select and rank in order of importance six values from the list. The reason for choosing such a large number in this case was that both personal and institutional values were involved. The resulting list was:

1. Family (Wife)
2. Productivity
3. Image/Prestige
4. Duty/Obligation
5. Self-worth
6. Friendship

He was then asked to separate what he considered to be the personal from institutional values and rank the personal and institutional values separately, producing this list:

Personal

1. *Family (Wife)*
2. Image/prestige
3. Self-worth
4. Friendship

Institutional

1. *Productivity*
2. Duty/Obligation
3. Self-worth

This list graphically portrays the conflict between the two types of values. Family (wife) and productivity were clearly competing for primacy in the conflict and productivity won out, even though family (wife) ranked first and productivity second in the single list. Dave's decision to invite his friend to dinner expressed, at least in this act, his preference for the primary institutional value over the primary personal value, although that is not the way he consciously wanted it to be. You might try diagraming and analyzing a conflict you are familiar with.

Conclusions

Difficulty is inevitable any time an institutional value imposes expectations on an individual in the personal realm that are in conflict with personal values. On the other hand when institutional values reinforce personal values harmony results. Today some work institutions are intruding into the home by offering the wife gifts if the husband reaches certain levels of productivity. Whether this promotes harmony or discord is problematic.

Only a highly skilled individual can cut through the intricate and many faceted relationships that tie personal to institutional values and only such a person can appreciate the respective impacts of each on behavior. In fact the coming together in a holistic fashion of a number of skills is what enables an individual to advance in this process of value development. These skills function as a sort of keystone in this theoretical construct of value development. Without them the structure comes tumbling down. For growth to be confluent skills in four areas must be developed.

Obviously the question of institutions and values is a complex one. This chapter is simply a beginning. Hopefully it will stimulate some to do research and raise constructive questions and strategies in relationship to those organizations with which they deal.

In the last analyses the question of how personal values relate and interact with institutional values is the age-old philosopher's question of whether values are subjective or objective. Institutions at their best are those environments that reinforce men to higher and more creative stages of consciousness.

If then we are to have a vision of a new world it must be one where we transcend the purely personal in value search and look toward the training of enlightened leadership and constructors of life-enhancing environments.

CHAPTER VII

BUILDING FOR A
CONSTRUCTIVE FUTURE

BLUME, Peter *Light of the World* 1932. Oil on Composition board 24 x 32 inches. Collection of Whitney Museum of American Art.

Someone might want to comment that model-building is merely proof of the statement: "A picture is worth a thousand words." This is only partly true. A picture that does not adequately take into consideration the forces that pertain to the situation may be false and therefore valueless. It has been my goal to introduce the technology of model-building as an important tool for man to use in meaningfully confronting multiple reactive and proactive changes in a way that helps reveal and sustain truth and values. It is a technology that can be used advantageously by those who wish to grow and solve problems by expanded use of logical and visual thinking.

Gordon L. Lippitt.

INTRODUCTION

To conclude I need to return to the beginning and reflect on what it is we have written here. First of all the reader has been presented with a model of how we view the development of man, his consciousness and consequently his values. What basis is there for thinking that such a reality exists—of what value then is this model—and where do we go from here? That is what this final chapter is about.

Some Personal History

Having worked in and been interested in value theory and practice for more than ten years I found myself being continually pressed by questions that some of the major authors such as Rokeach and Simon did not answer. For one thing they were not addressing the same questions. Kohlberg and Maslow came closer but were incomplete, especially in their practical ramifications.

Perception

The question had to do with "perception" arising out of several conflict experiences that I participated in and observed, usually in a cross cultural situation. Questions like:

1) Why is it that people having common values (on the surface) perceive these same values so differently, especially when there are cultural differences present?
2) What happens to people who work in institutions that are more rigid than the people themselves? Or what happens when the institutions are more open?

It seemed that in all cases people were talking about the same end values (education, service). But when one approached the how of a value then the perceptions of the individuals were radically different. This led me to write the three-volume work *Value Clarification as Learning Process* in which I attempted to resolve some of the dilemmas involved by pointing out that on the surface we often confuse value as behavior with value as an ideal or belief (imagination only).

For example a social-service agency may espouse the idea of working with unwed mothers. As a counselor interested in this value of service I joined the organization. One month later I found this was only an ideal, in fact we could only counsel people who paid high fees or else we would go bankrupt. I was disillusioned. The confusion was the fact that:

1) Service to unwed mothers was only an *ideal* not a behavioral reality.
2) To the extent that it was indeed a *value* it ranked low on the behavioral-priority list.

Concepts of value-ranking, and the clarification of behavioral values however only answered some of the questions.
Unanswered Questions:

There were still basic questions that seemed untouched especially in the nature of institutions. These questions had to do with the basic stance, the total way of perceiving the world by the persons involved.

Experience in Another Culture

A number of years ago I went to Venezuela to do a social services survey for the Anglican Church in Canada investigating the viability of Church-related services in that country. When the survey was completed a conflict arose over whether or not such services should in fact be offered. The conflict was *not over need*. Both the survey team and those in Canada agreed that there was a need for such things as university-related services. The point of conflict was:

1) The at-home group wanted to send an official delegation to Venezuela with a team of highly trained specialists who would then offer consultant services.
2) The survey team wanted no such official group stressing the Venezuelan apprehension and mistrust of foreign presence and Canadian willingness to be present until asked.

Obedience

Naturally members of the survey team had no real authority and were eventually asked to resign. My point is that there was a basic difference in perception. For one thing the leadership in Canada defined *obedience as our trust of them in the process, which meant that we should respect them and accept their wisdom based on age and experience. They also had clear responsibility for the final outcome, not we.*

On the other hand as inexperienced as we were we defined *obedience as trust in the survey experience and what we learned and concluded from experiencing that environment.*

Another experience in the United States has been typical of many I have had working in service agencies and had to do with professional/client relationships.

As a psychologist I was working in a small family-service agency with about fifteen social workers, education and family counselors.

Professional versus Client

Typically the agency had very rigid views of what therapy (healing) was. It usually required one-to-one counseling. The question of accountabilities came up and as a consequence the director of the agency said he would personally evaluate the work of each professional on the staff. Naturally it seemed to me basic questions needed to be raised:

Accountability

1) Should not the clients evaluate the staff?
2) Should not the clients have a voice in the mode of treatment and education the agency uses?
3) Who would evaluate the agency director?

Primary Questions

Again a heated conflict arose over who was in authority. But basically it was again a question of underlying perceptions. Both parties agreed that there was a *need* and a service being requested. It was not a value-making question of client versus professional. It was a question of *"Who is it that finally heals?"* the client assisted by the professionals or the professionals guiding the client? It was a question of: Is authority within or external?

The same value "healing" was defined from a different set of perceptions.

Over a period of time I began hopefully to get a little wiser and realized people weren't being stubborn or arrogant in their views. No, they were committed people. Their world

views were different. There was little or no communication between people holding different world views. They did not have
the skills to cope with each other.

A Model and a Method

From these concerns the Center for the Exploration of
Values and Meaning was started. Basically it is an institution-
in-process that continually tries to ask the underlying value
questions by observing data (anthropological method) in and
with itself and within the institutions with which it works. In
this regard Lippett has the following to say:

Lippett

One of the key elements in man's problem-solving is the factor
of perception. Perception is the process of becoming aware of
objects, relationships, or qualities outside or inside the individual who is doing the perceiving. Perception includes those processes of conscious cognition or awareness that is mediated
through the sensory nervous system. The intelligent and successful planner of change is aware of the critical factor of perception which must be understood and appreciated if he is to
carry out planned change activities with any degree of success.
A good model can enhance that perception.

The first six chapters in the book were a model gathered
out of our perception of the data of the environment. The environment consists basically of individuals in institutions and the
interaction between the two.

The theory of the development of consciousness then is
a model based on perception, how people perceive the world at
different stages in their life.

A CONFLUENT MODEL

When we say the model is confluent we do not simply
mean integration of skills with such things as emotional, imaginal and intellectual (affective and cognitive domain) sectors
of life but that it offers an opportunity to integrate the various
disciplines.

Cross Discipline

The research on this model was careful to bring together

people from the disciplines of science and medicine, social sciences, education, philosophy and theology. A lot of attention was given to the need for a cross-cultured and esthetic base.

Basically the model is developmental and obviously process oriented. Persons who have a static world view or see values as unchanging will have difficulty with a perception model such as this.

Over-all Meaning System

It is a change model. *It is an over-all meaning construct, intended to integrate the Sciences, Religion, Social Sciences and the Fine Arts.*

This does not mean it has the answer to all their questions, it means that it is itself a model that integrates—makes confluent—a variety of parts that are in fact a part of a whole. For example the four skills are not new. We have all the technology we need in those areas. *But* they need to be integrated into a confluent system in order for them to be maximally meaningful to people.

The Model in Process

The following diagram illustrates the process in which we are involved.

DIAGRAM 44

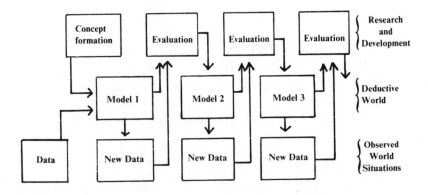

Model 1

The model that has been relayed in this book is the result of at least eight radical changes. It is not itself represented by Model 1. This diagram is simply a way of explaining the process.

Model 1 is the result of 1) concept formation and 2) data.

The data is presently collected and evaluated through:

1) Curriculum development
2) Consultation
3) Direct education

As early as 1972 CEVAM joined with persons from the department of education at Saint Louis University to initiate with the Dendron Publishing Company the project on Values and Meaning.

Later in 1973 the Lilly Endowment funded Project Values, a joint project between Saint Louis University and CEVAM directed by Dr. Richard Kunkel in Saint Louis, and myself in Indianapolis. Although greater than Project Values and Meaning, Project Values contributed much to the total project, which was aimed at developing a total curriculum grade one to adult in value development.

Curriculum Development

Presently grades one to three have been completed and the next phase is to begin. The curriculum based on this confluent theory of values tried to integrate the following components in each of the grades.

1. Integrating all four skills areas.
2. Integrating all the core values, stressing in particular the phase and stage that lined up with the particular grade level.
3. Making an effort to stress values immediately ahead of where the child is to open up the possibilities of development.
4. Integrating the subject matters of esthetics, science and social studies.
5. Effort was made to stress culture (global education) as integrative.

6. The history of ideas, as well as current world history, were seen as developmental and needing to be integrated into a child's personal development.
7. Skills such as moral development and value clarification were to be integrated into other skills in a balanced manner. For example: interpersonal and esthetic skills.

Consultations and Direct Education

By working in consultation with educational and other nonprofit institutions (hospitals, service agencies, religious groups) we have been able to apply the model for development through:
1) Leadership training and development
2) Teacher education and training to teachers in colleges of higher education.

As a consultative model, in helping an organization to grow, or in helping a Title III program design a two-year in-service program, the model:
1) Helped the clients diagnose their present behavioral reality (personal and institutional values and behavior).

But it also did something other methods too often fail to do:
2) See their reality in an over-all meaning structure: giving perspective to the value they had and allowing them to see their own deficiencies in terms of *skills needed* rather than as the result of inherent inadequacies.
3) It allowed the clients to see their reality in a time and development perspective. The *phase model gives people a sense of vision* with some concrete suggestions of how to grow by seeing growth as the integration of the four skills.

Example

One school district we worked with wanted to introduce a value-development component into a teacher education program. They decided that this meant working on the value of self-esteem (self-worth) of the teachers. The idea was to introduce experimental seminars and then measure teacher growth in one year.

Naturally there was resistance from teachers and the officials became discouraged. By working with the confluent model they were able to see that self-esteem is a part of a phase of consciousness related to many other values such as belonging, friendship, self-competence, prestige, being liked.

As such all the other values are related and therefore components of self-esteem. Such strategies as team pairings for classroom support, parental support in classrooms, the building of teacher committees, all increase security (one phase lower) and foster belonging and friendship, all valid growth components of self-esteem and less threatening to the system than *some* types of experimental learning.

Project Values under Richard Kunkel in Saint Louis is helping us to collect and assess data in three areas:

1) Direct-education workshops
2) Consultations (as above)
3) Curriculum development and its effect in the classroom.

Conceptual Team

All this data is then fed into the model we have developed. Periodically the concepts and data have been the topics of brainstorming by a group of cross-disciplinary consultants at CEVAM to refine and reform the model if necessary. In the last two years the team has included consultants from the publisher and Saint Louis University and other invited participants (see the Introduction).

Such sessions naturally produced more data which *was* and *is* continually being evaluated, especially through Project Values in Saint Louis and recently the Omega Project in Indianapolis. The principle evaluator of the data is Dr. Richard Kunkel, and of the Control and Method, Dr. Julius Elias, Dean of Arts and Science, the University of Connecticut.

And so it is that Model Two, Three and so on will be formed. It is then an anthropological method of gathering data, reflecting, constructing and testing new models.

What makes the model a valid process at all? The Chinese saying that "A picture is worth a thousand words" is the point of it all. A model is an attempt to symbolize in a practical manner the reality we try to grasp. 1) It is not valid unless it helps us to find meaning, to make sense out of the world. 2) It is not valid unless that meaning can lead us to practical creative consequences for ourselves and others.

Adapting Lippett's seven criteria for the valid function of the model as a search and research model.

1. Representation. It can be used to represent a complex situation helping persons to see new variables in a new way.
2. Guiding. It provides guidelines for growth and direction and perspective that is more holistic.
3. Interpretation. It can assist in interpreting and testing theory and in establishing a framework for experimentation and discussion.
4. Visualization. It gives a sense of vision as an aid to the teacher, consultant or change agent. It thus becomes a tool.
5. Prediction. In cases where experimentation is impossible it acts as a guide in predicting responsible outcomes and consequences. The value of its predictability of course will ultimately have to be tested.
6. Recreation. Building, formulating, constructing and making sense out of the world is fun, it is an act of leisure. The meaningful must be enjoyable.
7. Communication. The model as a symbol is a new language form. It is an art form and therefore by its nature can communicate in ways that other forms of language cannot. It decodes, synergises and miniaturizes complexities for its learner and introduces him to a new awareness of his own experience. It is a primary act of meaning making.

TRENDS

I would like now to spend some time on trends where we see this theory leading us. These will be introductions to areas that we are beginning to explore and hopefully an invitation for you to explore also.

First we will look at some further implications of confluence and then some directions for research.

What is a Value?

Simon, Raths and Harmon talked of the value process, the manner in which we choose a value, as being sevenfold. Something is a value when it is:

1) Chosen freely
2) Chosen from alternatives
3) Chosen after considering the consequences
4) Stated publicly
5) Prized
6) Acted on repeatedly
7) Acted on recently

Value Process for Systems

As we noted in the last chapter this definition of how we choose a value, although helpful, is naturally limited. The following process of valuing is one that deals more directly with the individual as system. It is a process that can be applied to value-ranking in the individual or within our institutional framework.

It is a fourfold process:

1) Contemplation
2) Generation
3) Reflection
4) Construction

1. *Contemplation:*

It is the activity of "being with"; it is an attentiveness to "what is." The stress is on *listening, clarifying, trusting* and *empathizing.*

The emphasis should be on "waiting patiently" and allowing the student or child to become, to share. The skill of value clarification would be a key for the seeing of another's values is a sacred moment and requires that the teacher have the abilities to first listen and empathize.

In teacher training trying to get the student skilled enough to see underlying values in an event or piece of behavior means teaching the teacher to relax and just "be with" another until they "see" the obvious. It means letting go of all

expectations and allowing the child or the event you are studying literally to become the teacher!

2. *Generation:*

Its first priority is hopeful imagining. This is the process
of "stretching" one's limits to see realistic alternatives from
what has been contemplated.

Once contemplation has taken place and values are perceived the ranking (prioritizing) of those alternatives and their
variations is of itself a generative process.

The major skills here are resourcefulness, brainstorming
and planning. A key to generation is the willingness to work in
close contact with others. For too often an executive who
seems to have excellent skills falls short because he lacks vision. Often this lack is tied to his inability to trust the creativity of others.

3. *Reflection:*

Its first priority is in meaning-making. This is the process of quietening the mind. It is a selecting after considering
consequences of the best possible alternatives. Stress should be
placed on order and meaning and the placing of things in
proper perspective.

Skills of personal authority and ownership, patience and
confidence are required. The choosing of alternatives from
what has been generated must be tempered with an ability to
confront one's limitations, so that the choices will be realistic
and not destructive or mere empty fantasies.

Reflection then is central to the process and like the
other categories is a part of a continuous on-going process.
However it needs to be made conscious to ensure that it happens. It is our evaluative and critical faculty at work and is essential to a balanced developmental life, individual or institutional.

4. *Construction:*

The first priority is to build something, to finish the job,
to complete the work creatively. This is a process of acting,
doing and producing. Stress is laid on the processes of decision-
making and committing one's self or group to a course of action.

The skills of manipulation and development of social and physical tools are required. It is the ability of a person or organization, having contemplated the reality and its limits, generated ideas, reflected and chosen a course of action to be able to project that idea into world and make it work.

For example if I am a history teacher in a high school and find that no one cares what I am teaching I might talk, listen and in fact contemplate my students' needs and interests. Second we might as a consequence brainstorm some lesson plans with those same students—reflect and choose two lesson plans. Construction would be the actual teaching of those lessons in the class.

The reason this probably would work is that contemplating their values is to key in on the basis of their motivation system. They are more likely to listen to something they have been a part of!

This instrument has been helpful to people trying to understand the latter process. First read over the four descriptions of contemplation, generation, reflection and construction and fill out the following diagram.

DIAGRAM 45

Value Process	Family Decisions	Personal Decisions	Professional Decisions	Social Decisions
Contemplation	%	%	%	%
Generation	%	%	%	%
Reflection	%	%	%	%
Construction	%	%	%	%

Looking at the four types of decisions try to put a percentage (1 percent to 100 percent) for each of the value processes as they usually are operative in decision-making.

The Phases and the Process

How do these four stages of value process relate to our world view? The following diagram will help explain.

DIAGRAM 46

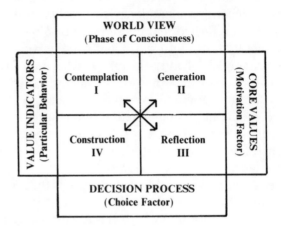

Personal and Institutional Disfunction

The inner ring shows the valuing process, the manner by which people choose priorities. This is a part of the confluent process and is itself a systems skill. Personal and institutional disfunction occur when any one of the four processes is absent.

When contemplation is absent persons or students feel unlistened to. An administrator or executive who has no generative skills lacks vision and will tend only to maintain the organization. The absence of reflection makes for serious misjudgments, and lack of construction simply means the job will not get done.

The arrows in the middle of the diagram simply indicate that all four sections are interrelated. Contemplation and reflection are never really separate. Reflection and evaluation are contemplative acts. Construction comes from generation, but what is constructed creates new awareness and therefore generates new ideas.

The outside ring relates the process to the phases of value development.

World View:

It bridges contemplation and generation as a priority, although it in fact relates to all four. Why these two most of all? Contemplation is *seeing what is*. Generation is related to the imagination and *what may be*.

World view as a phase of consciousness is always related to the present value stage (core values) as represented in one's behavior plus the values anticipated in one's imagination of what one would realistically like to be.

Therefore contemplation and generation are particular indicators of a person's world view and stage of consciousness. This value processing then as a day-to-day educational method and sequence is a way of developing values.

A great deal of research needs to be encouraged and curriculum developed that will help children contemplate and examine the myths of our society, the world views encouraged through television and advertising. This is particularly necessary when we consider generation and the option television is already suggesting.

Core Values and Motivation:

The core values (Chapter III) are seen and can be best utilized in the generation and reflection process. In our use of educational and training strategies we spend a lot of time teaching students to pull values from brainstorming sheets.

Example. Strategy: Generation and Reflection

Task: Teachers brainstorming on strategies for a high school class in values.

1. Have the teachers brainstorm (simply write words on a piece of paper representing ideas) around the question: "What are the value issues I experience in my students?" Stress it has to be the teacher's *experience* of the student—this is *generation*.

2. Pull out the underlying values (see Chapters III and IV) from the words on the list. Then have each teacher choose four values that represent their experiences of the students' values priority needs—this is reflection.

3. Have the teachers share the values and come to a consensus on four or five values and to prioritize them. Then define briefly each value by consensus.

4. Now repeat the process of generation. Take each value in order of priority based again on an observed experience that the students have of that value. Once you have your

list prioritize it, grouping those experiences that are similar (reflection).

5. Now taking the first group of experiences first ask the questions: 1) "If these kind of experiences are our students' experiences of this value, what would we want to add as positive experiences, if any?" 2) "How can we construct an educational strategy to repeat the positive value experience so as to reinforce that value and bring it to consciousness?"—This is construction.

This last strategy is just one process example; of course number five is really moving to construction. The final experience we feel should always be a balance of both intellectual and experimental (affective) components.

Now why are core values and motivation so closely connected? First of all what is generated includes the contemplative element—one is generating out of one's total value stance. Reflection here would be prioritizing so that the values one chooses are in fact the ones that *are the most important to the person.*

Values as we have seen in earlier chapters connect to my basic need and meaning system. In education and organizational development the question of motivation is very important, an area that needs much work. Maslow in positing his hierarchy of needs said there are D-cognitive values (deficiency) necessary for good mental health and B-cognitive or self-actualizing values. Maslow's self-actualizing values were for the most part Phase III with glimpses of Phase IV values. His point was that the real motivations were the self-actualizing values. As a hierarchy the values would be as follows:

DIAGRAM 47

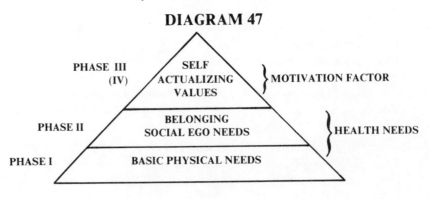

Frederich Herzberg, after doing extensive analysis in industrial settings on motivation had different results, but enough similar ones to make a comparison. He talked about "Dissatisfiers or Hygienic factors." They are as follows:

1. Status, salary, job security, personal life, company policies, on-the-job relationships and the nature of supervision. Interestingly enough these were not motivators but minimal indicators for the worker.

In order to bring about motivation Herzberg noted the following must be brought into action:

2. Challenging work, achievement possibilities, recognition and such things as visible growth and advancement.

As a consequence different organizational groups have tried to put Maslow and Herzberg together as follows (from the Telechemtrics Corporation):

DIAGRAM 48

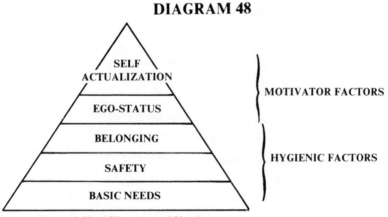

Maslow's Need Hierarchy and Herzberg

A consequence of all this for the administrator is that too high a stress on hygienic factors would give a lot of security but could actually reduce motivation. For example a tremendous amount of energy goes into dealing with tenure in public schools and universities—a system of security that attends to the hygienic needs but that quite often ignores the real motivational factors that according to this chart would be self-actualizing and ego needs.

One difficulty with the way Maslow and Herzberg are used in organizational development is that they actually don't fit together. Maslow's concern was with mental health, aiding individuals to grow in a healthy manner. On the other hand Herzberg deals primarily with what moves people in on-the-job situations. Both contribute valuable data on motivation, but a more holistic approach remains a vital need in motivational research. Our construct provides a framework for a more confluent consideration of motivation.

It is clear that looking at the phases, Phases I and IIa contain the hygienic factors. The central motivators would be out of Phase IIb and Phases III and IV; clearly more work needs to be done.

I feel that this phase construct points the way to some real progress in the motivational field. Here are some of the additional factors we feel have to be considered:

1) Motivation as it relates not only to the core values (needs) but as they relate to the integration of the four skills. We find that the sense of harmony that comes about from this integration is a key in the motivation itself. As an illustration let us take the Diagram 46 we had earlier and substitute for the four processes (contemplation, and so on) the four skills.

DIAGRAM 49

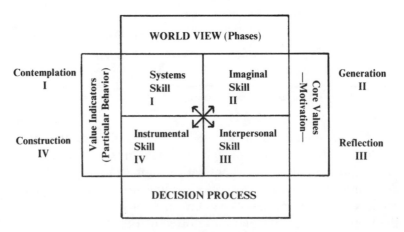

Again the world view actually takes in the whole diagram, but in fact the priority came out between systems skills and imaginal. Why? Because the systems emphasis integrated all external components in one's life and imaginal integrates (see Chapter V) all the internal with the external. Put these two together and one has a picture of one's phase of consciousness, the world view.

Moving then once again to the motivation factor imaginal skills are the indicators of the future one is willing to invest in.

The more enthusiastic and imaginative a teacher is the more he/she will be motivated when that energy has an outlet.

Man is a political animal. He cannot do anything really creative unless it is somehow interpersonal in nature. As Herzberg has pointed out good working relationships are a hygienic factor. But we have found that lack of a minimal level of friendship and intimacy means *loss* of meaning. This is still hygienic as a point of maintenance. However when you reverse them in an organization and put people with some imaginal skills (minimal not maximal) together in a good team setting and their motivation is increased tenfold—they become their own hygienic factor.

Clearly this is only a beginning in ideas; a tremendous amount needs to be done. It is also clear that integration of skill- and need-values as a confluent interaction has a lot to say about motivation. This is an area in which we ourselves are beginning to expand our work.

2) Motivation as a science must be related to the skills, directly to order and direction. The phases need to be programmed into leader training so that leadership can diagnose the following for individuals and the organization as a whole.

    1. Present phase stage

    2. Concreteness of next stage

    3. Long-term vision

Then as a consequence of the last item one can begin to plan on the basis of training leadership for the future phase experience. They key here is in so constructing administrators and classrooms for that matter that they reinforce advanced stages of development just enough to continually encourage growth.

Theoretically then this should increase motivation. We have strong indicators that this is so, but have not got enough data on this to be absolutely certain. I hope others will be encouraged to investigate this area also.

3) Decision and choice process in our earlier diagram bridged the gap between reflection and construction. Then this parallels on the skill diagram with interpersonal and instrumental skills as follows:

DIAGRAM 50

Construction	Reflection
IV	III
Instrumental Skills	Interpersonal Skills
DECISION MAKING (Choice)	

Simply put, after reflecting on alternatives one has to choose a course of action. This course is construction. In an institution at the skill level decision most often includes people; someone has to carry out the task. Minimally the task is going to affect others. This means interpersonal skills. Instrumental skills are needed to do the job (construct) like teaching a grade six class. Between doing the job and reflecting on what has to be done first is the decision-making process.

There are many elements that can be dealt with in this regard; here are some that we have used in leadership training sessions.

1) Decision making as the question of how one makes judgments on quality and expectation—the process of evaluating.
    a. Evaluation and individual accountability in supervisor relationships
    b. Evaluate methods and instruments in a group setting
    c. Evaluation methods for organization development. Evaluation is a formative program components.

2) Valuing as a decision-making process, such as Simon's seven criteria of the four processes.

3) Methods of role defining and goal-setting. Individual life goal-setting techniques. Institutional value analysis and goal-setting methods.

4) Force field analysis and SPIRO* methods of decision-making. Management by objective techniques.

5) General training in Value Clarification and group process skills.

6) Skill analysis: decision problems because skill deficiency is a major factor in personal development and creative institutional reinforcement of an individual growth pattern.

Two Additional Dimensions

In addition to the kinds of skills illustrated above two significant areas of training are indicated from the phases of consciousness that have some unique dimensions and need to be further researched.

1. Communication training for educators and those in leadership roles. By educators here I am referring primarily to those teaching at the adult level.

As we noted in the earlier chapters when there is more than one stage difference between two communicating parties the person at the earlier stage of development translates all that has been said in terms of his world view so that understanding is minimalized.

Those in leadership roles, school supervisors, agency directors and the like need to be trained in how to communicate well to people at different phases and stages of consciousness. You minimalize the freedom you give to a Phase I secretary—she needs controls and a system of accountability, an experience of supervision, that will make her secure enough to function well. You put different controls on a Phase III person or they would probably quit the job.

This is indicative of the new range of communication skills that leadership must acquire. In working with this we

*Stands for—specificity, performance, involvement, realism, observability.

have found that in order to learn the skills the person must have a minimal Phase III capacity and good imaginal skills to comprehend the vision that such skills demand.

2. Phases within phases. In most of our seminars the question is continually put to us: Are people not at different phases all the time? Our answer has been: People are generally at one phase and their behavior is characteristic of that phase. If they are Phase II people their over-all stance is social in its orientation.

Now a crisis will tend to move a person for a while. Sudden death and grief can move a person into Phase I or II in feelings. However one is generally growing through one phase for a long time. The clue to growth we have indicated is in the integration of skills. We consider a person to be in one particular phase until he gains minimal abilities in all four skills, at which point he will *in fact*, so we have observed, be moved into the next phase. At this point the general behavior characteristics will have changed.

What we are now working with is a concept of phases within phases; consider the following diagram:

DIAGRAM 51

MINIPHASES

	Phase i	Security: Coping, Skills are low. Affection.	**Phases I and II**
	Phase ii	Self-Worth Competence High Expectation Concern	
Phases III	Phase iii	Being Self: Learning to Construct	
and IV	Phase iv	Interdependence/high community cooperation	

The idea is that the miniphases represent what an individual goes through at each major phase after Phase II. That this miniphase is also what coincides with the stage of normal group development, expanded the diagram would be as follows to include group laboratories development:

DIAGRAM 52

Mini Phases	Characteristics
Phase i	Security. Learning to cope with new authority of a major phase. *Sharing* minimal information uncertain about future
Phase ii	Self-worth and competence. Stress on *belonging* to new major phase group. High expectations. Emphasis on sharing. New friends and grouping.
Phase iii	Being self: Learning to be independent by constructing, or making one's own way. Confronting authority. Letting go of expectations
Phase iv	Interdependence: High Cooperation and willing to work in team. Confrontation and intimacy move nations

This would be an additional skill the leaders would work with. A person at Phase III is going to be insecure but that does not mean he is experiencing Phase I although he may have some of those feelings.

Again the construct is a director, a timing model, a pointer to the future, a place where work needs to be done.

4) Particular Behavior as Value Indicator.

DIAGRAM 53

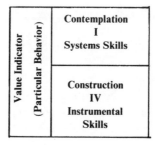

And so we have come full circle. This last section indicates the behavior we observe, our particular individual skills and the way we deal with systems. It is really the fruition of our work and the conclusion of the book.

CONCLUSION

What the model is that we have presented is our construct for the time being. It is also a way to contemplate the world we live in. For a model is not a way of viewing the world; rather it is a limited vision of the world. It is a way of gaining access to the mystery we strive to understand, not to control it, but only to "see" and "be" with it.

Much work has to be done. And we at least are willing to help those researching these areas in any way we can. Some of the areas of need that we are suggesting for research in relationship to the confluent theory of values are:

1. Development and standardization of new testing instruments and evaluation methods that will take into consideration all the phase values and skill integrations.
2. Critical studies of major values areas: genetic engineering and phases of consciousness.
3. Phases and the history of science: problems of world view and observation.
4. Vision, ecority (ecology, harmony, technology) and phases of consciousness.
5. Leadership development and the phases
6. Metaethics: history of ideas, behavior and value development
7. Higher education: its vision towards some helpful constructs
8. Phases: A theology. Is it really a hierarchy?

City as Model

In the beginning of the book I quoted from Lewis Mumford's *The City in History*. I would like to do so again. For Mumford the city is a constructed model of man's perception of the universe. He has the following to say:

> The final mission of the city is to further man's conscious participation in the cosmic and historic process. Through its own complex and enduring structure, the city vastly augments

man's ability to interpret these processes and take an active formative part in them, so that every phase of the drama, it stages shall have, to be the highest degree possible, the illumination of consciousness, the stamp of purpose, the color of love. That magnification of all the dimensions of life, through emotional communion, rational communication, technological mastery, and above all, dramatic representation, has been the supreme office of the cities in history. And it remains the chief reason for the city's continued existence.

Someone said once authors only speak of vision within the limits of their own! Our vision stops at Phase IV as an evolutionary possibility. But that is only because that is as far as I can see. We would assume there is a beyond, so what does such a model as the confluent theory of values represent?

For me it is like the city. It is a construct to help people make sense out of the complexity pressing upon them. It is a recognition that complexity is not bounded by arbitrary disciplines of science, religion and social studies. So it is a discipline that tries to move toward the integration of those studies, bringing all their data into a central focus, values.

This city, this confluent theory, hopefully will be a reinforcing environment, a tool that will help some maybe just someone to see the phases beyond.

Beyond Phase IV and ecological control of our bodies and this planet would be the universe, a looking toward a postgalactic man. Already there are a few who have seen and been affected by travel in space. Those days are not surely so far away.

Man must prepare to be responsible not only for this little world of ours but one beyond. For it is only as we have a large vision that our constructive present can be creative and life-enhancing to all the men.

BIBLIOGRAPHY

GENERAL

Allport, Gordon W., *The Nature of Prejudice*. New York, Anchor Books Edition, 1958.

Asch, Solomon E. and Henle, Mary, eds., *The Selected Papers of Wolfgang Kohler*. New York, Liveright, 1969.

Beck, C.M., Crittenden, B.S., and Sullivan, E.V., *Moral Education*. Toronto, University of Toronto Press, 1971.

Bell, Daniel, *The Coming of Post-Industrial Society: A Study in Social Forecasting*. New York, Basic Books, 1973.

Berger, Peter L., *The Sacred Canopy: Elements of a Sociological Theory of Religion*. New York, Doubleday, 1967.

Bronowski, Jacob, *The Ascent of Man*. Boston, Little, Brown, First American Edition, 1974.

Brown, George, Professor of Education, Santa Barbara, California, Unpublished Manuscript.

Cantin, Eileen, *Mounier: A Personalist View of History*. New York, Paulist Press, 1974.

Carroll, Lewis, *Alice's Adventures in Wonderland*. London, Macmillan, 1963.

Clark, Kenneth, *Civilisation: A Personal View*. New York, Harper and Row, 1972.

Frankl, Viktor, *Man's Search for Meaning*. Boston, Beacon Press, 1963.

Freire, Paulo, *Education for Critical Consciousness*. Translated by Myra Ramos. *The Pedagogy of the Oppressed*. Translated by Myra Ramos. New York, Seabury Press, 1971.

Fromm, Erich, *Escape From Freedom*. New York and Toronto, Rinehart and Company, Inc., 1941.

Frondizi, Risieri, *What Is Value? An Introduction to Axiology*. Translated by Solomon Lipp. LaSalle, Illinois, Open Court, 1971.

Glasser, William, *Reality Therapy: A New Approach to Psychiatry*. New York, Harper and Row, 1965.

Goulet, Denis, "An Ethical Model For The Study Of Values," *Harvard Educational Review*, Vol, 41, no. 2, 1971.

Hall, Brian and Osborn, Joseph, *Nog's Vision*. New York, Paulist Press, 1974.

Hall, Brian, *Value Clarification As Learning Process: A Guidebook*. New York, Paulist Press, 1974.

Haughton, Rosemary, *On Trying To Be Human*. 1966. Springfield, Illinois, Templegate, 1966.

Havighurst, Robert J., *Developmental Tasks and Education*. Third Edition. New York, David McKay, 1972.

Illich, Ivan, *Interpersonal Relational Networks*. C.I.D.O.C., No. 1014 *Tools For Conviviality*. New York, Harper and Row, 1973.

Kimper, Frank, Professor of Pastoral Counseling, Claremont, California, Private Paper, 1969.

Kohlberg, Lawrence, *The Concepts of Developmental Psychology As A Central Guide To Education: Examples From Cognitive, Moral and Psychological Education*. Institute for Human Development, Harvard University.

Lippitt, Gordon L., *Visualizing Change: Model Building and the Change Process*. Fairfax, Virginia, NTL Learning Resource Co., 1973.

Luthe, Wolfgang, and Schultz, Johannes, *Autogenic Therapy*. Vol. I. New York, Grune and Stratton, 1970.

Maslow, Abraham, *Toward A Psychology of Being*. Second Edition. Cincinnati, O., Van Nostrand Reinhold, 1968.

Milne, A.A., *The House at Pooh Corner*. Revised Edition. New York, E.P. Dutton, 1961.

Minuchin, Salvador, et al., *Families of the Slums: An Exploration of Their Structure Treatment*. New York, Basic Books, 1967.

Mounier, Emmanuel, *The Character of Man*. Translated by Cynthia Rowland. New York, Harper Bros., 1956.

Moustakas, Clark E., *The Self: Explorations in Personal Growth*. New York, Harper and Row, 1956.

Mumford, Lewis, *The City In History*. New York, Harcourt, Brace and World, 1961.

Oden, Thomas C., *Game Free: A Guide to the Meaning of Intimacy*. New York, Harper and Row, 1974.

Phenix, Philip, *Man and His Becoming*. University of Puget Sound, Tacoma, Wa., The Brown and Haley Lectures, Twelfth Series. New Brunswick, N.J., Rutgers University Press, 1964. *Realms of Meaning: A Philosophy of the Curriculum for General Education*. New York, McGraw-Hill, 1964.

Progoff, Ira, *The Symbolic and the Real*. New York, McGraw-Hill, 1973.

Raths, Louis, et al., *Values and Teaching: Working With Values in the Classroom*. Columbus, O., Charles E. Merrill, 1966.

Rescher, Nicholas, *Introduction to Value Theory*. Englewood Cliffs, N.J., Prentice-Hall, 1969.

Rogers, Carl, *On Becoming A Person*. Boston, Houghton Mifflin, 1970.

Rokeach, Milton, *The Nature of Human Values*. New York, Free Press, 1973.

Satir, Virginia, *Conjoint Family Therapy*. Palo Alto, Calif., Science and Behavior Books, 1967.

Schiller, Friedrich, *Naive and Sentimental Poetry* and *On The Sublime*. Translated and edited by Julius A. Elias. New York, Ungar, 1966.

Schlegel, Richard, "Quantum Physics and Human Purpose," *Zygon*, Volume 8, nos. 3 and 4, September—December, 1973.

Soleri, Paolo, *Arcology: The City in the Image of Man*. Cambridge, Mass., M.I.T. Press, 1969. *The Bridge Between Matter and Spirit Is Matter Becoming Spirit*. New York, Anchor Books, 1973.

Sperry, R. W., "Science and the Problem of Values," *Zygon*, Volume 9, no. 1, March, 1974.

Terkel, Studs, *Working*. New York, Pantheon Books, 1972.

Thera, Nyanaponika, *The Heart of Buddhist Meditation*. New York, Samuel Weiser, 1970.

Townsend, Robert, "Don't Just Do Something," *Center Magazine*, Volume 2, 1970.

Wagner, Richard, *Environment and Man*. New York, W.W. Norton, 1971.

Wheeler, Harvey, *Center Report, 1974*. Center for Democratic Institutions, Santa Barbara, Calif.

Wigginton, Eliot, ed., *The Foxfire Book*. New York, Anchor Books Edition, 1972.

ANNOTATED

(Books worth special consideration)

Bronowski, J. *The Ascent of Man*. Boston: William Brown Company, 1973. Like Clark's book, *Civilisation*, this is taken from a BBC television series. There is an excellent set of illustrations from the original television series. In this work Bronowski traces the history of ideas with a particular emphasis on science. A developmental view of man which goes beyond the social sciences this book makes fascinating reading and is a real contribution especially to those readers who do not have a strong scientific background.

Clark, Kenneth. *Civilisation*. New York: Harper and Row, 1969. From the public education television series of the same name Clark's book tracing the history of western ideas interweaves an incredible amount of information from the social sciences, philosophy and the history of ideas. Art illustrations in the book interface beautifully with the language to communicate deeply rooted values mainly through symbol. Highly recommended for the reader who wants to trace the sequence of human development through history and art.

Flynn, Elizabeth W., and John F. LaFaso. *Designs in Affective Education: A Teacher Resource Program for Junior and Senior High*. New York: Paulist Press, 1974. By the authors of *Group Discussion as Learning Process*, this interesting compilation of strategies cuts across a whole range of subject matters from interpersonal relations and moral choosing to strategies in science and esthetics. An excellent resource for those who are interested in confluent education and are looking for a variety of strategies in skill and content at the Junior and Senior High School level.

Freire, Paulo. *Pedagogy of the Oppressed*. Translated by Myra Bergman Ramos. New York: Herder and Herder, 1968. Illich calls this work "truly revolutionary." The ideas in it helped gain the author an "invitation" to leave Brazil, his homeland. The work is a strident assertion that everyone, no matter how "illiterate" or "ignorant," is capable of much more than a cursory comment on his world.

Frondizi, Risieri. *What is Value?* LaSalle, Illinois: Open Court Publishing Co., 1971. This book is about the value issue and its relationship to the history of ideas. It is an introduction to axiology and a must for those who want to examine values from the point of view of a philosopher. An invaluable resource, this book deals with the problem of whether values are objective or subjective, or both. It was written by a creative author who makes concrete suggestions for creative integration in resolving the problem.

Hall, Brian. *Value Clarification as Learning Process: A Sourcebook for Educators*. New York: Paulist Press, 1973. This book created for adult educators provides a comprehensive and in depth statement of the theory of value clarification. Value clarification is a methodology that has been around for a long time and relates to all areas of life. The book takes a look, not only at materials appropriate for the classroom, but also relates to adult value issues such as work and leisure.

Hall, Brian: *Value Clarification as Learning Process: A Guidebook for Educators.* New York: Paulist Press, 1973. This book was created for teachers and student teachers to provide a multitude of designs and strategies in the value clarification process. It can be used both for teacher formation and for actual classroom settings. The book is an invaluable resource for in depth approaches to value clarification.

Hall, Brian, and Maury Smith. *Value Clarification as Learning Process: A Handbook for Christian Educators.* New York: Paulist Press, 1973. Written especially for the Christian educator, the primary emphasis of this book is on parish programming. It stresses the relationship between the value clarification process and Christian education. Materials on group dynamics and parish team building are included in this work along with a large section on values as they relate to the problem of volunteerism.

Joyce, Bruce, and Marsha Weil. *The Models of Teaching.* New Jersey: Prentice-Hall, 1972.   1) This book is especially recommended for professional educators. 2) It describes a wide variety of teaching methods, the values stressed by each method, and the likely consequences of utilizing each methodology. The conclusion of the authors is that teaching should always integrate a variety of approaches and should not be monolithic. This wonderful little book stressing alternatives for educators is a must for anyone interested in values education.

Krathwohl, David R., Benjamin S. Bloom, and Vertram B. Masia. *Taxonomy of Educational Objectives; The Classification of Educational Goals.* New York: David McKay Company, Inc., 1974. Definitely not for the casual reader. The work offers a highly technical discussion of values and education.

Maslow, A.H. *The Farther Reaches of Human Nature.* New York: Viking Press, 1971. This Esalen book was completed after Maslow's death. It does not read as a unified document but it is almost an encyclopedia of information. For those who are interested in the work of Abraham Maslow, on values, human needs, human development, and ultimate potential this work is indispensable.

Moustakas, Clark E. (Editor). *The Self: Explorations in Personal Growth.* New York: Harper and Row, 1956. The issue of what the self is and of how this deepest part of our inner being relates to the world as a chooser of values is dealt with in this compendium of articles collected and edited by Clark Moustakas. Articles by Jung, Rink, Fromm, and Allport are included. For persons interested in studying personal growth in depth this is an invaluable book. It would be useful for college seminars.

Nash, Paul. *Authority and Freedom in Education: An Introduction to the Philosophy of Education.* New York: John Wiley and Sons, 1966. An introduction designed to show how the theme or problem of authority and freedom in education can be approached through the use of practical dialectic. It has an excellent treatment of work and leisure in education.

Oden, Thomas C. *The Structure of Awareness.* Nashville, Tennessee: Abingdon Press, 1969. Certainly not for those who have "dropped out" of society; more for those seeking deeper awareness, hungering for a more intimate taste of human existence. A "celebration of now." It is a basic book in values.

Parsons, Talcott, and Edward A. Shils. *Toward a General Theory of Action.* New York: Harper and Row, 1962. A worthwhile collection of papers discussing the interactive process between person and system. The book is heavy reading; it has tremendous amount of information on values and systems. For the serious reader it is an important resource.

Phenix, Philip H. *The Realms of Meaning: The Philosophy of the Curriculum for General Education*. New York: McGraw-Hill, 1964. For the educator in particular, but for people in general who are interested in values, this work of Philip Phenix is an indispensable resource. Phenix for years has been advocating a confluent approach to education, particularly through the development of appropriate school curricula. Phenix constantly refers to the necessity of confluent skills particularly in the area of cross-disciplinary action. He confronts questions of meaning and of meaninglessness in society and stresses the necessity of developing the imagination along with a host of other skills so that human development can occur synergetically. Phenix is particularly helpful relating values to science and education.

Proshansky, Harold M., William H. Ittelson, and Leanne G. Rivlin, eds. *Environmental Psychology: Man and His Physical Setting*. New York: Holt, Rinehart and Winston, Inc., 1970. A thorough presentation of the concepts, approaches, findings, and methodological issues that characterize the still-to-be-defined field of environmental psychology.

Raths, Louis E., Merrill Harmin, and Sidney B. Simon. *Values and Teaching: Working with Values in the Classroom*. Columbus, Ohio: Charles E. Merrill Publishing Company, 1966. Value theory and the teaching strategies associated with it are presented in this book, as well as an outline of a theory of values and a methodology for the clarification of values. It is a classic in values that everyone interested in the subject should have read.

Rogers, Carl E. *Freedom to Learn*. Columbus, Ohio: Charles E. Merrill Publishing Company, 1969. This is for educators and it is appropriately enough about learning—LEARNING—insatiable curiosity, discovering, drawing in from the outside; not "the lifeless, sterile, futile, quickly forgotten" charade which has been passed off as education for too many years.

Rokeach, Milton. *The Nature of Human Values*. New York: Macmillan, 1973. Rokeach has been working on values particularly from the point of view of data gathering and statistical anaylsis for a number of years. He has much information to offer the serious reader.

Simon, Sidney B., and Howard Kirshenbaum. *Readings in Values Clarification*. Minneapolis, Minnesota: Winston Press, 1973. This recent addition to values literature by Simon and Kirshenbaum is indispensable to entering the area of value studies. The book includes articles by Westerhoff, Kohlberg, and Rokeach. An excellent book with a wide range of theoretical and strategic suggestions for using value clarification.

Sizer, Nancy S. and Theodore R. *Moral Education*. A collection of lectures by James F. Gustafson, Richard S. Peters, Lawrence Kohlberg, Bruno Bettelheim and Kensiton. Cambridge: Harvard University Press, 1970. An interesting series of readings in the area of moral education. Of particular importance is Kohlberg's article on moral development. Those who want to understand a confluent theory of values development should read this article.

SUPPLEMENTARY

Adams, T. "A model for teaching valuing." *The Humanities Today,* April, 1971, 507-509.

Allport, G. *The Individual and His Religion*, New York: Macmillan, 1962.

Assagioli, Roberto, M.D. *Psychosynthesis*. New York: Hobbs, Dorman and Co., 1965.

Baier, K. *The Moral Point of View*. New York: Random House, 1965.

Baier K. & Rescher, N. *Values and the Future*. New York: The Free Press, 1969.

Barr, R.D. *Values and Youth—Teaching Social Studies in an Age of Crisis—No. 2*. Washington, D.C.: National Council for the Social Studies, 1971.

Berkowitz, L. *The Development of Motives and Values in the Child*. New York: Basic Books, 1964.

Bronowski, J., 1965. *Science and Human Values*. New York: Harper Torchbook, 1972.

Chanzan, B. Soltis, J. *Moral Education*. New York: Columbia Teachers College Press, 1973.

Childs, J. *Education and Morals*. New York: John Wiley & Sons, Inc. Science Editions, 1967.

Cox, Harvey. *The Feast of Fools*. Cambridge, Massachusetts: Harvard University, 1969.

Crittenden, B. *Form and Content in Moral Education. Monograph Series No. 12*. Toronto: Ontario Institute for Studies in Education, 1972.

Dale, E. *Building a Learning Environment*. Bloomington: Phi Delta Kappan, 1972.

Delgado, Jose M.R., "Science and Human Values," *Zygon* 5, 1970, 148-158.

Erikson, Erik H. *Childhood and Society*. New York: W.W. Norton and Co., Inc. 1950.

Fenton, E., Kohlberg, L. *Moral Education*. Report given at ASCD National Curriculum Study Institute. Portland, Oregon, December 8-10, 1974. Summary by Glenys Unruh.

Fitch, James Marsden. *Environmental Psychology*. New York: Holt, Rinehart and Winston, Inc., 1970.

Freire, P. "Cultural Action for Freedom." *Harvard Educational Review* and Center for the Study of Development and Social Change. Monograph Series, No. 1, 1970.

Fromm, E. *The Sane Society*. Greenwich, Conn., Fawcett Publishers, 1955.

Greenwald, Harold. "Play and Self Development." *Ways of Growth*. Edited by Herbert A. Otto and John Mann. New York: Pocket Books, 1971.

Goulet, D. *The Cruel Choice*. New York: Atheneum, 1971.

Gulick, Addison, 1968. "A biological prologue for human values." *Bioscience*, 18: 1109-1112

Harmin, M., Kirschenbaum, H., Simon, S. *Clarifying Values Through Subject Matter—Applications for the Classroom*. Minneapolis: Winston Press, 1973.

Harmin, M., Simon, S. "How to help students learn to think . . . about themselves." *The High School Journal*, March, 1972, 256-264.

Hawley, R., Simon, S., Britton, D. *Composition for Personal Growth—Values Clarification Through Writing*. New York: Hart Publishers, 1973.

Hudson, L. *Contrary Imaginations*. New York: Schocken Books,1966.

Hutchings, Edward and Elizabeth, editors, 1967. *Scientific Progress and Human Values*. New York: American Elsevier.

Illich, I. *Deschooling Society*. New York: Harper & Row, 1972.

Illich, I. *After Deschooling, What?* New York: Harper & Row, 1973.

Kohlberg, L., Kramer, R. "Continuities and Discontinuities in Childhood and Adult Moral Development." *Human Development* 12: 93-120 (1969).

Kohlberg, L. "Continuities in childhood and adult moral development revisited." Chapter 45 in L. Kohlberg & Turiel (eds.) *Moralization, The Cognitive Development Approach.* New York: Holt, Rinehart & Winston, 1973.

Kohlberg, L. "Stage and sequence: The cognitive development approach to socialization." Chapter 6 in D. Goslin (ed.) *Handbook of Socialization Theory.* Rand McNally & Co., 1969.

Kohlberg, L. "The child as a moral philosopher." *Psychology Today*, September, 1968, 25-30.

Kohlberg, L. "Stages of Moral Development as a Basis for Moral Education." Harvard University.

Kohlberg, L., Mayer R. "Development as the Aim of Education." *Harvard Educational Review*, Vol. 43, No. 4, November, 1972.

Lassey, W. *Leadership and Social Change.* Iowa City, Iowa: University Assoc., 1973.

Lockwood, A. *Moral Reasoning.* Columbus, Ohio: Xerox Education Center, 1972.

Maslow, A. *The Farther Reaches of Human Nature.* New York: Viking Press, 1971.

Maslow, A. *Religions, Values and Peak-Experiences.* New York: Viking Press, 1964.

Murphy, M. *The Murphy Inventory of Values.* San Diego: Pennant Press, 1969.

Nelson, J. *Values and Society.* Rochelle Park, New Jersey: Hayden Book Co., 1974.

Nelson, J. *Introduction to Value Inquiry.* Rochelle Park, New Jersey: Hayden Book Co., 1974.

Oden, T. *Structure of Awareness.* New York: Abingdon Press, 1969.

Ostrander, R., Dethy, R. *A Values Approach to Educational Administration.*

Piaget, J. *Moral Judgment of the Child.* New York: Free Press, 1965.

Piaget, Jean. *Six Psychological Studies.* New York: Random House, 1970.

Reich, Charles A. *The Greening of America.* New York: Random House, 1970.

Rokeach, M. *Beliefs, Attitudes and Values: A Theory of Organization and Change.* San Francisco: Jossey-Bass, 1972.

Simon, S., Howe, L., Kirschenbaum, H. *Values Clarification—A Handbook of Practical Strategies for Teachers and Students.* New York: Hart Publ., 1972.

Skinner, B.F. *Beyond Freedom and Dignity.* New York: Alfred A. Knopf, 1971.

Teilhard de Chardin, Pierre. *The Future of Man.* New York: Harper & Row, 1969.

Teilhard de Chardin, Pierre. *The Divine Milieu.* New York: Harper and Brothers, 1960.

Toffler, Alvin. *Future Shock.* New York: Random House, 1970.

Van Der Poel, Cornelius, *The Search for Human Values.* New York: Newman Press, 1971.

Webster, M., Socieszek, B. *Sources of Self-Evaluation.* New York: John Wiley and Sons, 1974.

Wilkinson, John, Editor, 1967. *Technology and Human Values.* Santa Barbara, California Center for the Study of Democratic Institutions.

INDEX

267